W9-AMO-892

BUT NOBODY WANTS TO DIE

or (the eschatology of bluegrass)

[RELEVANTBOOKS]

Published by RELEVANT Books
A division of RELEVANT Media Group, Inc.

www.relevantbooks.com
www.relevantmediagroup.com

Design by RELEVANT Solutions
Cover design and interior illustrations by Gary Dorsey
Interior design by Jeremy Kennedy

Library of Congress Control Number: 2006926599
International Standard Book Number: 0-9777480-0-6

For information or bulk orders:
RELEVANT MEDIA GROUP, INC.
100 SOUTH LAKE DESTINY DR., STE. 200
ORLANDO, FL 32810
407-660-1411

06 07 08 09 9 8 7 6 5 4 3 2 1

Printed in the United States of America

For those we have lost

CONTENTS

IRELAN
(northern Ulster reg
OKLAHOMA CITY
MEMPHIS, TN
(ELVIS!)
DALLAS, TX
CHICAGO, IL
LITTLETON, CO
ROSINE, KY
NEW YORK
(Lennon, 911, etc
Appalachians
East Coast
AMERICAN SOUTH
WACO, TX
TYLER, TX
ORLANDO, FL
(Gulf of Mexico)

EDINBURGH, SCOTLAND
(Lowlands (The River Tweed), Highlands)
LONDON
GERMANY
(mathematicians!)
PARIS
(site of Princess Di's death)
ITALY
(violin makers)
CENTRAL AFRICA
- Senegal - Gambia

AN INTRODUCTION

or

(Hello, My Name Is)

Traditionally speaking, the introductory section of a book is a space for the author, or in this case, authors, to summarize what a particular piece of writing is written in regard to, or to present a collection of ideas that set the scene for what the author or authors will attempt to convey to the reader. We, in fact, do wish to do that here, but we would also like to be slightly atypical and take the opportunity to use our introductory section to formally present ourselves to you the reader, so we may become acquainted on some level before our journey begins—a proper introduction if you will. (Atypical people are known for doing really cool atypical things like this.)[1] The journey on which we are about to embark requires companions. It would be much too sinister to go this alone and, as a matter of fact, this simple sentiment just so happens to be one of the few items we are hoping to force into your chest with our small collection of words—we need companionship—the company of friends.

It is not our intent to obligate you to favor us, but we must

---

1. Other words that could function contextually in place of *atypical*: *Indie, Pomo, Magical-Realism* (actually that one doesn't work at all, but we thought it best to go ahead and get it out there now before it was too late), or *Hipster-Twentysomethingish*. So please note the authors for being like seven times more indie than the next guy. No. Seriously. We're so, so indie.

acknowledge that we have you at a disadvantage. You see, due to the nature and limitations inherent in the communicative medium of books, you have not the opportunity, by way of formal introduction, to present yourself to us. But we will disregard this glaring flaw in our introductory process here and proceed by making a number of assumptions about you, given that you either bought or borrowed this book, or, in the least, have had the incredible good fortune of it currently resting in your hands. (If, perhaps, this book came to you by means dubious and debatable, we, the authors, would prefer not to know about it. However, if that is the case, which by the way we are making no assumptions or judgments about, we applaud your disregard for social norms and admit freely that while we do not condone ignorance of the law, we admire the vigilante spirit.) This simple act alone (your eyes upon this page) leads us to believe a number of things absolutely.

1. You are both intelligent and good-looking, with a high aptitude for mathematics and cartography, are exceptionally well rounded, possess great athletic ability and a keen sense of style. (We based this first assumption solely upon the fact that this guy named Steve told us he was sure to buy this book upon its release; so if your name is not Steve, please proceed to number 2.) Or ...

2. You are like myself and my coauthor, both introverted and reclusive; consider the reading of books the sum total of your obligatory societal interaction; are plagued by sizable personal space issues and met all too frequently with environments besetting to prey upon them; have absolutely no retentive capacity for the concepts concerning numbers and figures and their various summations, subtractions, multiplications, and divisions; are incessantly nervous yet unable to declare exactly why; enjoy comic books and microwaved marshmallows; and, of course, eat only with a spoon, as pointy objects make you anxious.

All this we can assume by the simple fact that you are reading this sentence now. And thus we shall freely extend our hand of companionship to you, at least for the brief period of time it takes for your eyes to follow these words to their end.

Yet you know nothing of us, outside of what you know of yourself, for we are like you. But it's been said that the self is the most difficult to truly know, so we will present ourselves in hopes that you may recognize a portion of yourself and, upon doing so, lightly take our hands into yours for the journey to begin.

But, enough concerning the second person pronoun! It is time for us, the authors of this book, to formally say hello.

My name is David. I am the one currently typing. I am a musician in a band that just so happens to bear my name and that also happens to bear my coauthor, Mike Hogan, as one of its fellow contributors. Of course, you could have perused the back of the book for a nice little spiel indicating as much, but there you would not have found the following anecdote: We had at one time in our possession a band name formula that would have shown itself foolproof. It involved a number, a mammal, and a color, not necessarily in that order. But, alas, our current name found us before we could enunciate something so profound as what this formula would have dictated. The honest truth of the matter is that none of us in the band can really pinpoint how or when our current name came to be. We did, however, have the cunning cleverness of choosing not to use a definite article in it. That's largely due to our wanting to make a statement. We wished for a name that really said something. To discard the definite article is a bold, daring move, one that should not be overlooked. So I would suggest you note the authors for both their musicality and their bravery—equally authorial qualities fit for the making of two fantastic travel companions. And when I say *authorial companions*, I do intend to indicate Mr. Hogan, whom I will henceforth refer to as merely Hogan, and myself.

Now, being that there are multiple authors, we realize there is great potential for small amounts of confusion to arise. For instance, one may be reading a passage and wondering all the while, who exactly is responsible, Crowder or Hogan? This could prove to be irritating, in turn, generating the prospect for reading to grow difficult and unsettling.

[Okay. Something terrific just transpired that I must immediately inform you of! Moments ago, while hard at work on this very introduction, an email arrived from the powers that be concerning the cover design of this book. We had been working meticulously with our friend and brilliant designer, Gary Dorsey, on said cover and had reached what we thought to be a climactic zenith of sheer pleasure and excitement when we kindly requested that Gary send it on to the "higher-ups" to see what they thought—you know, see if this thing would sell or not. It seems, despite great claims among the public concerning the necessity of judgment being held in the discussion of books and their respected covers and the goodness or foulness held therein,[2] the consumer's judgment is often fickle, and at times both quick and terrible, when determining exactly what to pluck from a bookstore shelf. And truly, the "higher-ups" know things the rest of us live in the oblivious unawareness of. Things like font types and sizes and which colors said fonts should be in to cause you, the consumer, to instantly feel the need to spend your hard-earned money. Apparently, someone felt my coauthor's name was unnecessarily large, and an appeal for it to shrink in size and for mine to span the entire width of the front of this book was made in the form of an electronic mail message that just entered my inbox. This is due to the wiliness of said powers and their insight into you, the buyer. And if this insight proves true, it renders this introduction a complete and utter waste of your time because you obviously know me. So if in fact you purchased this book due to your astute observation of such a profound moniker

---

2. It seems that the expression "Don't judge a book by its cover" has no traceable origin. According to the *Random House Dictionary of Popular Proverbs and Sayings* by Gregory Y. Titelman (Random House, New York, 1996), this phrase, with the intended meaning of not judging things by their appearance only "originated in the United States"; was "first attested in the journal 'American Speech' (1929)"; and "has been used in Britain since 1954 ('Murder in Haste' by H. Gardiner). The proverb is found in varying forms." So in summary: it appears that misleading covers are a relatively new phenomenon in the history of the written word, and it was most likely some savvy American who authored a sufferable book with a brilliant cover who is at fault.

of consequence as DAVID CROWDER emblazoned across the front of this book in a large, legible font, forgive me my unnecessary introductory ramblings here and please skip immediately to the summation pages of this book beginning on page 246. The bulk of this book is not for you.]

But back to the problem at hand.

As I was noting before the momentary interruption, there are in fact *two* authors. And this, as I previously mentioned, could prove troublesome for the reader, and we most definitely do not wish to be troublesome. So we, the authors, brainstormed a number of possible solutions that might help eliminate confusion as to which of us you are reading. One idea was that any time I was responsible for what you are reading, it would appear in a very large font. And it would follow that anything written by Hogan would appear in a very tiny font. Then there was the clever suggestion that we simply change the title of the book to: *This Book Was Written by David Crowder*. But the twist would be that Hogan would write it. Of course, this would be noted in very tiny letters at the bottom of the cover. So it would look like this: Where the existing title appears, there would be instead—
This Book Was Written by David Crowder.
Then at the bottom, where currently the coauthors' names reside (one in a much larger font than the other), it would read: By Mike Hogan. Then Hogan could write the whole thing, and I could be playing golf right now. Then we came upon the idea that was finally implemented: We would solve the problem by having the foresight to create a bit of space here in the introduction for you to get to know us a little. We would give you insight into our respected characters and personalities. Thus, when you are reading a particular passage, you will have a clearer suspicion of the one responsible. So here goes ...

I am sad. Therefore anytime you read something sad, you should attribute it to me.

Hogan is also sad but less sad, so anything less saddening is mostly his fault.

I have the propensity for inflationary commentary and overexaggeration, so anytime you read something that is too definitively vast or impractically impossible to take in, such as the inestimable depth of sadness in both of the authors, I can be attributed.

Hogan, conversely, has a tendency toward irony and understatement, so when you read something like "David is sad," it is most definitely Hogan who wrote it.

I enjoy tea.

So does Hogan.

So that will be confusing if you encounter something similar to,

> I found myself squinting, while holding a now cold cup of tea that was still shaking in its saucer, outside a rather smallish cafe, and I was attempting a determination as to whether the sun's yellow was welcoming or taunting me. Yellow was too happy a color for today. Something as large as the sun should not be so happy. Not today. And it was spreading its yellow everywhere. And the tea should have still been hot, and there should have been more of it. The cup was easily half empty. Yes, the sun was most definitely taunting.

It would be almost impossible to tell whether Hogan or I had written this except by noting one particular sentence toward the very end pertaining to the cup being half vacant. Most definitely written by Hogan.

He is a pessimist. He often sees things from a "half empty" perspective. Anytime you read something from this jaded, cynical vantage point, it is Hogan.

I, on the other hand, find that the cup is merely too small. It is not the liquid that should be called into question, but the container. It is the whole that is flawed and in need of disposal. The cup should, as a result, be shattered to bits there on the yellow concrete.[3]

Then there is the detail that Hogan is our violinist, DJ, and resident

---

3. At this moment please make quick reference to the few sentences appearing earlier in the introduction suggesting one of the authors holds unhealthy inclinations toward overexaggeration and boasts a predisposition toward drama. The annotated sentence should therefore be reread in light of that.

musicologist. His retention of band names and their respective album releases and the historical impact and implications of such entities on the general public is nothing short of fantastic. His brain works in an archival way of sorts, with the filing and retrieval of these mostly useless[4] bits of information transpiring in such a flurry as to produce an almost audible low humming noise if he leans over and allows you to press your ear against the crown of his head. Therefore, when you find reference to a particular genre of music and the history contained therein, you should initially consider Hogan to be responsible. Unless it is tragically sad. Then it could be either of us.

It hasn't always been like this.

Granted, we can't exactly remember not feeling the weight of this sadness, but I insist there once was a time that we did not. And not to say that there aren't now instances of terrific joy would be one more example of unnecessary drama. But there is most definitely a weight—the suffering weight of a collective grief, perhaps. One might suggest this book is the plain fault of our heads' and hearts' locale over the past number of years. It seems we've been having the same conversations over and over. People in the proximity of our affections keep dying. For a while it seemed cancer was the antagonist. We found ourselves in the cyclical ebb and flow of onsets and remissions, the real-life drama of ignited hopes and extinguishing disappointments, and then eventually we would reach the seemingly inevitable moment of final transpirations. And again there would be the same conversations. Condolences. Commiseration. Hugs and handshakes. Looks of concern and care. Sympathy. We were getting good at these conversations. We could perfectly intonate names in a way that brought calm and assurance while reading them out loud from little white florist cards attached to flowers in the viewing rooms. "Oh. The Smiths. That is so kind of them. _______ just loved them." I began to realize that the flowers were there to distract. At first I fell for it. They stole my eyes from the open casket where my friend or family member lay with their blatant bright greens and reds and yellows and whites and gave me something to look at

---

4. Useless, unless of course you find yourself writing a book pertaining, in some loose sense, to a specific genre of music.

and talk about while my insides strengthened. Then all the rooms started smelling the same. Consequently, it then seemed to me that the flowers were exerting great effort toward filling the room with something of the living but failing miserably at it. It's frightening when you can feel flowers trying too hard. They weren't really alive even. Just acting like it. They were no longer pulling life from the ground and sky, but stuck in a dimly lit room dying next to the dead. And this was supposed to make me feel better.

But cancer had a pace that we had adjusted to. It gave you time to brace for the smell of flowers. Time to get yourself composed and ready.

Then a new antagonist entered our story.

Electricity.

On October 30, 2005, Kyle Lake, my very close friend and pastor of the church I helped start and am still a part of, was electrocuted and died while baptizing a friend of ours during the Sunday morning service. Things inside us began to spill over, and we started collecting them in this book.

We have chosen bluegrass music as a means to discuss death and the soul, our grief and mourning and the resulting hope that was born out of it. Hogan once told me, on a particularly tragic day, that he had a very sinking feeling that there just wasn't much of anything to live for here on Earth. That even the good stuff was so fleeting, so very easily stripped from you, that he felt existence created suffering too great for one planet to contain. He was just being honest and vulnerable in a rather dark moment. Forever the pessimist. But I suggested that maybe it's not that there is not enough here to live for, just that *here* is not enough. Maybe it's the container that's flawed. The thing about grief is that it makes it terribly difficult to see further than the feelings that are in your chest. It sets a tint over your world. Everywhere you look is colored and blurry from the heart's sinking. You say things you wish you could take back. He tried to tell me later that he didn't know what he was saying. That he was just spewing words because he was sad and didn't have any that were lighter than those that landed on me. I'm sure there are more words like the ones that fell from his chest here in these pages, but maybe this book can be your bluegrass.

There is an eschatology[5] to bluegrass music that holds both suffering and hope. Both are inherent and necessary items within it.

And so we begin with a premise: the "high lonesome sound" of bluegrass music was born from pain yet, despite such dismal roots, has hope at its core. We are not scientists; therefore, we are not scientific in the formation or conception of this premise or in the execution of proving it. But we will tell the story of bluegrass. And you can hear that it is truth. That it is, in fact, pain that birthed this high lonesome sound. In the living of life here on earth, there is most assuredly present a large amount of joy, but there is also a given amount of pain. Bluegrass is a shaking, shimmering echo of this—our reality.

Have you ever sat quietly in a dark room with only the green glow of stereo lights cracking the black while Ralph Stanley's voice pours lonely from speakers, moving the molecules of air toward you?[6] You can feel your heart start to fold in on itself as your eardrums unsettle from black stillness into melancholic motion by the changing air pressure, their beating shooting tiny packets of electric pulses sorrowfully through the interior of your skull. Apparently neural impulses travel anywhere from two miles per hour to two hundred miles per hour. Pain impulses travel at the slowest of these speeds. I'm not a scientist, but that's what scientists have measured. They say that the sensation of touch travels faster. They say if you stub your toe, you feel the pressure of the object almost immediately, but the pain doesn't hit until two or three seconds later. I'm not sure that I wholly believe them. I've stubbed my toe and felt the momentary delay before falling fetal to the floor or hopping around on the one good leg contemplating how one tiny portion of my body could provoke such ridiculously large objections, but my perception is that emotional

---

5. **es-cha-tol-o-gy** *n.* the part of theology concerned with death and the final destiny of the soul and of humankind.

6. Odds are you have not. I mean, for one, who does that ...? And secondly there is a good chance you may have even found yourself muttering the words "Who is Ralph Stanley?" while reading that sentence. Personally, I first came upon Ralph's name, not through his music, but through a tattered sticker affixed to a beat-up guitar case. It suggested the following in bright, bold yellow lettering against a firm black background: "Ralph Stanley for President." I am now of the opinion that this is not too terrible of an idea.

pain moves at electric light speed. Here, watch. Think of a person close to you. The *closest* to you. The one you find it most difficult to picture existence without. Then imagine them gone. Gone as in no longer living and breathing the same air as you. Ever. Feel that? It is practically immediate. Heartbreak happens promptly. At electric speed your world is dissolved. But if it's true—that touch travels faster than pain—then maybe we need those around us to pull in close, to beat it to the punch, or to brace us before we're shattered.

Listen to Ralph's voice one night in the dark. You will feel the weight of mortal humanity in it. There is pain in that voice, and it moves fast. Have you heard the banjo of Earl Scruggs? It will quickly break your heart. I promise. Both are voices from a tradition that suffered communally.

This book is a study of grief and the soul. It is a book about the pain that absence can bring. It is about the sharpness of memory that eventually dulls into something we both fear and pray for. It is a book about dying. The kind of corporeal dying that every one of us will one day experience and the kind of dying that must happen at some point before that moment of mortal death in order for true living to begin. Everybody wants to go to heaven, but nobody wants to die. And heaven, if we're to believe what was proposed by a man two thousand years ago, is a kingdom coming and a kingdom here and now; something for the present, not reserved entirely for the ever after. Right now we exist somewhere between here and there, and bluegrass carries the high lonesome song of our condition in its soul. None of us are getting out of here alive, but we will conclude that death is not the ultimate calamity. We will conclude that community is necessary for truly living despite even the pain potentials it creates.

To live solitarily is to be avoided. Touch travels faster than pain. Death does not win. It is the beginning.

PROLOGUE

There are some deaths, which upon occurrence, arrest the considerations of the public at large. There is something concerning them—be it the public visibility of the individual, or the curiously unusual or wholly universal circumstances surrounding the death—that coerces our eyes and empathies in their general direction.

For me, the first cognitive recognition of this phenomenon was while sitting at the bar with my wife at the Red Lobster in Waco, Texas. We were waiting on a table. It was September 1, 1997. The televisions scattered around us announced that an English princess had died. Grief ignited. A planet wept. And I cried right along. Sitting there with cheese sticks and a Dr Pepper, I cried. Which was weird; I didn't really know the princess.

The New York Times reported that the posture of the massive crowds of mourners appeared to hold "something more Latin than British ... the intensity of people's words and actions; a largely Protestant culture that epitomizes restraint and values privacy was galvanized by a need to display its powerful emotions publicly."[1]

---

1. *The New York Times*, September 7, 1997, internatl. ed.: 1.

As a funeral procession advanced through the corridor of overt grief that lined Kensington High Street winding toward Westminster Abbey, we joined the crowd through television sets and radio broadcasts, newspapers and magazines. Physical distance overcome by empathetic proximity, or the transferable nearness of emotional presence. Our conversations became occupied with the grieving of a stranger. Death bringing unity. Uniting us. Pulling us together. If only to bewail someone we did not really know. In excess of a million bouquets, garlands, sprays of flowers, cards, and signs bearing our sentiments lay resting in front of royal palaces. Questions came from the mourners: How could someone attempting such good die so dreadfully in twisted metal and concrete? Did it have to come so unforeseen and immediate? Was this real? Was she really gone? How can she be gone?[2] Their princess who would never be their queen.

Within minutes of four pistol shots being fired outside a New York City apartment located at the corner of Seventy-second Street and Central Park West, crowds gathered outside the historic Dakota residence and the Roosevelt Hospital mourning the death of John Lennon. There was Columbine. There was Oklahoma City. There was another New York day, in another September of a more recent year—more twisted metal and concrete. More crowds. More collective tears.

There are these moments when we all cry at once.

You know how sometimes in the middle of the summer when rain has been scarce and the sun has been hot, the ground dry and cracked, and a storm hits? The water comes fast and in torrents, sounding its arrival with claps of thunder and cracks in the sky. It's all too much for the soil to hold, and then suddenly, violently there is a flood. Grief arrives with this force. It is itself a force, coming on unstoppable, leaving no one safe from it. Once upon a time, we almost drowned from the grief of God.[3]

If the earth were in fact a glass, there are these general instants of grief when it seems too utterly small to contain what is collected

---

2. Kurt Fosso, *Buried Communities*, p. ix.

3. Genesis 6:6-7

among us, and the probability exists that the gathered tears will spill over.

In his book *Buried Communities*, Kurt Fosso writes,

> The loss of a family member or close friend can easily spark a desire for the social possibilities afforded by sharing one's grief with others, particularly when that grief is felt to be burdensome or even unbearable. It seems clear from these social manifestations that for such grief to be shared there must be something common to those who gather together, whether what is imparted is grief for the deceased or the unique problems of grief itself. One widower or widow or friend or neighbor seeks out another for comfort and for the particular kind of social cohesion offered by mutual mourning ... that sense of shared, personal loss.[4]

Commonality is significant to our belonging; to share similar characteristics or homogenous qualities with those around us brings a profound sense of comfort. In a moment of public tragedy it seems it is enough just to be human; that our condition here, situated on planet Earth, with flesh and bone and blood and breath, is a struggle common enough to include us all. A death that captures a public's attention and holds a story line compelling or intimate enough to provoke a public's mourning brings with it assurance of cohesion, declaration that we are not alone in our human experience. If only in the sense that we all have the capacity to bear loss, that we all have the capacity for human attachment, that we can be bound with things invisible to the point that a severing of this invisible bond rips at the heart and pulls at us collectively. It is as if to look around and ask, "Do you feel that? Can you feel these various things coming apart in your chest?" Community erupting from tragedy. It is the need for another to share in loss, to know that the feelings are common, and to give surety that we will somehow be alright.

Due to the bizarre circumstances surrounding it, the death of

---

4. Fosso, p. x.

Kyle Lake and his subsequent burial on All Saints' Day quickly became national news. It was extraordinarily odd to view his name running along the bottom of *Headline News* with the word *electrocuted* following closely behind it. Kyle was not a visible public figure in the same sense as Princess Diana or John Lennon. He was simply the humble pastor of a small church in a fairly small Texas college town. He was the author of two modest-selling books.[5] He was a thirty-three-year-old husband and father of three children—one five-year-old daughter and two three-year-old twin boys with the blondest hair you've ever seen.

There could be nothing that would attract mass media attention outside of the freakish oddity of the way he died. For a pastor to die of electrocution while standing in the Christian symbol of new life was nothing short of paradox. And it was a public death in the most real sense, one transpiring in full view of a wife and congregation who loved him entirely. I'm certain these are the reasons it was picked up by the Associated Press and CNN and why, a few weeks later, my cab driver in Washington, D.C., was asking about it when I mentioned I was from Waco. I, however, chose to believe that the world knew what had been collectively lost that morning, and that's what the fuss was all about. When a person plays a role of such mass and significance in one's life, one assumes that the whole of creation feels the moment of his exit too, that the severing is as severe and deeply felt.

I thought for sure you were sitting in a Red Lobster somewhere crying with me.

---

5. *Understanding God's Will: How to Hack the Equation Without Formulas* (RELEVANT Books, October 31, 2004) released the day after the day he would die a year later. And *(re)Understanding Prayer: A Fresh Approach to Conversation with God* (RELEVANT Books, October 11, 2005).

THE END ...

it was the best day yet. there were still a few solitary clouds left over from the hurricane that had passed through orlando just days before. but now there was sunshine. way more sun than clouds. and it felt good on the skin. the air was just happy. the space around the clouds between the sun and me was full of blue. the deepest of blue. and where the blue met the ground, the grass was perfect. i could feel the blades folding under my shoes. giving in to my weight and letting off with vivid clarity the distinct golfing smell of crushed green as i walked toward the pyramid pile of balls. the molecules around me were inventive and resourceful. pulling from all of these things to amend the surface of my feelings. pulling them up from my dulled insides to the more susceptible exterior of my person until the most minuscule hairs on the outermost portions of my skin were acute and ready. i could feel everything. my friends shane, jack, and jason were with me. our movements were animation. our expressions painterly. someone ... an artiste of immense capabilities ... had whipped this day up. my heart hovered in ascendance. it was rising in my chest. i pulled out my nine iron and scooted a ball along the short tattered grass toward me. i watched as jason swung and his ball flew against the blue that was in between the clouds and the sun and me.

"this is going to be great," i said. and i meant it. completely. *great* was such a ridiculous word, but it was all i had. and i believed 100 percent that today would be an exceptionally brilliant day. then my phone rang ...

HISTORY OF THE SOUL

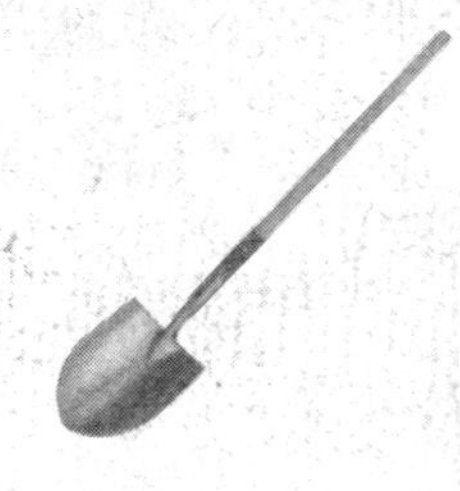

— PART 1 —

PHILOSOPHICAL JOURNEY TO THE CENTER OF THE SOUL

or

The Weight Is a Gift, Part 1

The opening statement of a rather large, intimidating volume called *Flesh in the Age of Reason*, by one Roy Porter, reads as follows:

> Who are we?
>
> Our contemporary Western secular sense of identity stems directly from transformations occurring in the centuries since the Renaissance. These developments are often characterized as the "death of the soul"; but inseparable from such a process, and no less salient, has been the reappraisal of the body. The two have been symbiotic in the refiguring of the self.[1]

If you are able to sift through the quote without the use of a dictionary and a college professor, you'll be able to get the gist of what this mammoth book is all about, namely the "death of the soul,"

---

1. Roy Porter, *Flesh in the Age of Reason*, page 2.

the rise in importance of the physical body, and how those two things together have become the lynchpins of the ever-evolving pastime of self-discovery. Or more simply, "Who are we?" Seeing as how Porter passed on before the book was published, we can only hope that he found what he was looking for.

But that question—*Who are we?*—holds a lot of weight. Sometimes the answer is simple. If you ask a group of thirteen-year-old girls dressed in matching cheerleader uniforms who they are, they will most likely give you the answer you would expect, though with a little more spunk and eye rolling than necessary. But if you were to ask the same question to a university philosophy student, the answer would become more complex.[2] All in all, it's just an awkward topic. Perhaps it's because most of us don't spend a vast amount of time contemplating the soul. And why would we? We already have more distraction in our lives than we can shake a stick at (which would only serve to add yet another diversion, that of stick-shaking).

What Porter's opening statement does, however, is beg the question: is the soul really dead? And it's not just Porter who has made note of this. It is by no means a new sentiment. But if it is true, if we live in a society that has lost its belief in the soul of man, it changes everything, both for the living and the dying. So, in an attempt to sort this one out, let's look at a brief history of the soul.

To avoid this becoming too academic or dry, try thinking of what follows as an adventure movie through history or one of those Magic School Bus programs that the kindergarten kiddos seem to enjoy, only with the ghost of Roy Porter peering over our shoulders. So here goes ...

THE MAGIC SCHOOL BUS AND THE JOURNEY THROUGH THE HISTORY OF THE HUMAN SOUL![3]

---

2. Yet equally annoying.

3. Hogan's wife, who is currently a teacher in the public school system, informs us that the Magic School Bus books are, in fact, popular amongst the kids but difficult to read in a group setting. There are apparently small bits of information scattered throughout, making the pages dense and complex. The same may be said here.

THE BEGINNING: Primitive man is thought to have a tribal mentality, making authentic individuality impossible. This is because every aspect of life is seen through the eyes of the community. Magic and the supernatural apparently played a big part. (Centuries later, some of these aspects will be acquired as buzzwords for the emerging church. Buzzwords to follow would be: *Socratic, Midrash, metanarrative, coffee, candle*, and *Guinness* to name a few.[4])

THE GOLDEN AGE OF GREECE: Individual consciousness emerges. Ideals of goodness and truth abound in the teachings of Socrates and other philosophers of the day. Although it sounds good at first, people start to get their feathers all ruffled because this does not jive with their traditional communalistic thoughts. The advanced and progressive Athenian government, which was no small influence on our great nation, executes Socrates by forcing him to drink the poison hemlock. (Interesting to note, hemlock comes from a plant called *Cicuta virosa*, a perennial with little white flowers that cluster in the shape of an umbrella. Inside the stalk and roots of the flower is a yellow resin from which the poison is made that is said to smell of parsnips, carrots, or mice. The poison affects the central nervous system and causes abdominal pain and vomiting. We would wager that sucking on a mouse would inflict similar symptoms.)

In the art world, Sophocles, Euripides, and other guys with last names ending in "es" wrote long dramas where everybody dies in the end, usually because the main character had the gall to step out and do something *on his own* rather than listen to the gods. These are called tragedies, not only because every character meets with dismal doom, but also because every high-school student in America is forced to read them and to learn applicable vocabulary such as *hubris*.[5]

THE AGE OF FAITH: Christianity begins its spread across the world. On the one hand, this is a huge advancement for the soul. Life after death? Sounds good. On the other hand, the early Catholic

---

4. Zinger #1.

5. Zinger #2. Could it be the authors' own hubris that subjects you to such jokes? Only the gods truly know!

Church wasn't so keen on this whole self-exploration thing for the sake of self-exploration. The way they saw it: original sin occurred because of an individual desire of forbidden knowledge.

It didn't help that the medieval period was in full swing, and along with it, the whole caste system of master and servant, lord and serf, blah, blah, blah. The upside of this time period? Sweet architecture and stories of knights and chivalry. The downside? Modern-day man will read *The Da Vinci Code* and traipse around European churches of the period wearing fanny packs and ignoring the "No Pictures, Please" signs.[6]

THE RENAISSANCE AND THE REFORMATION: At the same time Columbus was busy discovering the New World, the Renaissance was getting under way in Italy. "Man" (Porter makes a note here to confirm that *man* means literate, gifted, elite males, and I am not one to argue with him) begins to make great strides in self-discovery by deciding he has *had it up to here* with the Church, conformity, and the customs of his forefathers. In modern times, this would be the equivalent of your older sister going off to her first year of college and coming home over Christmas break for the first time with dyed black hair, a nose ring, a book on Buddhism, and some newfound contempt for the way she was raised.

During this time, mankind puts himself on a pedestal as the pinnacle of creation, master of the world. New forms of self-centered art like the self portrait and the autobiography emerge.

Meanwhile, Martin Luther was busy with the Reformation. Rather than killing the soul off, the reformers were busy adapting the soul for the newly shaped world of personal self-expression by suggesting that salvation came from a personal journey and faith. Cessation or adaptation. The soul was torn in two directions, which must have hurt.

---

6. Zinger #3. We are on a roll, here!

IM CONVERSATION 1

hey I've got an idea! **:DAVID**

HOGAN: OK

ok, so we have the soul stuff and the bluegrass stuff, right? **:DAVID**

HOGAN: Yeah

and there will be columns **:DAVID**

HOGAN: Yeah

well we could include an instant message exchange **:DAVID**

HOGAN: What do you mean?

we could put stuff like this exchange in. you know just put this stuff before the columns **:DAVID**

HOGAN: What stuff?

stuff we'll write. **:DAVID**

HOGAN: What would be the point?

to discuss stuff. you know, put some pieces together. **:DAVID**

HOGAN: It doesn't seem like including this exchange would be putting anything together.

yeah it would. we would have just told the reader that we're including instant message exchanges. **:DAVID**

HOGAN: The reader would know that already.

what? **:DAVID**

HOGAN: If you're reading an instant message, you don't need to be told you're reading an instant message exchange.

yeah you do. **:DAVID**

HOGAN: No you don't. It's like watching television and the television says, "you're watching television."

no, it's like watching television and it says, "you're reading a book." **:DAVID**

HOGAN: What?

and then we could explain that at times the real thoughts of you or me could break in. **:DAVID**

HOGAN: What do you mean by real thoughts?

you know, what we're really thinking. **:DAVID**

HOGAN: So far I have typed everything that I am really thinking.

This is a ridiculous idea. But if I disagree he'll probably just write the book by himself.

no. you know how there is always a given amount of posturing in any exchange of language **:DAVID**

always trying to present your best self, even when you're supposedly being vulnerable **:DAVID**

being vulnerable just to look good. **:DAVID**

HOGAN: No, I think it's a great idea.

but in instant messaging you don't have as much time to put your best foot forward. you know you say things you regret. **:DAVID**

HOGAN: Yeah, like earlier when I was acting like this might not be such a great idea. I think it's a great idea.

It's really a pretty pathetically obvious literary device. So I guess "instant message" could be the new "letter of correspondence." I'd like to know the number of books that have supposed "letters" in them. An author wants to write in first person, draw the reader in, so ... here comes a letter.

it would be sort of like using a letter. **:DAVID**

HOGAN: I love it when there are letters in a book. A really clever literary device, the letter.

yeah! yeah! I LOVE LETTERS!!! **:DAVID**

HOGAN: Yeah, me too.

but then you know if we let ourselves write what we're really thinking in bold or something **:DAVID**

you know and italicize it **:DAVID**

or something so the reader knows it's not part of the instant message exchange **:DAVID**

HOGAN: Yeah, that's a really good idea.

Thanks a ton for the suggestion. You're an absolute genius for thinking of something so glaringly obvious that I'd already done it.

i'm really excited about this. **:DAVID**

HOGAN: So should we say anything about the first chapters then?

what do you mean? **:DAVID**

HOGAN: Well you suggested that the exchange serve as a means to discuss the previous content?

yeah, but i think if we explain that we're doing this instant message thing we'll have done enough. no need to become overly ambitious. **:DAVID**

HOGAN: Well I think we're safe then.

what do you mean? **:DAVID**

HOGAN: I don't think we've been too ambitious here.

we don't have to do this if you don't want to. **:DAVID**

HOGAN: No. I think it's a great idea

Please tell me there's not going to be a letter in here somewhere.

ok **:DAVID**

HISTORY OF BLUEGRASS

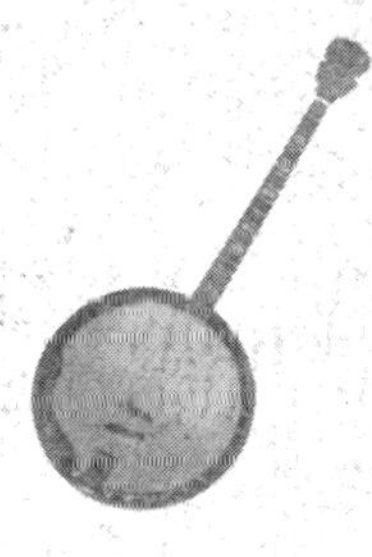

— PART 1 —

AN INTRODUCTION TO BLUEGRASS

or

The Perils and Trials of Transatlantic Voyages

"Oh God, please help me! Someone help me!" He was turned sideways in his seat, eyes wide, nose crinkled up in a ball of wrinkles and nostrils, with a mouth performing the impossible feat of frowning, grinning, and gaping open in slack-jawed astonishment all at once. "Seriously, *what is that*? Can you smell this woman next to me?"

The woman in question was a large, spherical lady of undetermined age and ethnicity that was wedged in the seat next to them on an overcrowded plane flight over international waters. Their friend Jeremy's voice was the one heard pleading through the din of boarding passengers in gag-whispered, scarcely discernible utterances for intervention. If invited to wager a guess, they would have put forward she was German. They have known a good number of Germans, all of which seemed well groomed, free of offensive odors, and very good at math for some reason. Not only was the woman in question the antithesis of well groomed, but there was serious doubt as to whether she could crunch differential equations or explain the complexities of "nozzles," which one of Hogan's old roommates (an engineering major) happily did at all hours of the day. *He* was German. Maybe.

The matter simplified itself a little when, shortly after the thickening ether around them had been duly noted, the round woman grunted, shifted faintly in her seat, and, as if by magic, pulled from thin air and opened a plastic container containing ... brown. Who knows what this "food" stuff was? But the best description was: brown. The air blossomed with a whole new catalog of odors. Now they were the ones gagging a modest amount at the pungent assortment of body odor, mysterious hints of chili-cheese Fritos, and the insinuation of festering stool, all in a garlicky base. At that exact moment it became clear that she was in no way German. No, what they were dealing with was distinctly Eastern European.

And the flight to London had barely even gotten under way.

The aforementioned, while true, has absolutely no real bearing on the story. To be honest, it happened two years prior to this story's beginning. But there are two reasons it is mentioned here. The first is that the woman portrayed above did in fact smell awful, and she did indeed indulge in an enigmatic cuisine off and on over the course of eight hours that made them long to swallow their own tongues. She also snored. This is funny, and anyone who is capable of putting out such an odor as to still be remembered years later deserves to be honored in print. The second reason is to show just one of the laundry list of perils (one being: Forced Proximal Travel Companions) a person can experience while traveling to a different country.

If you're lucky, you're the type of person who can step foot on a plane, fall asleep, and have no recollection of the suffering taking place around you. The cramped legs, sore backs, bad food, worse in-flight movies, and, of course, Slovakian gasbags. The authors, however, are neither lucky nor do they have the foresight or fortitude for prescription pills thrown back with mini adult beverages and are therefore forever doomed to suffer slouching in uncomfortable seats, eyes peeled open, lower backs screeching in pain, and nostrils at the ready. For them, the plane ride from Dallas to Great Britain seemed to

take

for-

everrrr.

You can imagine their enthusiasm for a whirlwind three-day trip to Scotland knowing the following was in store: Get on a plane. Get off a plane in a foreign land. Attempt sleep a few hours. Play music. Attempt to sleep a few more hours. Get back on a plane. Get off a plane. Go home. Now, don't think there wasn't excitement at having the opportunity to play a show in Scotland, because there was. They were more worried about the next few days of their lives becoming a blur or disappearing completely from their memory in a jet-lagged haze, as they found themselves waking up back in Texas wondering what the heck happened and, more importantly, where the plaid woolen scarf came from.

Hogan had been to Scotland once before on a family vacation when he was about ten. His memories include a cluster of fluffy sheep, Jefferson Starship blaring from a pub's jukebox, and very, very cold water in Loch Ness. He was therefore surprised to find that on their descent into Edinburgh it looked nothing at all like a foreign land. In fact, it looked downright ordinary. It could have just as easily been North Carolina. Nothing against North Carolina, mind you; it's quite a lovely state, and they make a great peanut brittle. Or is that North Dakota? Or Kentucky? It's Kentucky.[1]

Maybe if there had been tiny sheep dotting the landscape like cotton balls. Maybe if his in-flight iPod playlists had included Jefferson Starship. Maybe if Nessy herself had met them at the tarmac with a bag of golf clubs in one flipper and haggis in the other, perhaps then Hogan would have recalled the childlike wonder he thought he had at age ten. Regardless, they hadn't slept in twenty-four hours, their eyes were still watering from the whole Slovakian encounter, and here they were, after all of that suffering, in North Carolina.

---

1. Kentucky also produces the fine beverage Ale 8-one, which tastes like an alternative version of ginger ale. The logo is simple and appealing, and has appeared in grocery stores across the bluegrass state as well as on a T-shirt worn by the main character in Cameron Crowe's film *Elizabethtown*, which is incidentally sort of about death. Weird how that all fits together, isn't it? Oh wait, you don't know yet. Sorry.

Things began to look up when the guy who was to retrieve them from the airport arrived.

Enter Justin Dowd, a large, full-bodied Scotsman whose accent sounded remarkably like a mix between Mike Myers' father in *So I Married an Axe Murderer* ("Look at the size of that kid's head ... it's like an orange on a toothpick!") and Groundskeeper Willy from *The Simpsons* ("Arrrgh, that's ma retirement grease!"). His job, at least at the moment, was to take the band and their gear to the hotel where they could slumber away their transatlantic hangover. He did his job capably, with enthusiasm and then some. Along the way he treated them to a discussion on the rising property values of the Scottish countryside, why small British cars are the way to go, and why most Scots have a vendetta against Mel Gibson. ("A few years ago a monument of William Wallace was erected in the town, which just so happens to look exactly like Mel Gibson! People come from all over the world to see one of our national treasures, one of the greatest Scots in history, and what do they get? An Australian in a kilt! *Bah!*")

When you meet a guy like this, you can't help but ask a batch of pointless questions, like "What do you guys think of the Irish?" Frankly, it is difficult to say who asked him this or why, but it seemed important at the time. He delivered his retort straightaway with great passion: "Oh, we love the Irish. Celtic brothers, ya know!"

Errr, well, no. But the authors took his word for it. He was so passionate they had no choice. (This is a Scottish quality. Even when you can't make out a word, you find yourself nodding in agreement. For example: "Eh, would you enjoy a bite of this baked sheep's stomach filled with its own intestines and heart? It's a delicacy!" Response: "Yeah, sure, sounds amazing! I have absolutely no idea what you just said!" Fork to mouth.)

The Scots and the Irish have a long and storied history. On many occasions the two have come together over a mutual loathing of the English and their monarchy. It's a history that involves fighting, farming, dancing, oceanic travel, persecution, hardship, and the creation of what would become one of America's most influential and unique art forms: bluegrass.

IM CONVERSATION 1.1

HOGAN: So what should we say about the columns?

what would you say? **:DAVID**

HOGAN: I don't know.

no. this is great. i don't think we need anything about the columns. **:DAVID**

I feel a weight when I think about the columns.

HOGAN: I hear music when I think about the columns

really!? **:DAVID**

HOGAN: I don't know, it's weird. Every time I think about the columns, I hear a cello.

that's really weird **:DAVID**

HOGAN: I know.

HOGAN: I wish we could write musical notes into the pages that would play what I'm hearing for the reader while they were reading it.

maybe we could. it could be like watermarking. you know, in the page, but not visible. i've already asked if we can get that special icelandic paper. **:DAVID**

HOGAN: What did they say?

they said it would be tough and would depend on the number of illustrations, for pricing and such. **:DAVID**

HOGAN: We need that Icelandic paper man!

i know. you can feel the weeping under your fingers. **:DAVID**

HOGAN: Let's use it only in the column sections.

yeah! hooray for icelandic paper! holding weeping and music. **:DAVID**

I hear cello too.

COLUMNS, PART 1

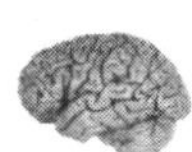
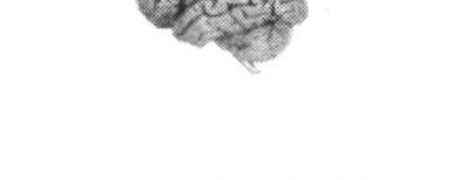

"I CAN'T FIND A PEN."

She said this while opening and closing the drawer closest to the sink. The one that held the forks and knives and other various shiny pointed things.

"Why is she looking in the silverware drawer?"

Sarah whispered this across the table to her friend Daniel, who was sitting with his arms folded. He was smiling. This was obviously funny to him.

HE OPENED HIS EYES. THE sun was bright coming through the curtains. They weren't curtains really. Just long clear pieces of plastic hanging from the nails he had hammered in a perfectly straight line above the 3 windows of the bedroom. The nails were spaced exactly 3 inches apart. One window faced east. Two were side by side facing the south. The eastern window was the largest: 7 feet tall. 7 feet wide. That meant there were exactly 28 nails above it. The southern windows were each 7 feet tall. 4

ONCE, LONG AGO,
there was a little boy named Steven.

In those days, Steven was not such a common name. In fact, so far as forenames were concerned, he was the first.

No, up to this point there had never been another him; he was something the New World had never seen.

Now, there are lots of Stevens. You probably know one even.

"She means to say *fork*."

Daniel most definitely thought it humorous that his grandmother was saying *pen* while referring to a fork. Finding it amusing helped. He could choose humor or sadness when the confusion came, but the two were getting harder to tell apart.

"They're in the dishwasher, Grandma."

"What?"

"I said, 'They're in the dishwasher!' We're out of forks! You'll have to get one out and

feet wide. That meant there were 16 nails above each of them. The foot of his bed was closest to the eastern window. The light coming through it was just now touching the tops of both of his feet. Which meant the day could begin. The radiance on his feet is what woke him each morning. If it were overcast he would not wake. Once it rained for 14 days straight. That was the last time he could remember his feet having had the time to heal. Through the plastic he could feel the heat of the light. Soothing what it touched. That's why the curtains were clear. To let the light in. He took a deep breath. He held it for 4 seconds. He reached over

But this particular boy was the beginning.

No past.

Only future.

Steven's favorite color was grey, but to be fair, it should be pointed out that it was the only color the little boy could see. It came, of course, in all shades, but it was still grey nonetheless—light grey skies with dark grey clouds and a lighter grey sun. If you were to ask him, "Steven what is your favorite color," he would most assuredly answer, "Grey. Grey is my favorite!" He knew no better.

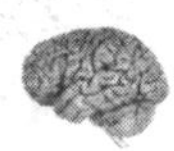

wash it in the sink."

She scowled in their direction. She could tell Daniel thought this was hilarious, despite his trying to hide it.

The stroke had rearranged her memory. The places she had formerly stored words and their respected meanings had been reordered in a way dissimilar to what had existed previously.

"You can't be serious?" Sarah whispered.

"Yeah. It's weird. There's a medical word for it, but I can't remember it."

and touched the nightstand 4 times. He loved this part of the day. When he was awake but his feet weren't yet on the ground. He swung them over to his right until they were hanging off the southern side of the bed. He let them fall slowly toward the floor. The bottoms of them came to rest against the fresh white towel he had laid out the night before. And which would now be stained red. His jaw muscles tightened. He never got used to this moment of pain. Deciding to put his feet on the ground. The thought crossed his mind that it hurt as badly now as it did in the beginning. He smiled. The look on his face was that of complete and utter

He had the bluest of eyes; he would, of course, describe them as *light grey*.

People would tell him, "Little boy, there is no grey; there is only black and white."

"I don't think it's that simple," he would quickly respond, for he knew—obviously—that the black necessitated the complete absence of light and the light—obviously—was everywhere ... that is, if you looked hard enough.

The little boy Steven had the same dream every night. He

The word he could not locate
was *aphasia*.

"So, like, how many words are
messed up?"

"I don't know; it keeps
changing. And there's getting to
be more and more. It's hard to
keep up."

"That's just crazy!"

"No, it's for real. It's like a
system of filing drawers or
something. It's as if you put a
word away, stuck it in a drawer
so you'd know right where it
was when you needed it, but

satisfaction. A tear fell down his left cheek. He clapped his hands 4 times and stood up. He felt his perpendicular weight settle into the towel as it soaked up the fluids that had gathered overnight. He looked at his hands. Still stinging from the 4 quick claps. He shook them. He pulled open the top drawer of the nightstand. It was full of thin cellophane packages of stark white gloves. Stacked 7 deep. In 3 rows. He touched the top of each stack 1 time. He picked up the top plastic package on the right. He broke the seal. He pulled the white gloves out and laid them down side by side on the nightstand. He tenderly stepped on the silver pedal of

would fall asleep and dream he was awakened, right as the dawn was breaking. He would be falling through the light grey sky, through darker grey clouds, toward the even darker grey ground. He could see the light grey faces of thousands of people staring up at him. And as he fell further and further, as they screamed closer and closer, as soon as he could see into the deep blacks of their pupils, a thought would blister into his little boy mind:

"They were wrong. There is no black and white ... There is only black."

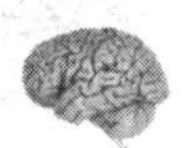

then, while you weren't looking, someone came and moved the drawers around. They look like the same drawers, but the one that was on the top is now on the bottom. So if you wanted that particular item that you had stuck in the top drawer, you'd go right to the place you *knew* you'd put it and you'd open the drawer, but there'd be something else in it. You're *sure* you're at the right place, but you also suspect you've got the wrong thing. But you keep closing and opening that same drawer because that's where it's supposed to be. Make sense?"

"No! Not a bit. That is so weird!"

the silver can that sat next to the nightstand and tossed the empty cellophane in. He watched as it floated down to rest on top of the others. He loved this sound. Of cellophane landing. Crinkling softly. The silver can was getting full. Mary would have to empty it soon. He let the lid fall closed. He stared at the two white gloves sitting on the nightstand. He reached down. Picked up the one on the right. His jaw clenched. Carefully he slid it on. He took the other glove and slid it on. He clapped 4 times, then began to disrobe. Folding his previous night's clothes. Creasing them neatly before placing them on top of the linen-less bed. Mary, the

Then one night, immediately following this thought, there was a flash, as the world burst alive into vivid color. For an instant his insides filled with dark reds. Brilliant oranges. Glowing greens. Color. It was everywhere. But it was too late. He fractured there over the city, splitting apart, draping his grey over everything. Grey upon grey upon grey. The light went out as he thought to himself, "We shall finally perish here together in the black."

From that night on, every time he dreamt, he would get a glimpse of a world different than the one he took in during his

Daniel watched as his grandmother leaned over the dishwasher; it was gapping open like a mouth in awe at her.

She used to be brilliant. Taught advanced microeconomic theory in the city, a tenured professor at NYU's Stern School of Business, was published, had retired only a few years ago.

"I'm going to university. You kids behave."

Her mouth sort of melted away on the left side. About a quarter of an inch before the upper lip met the bottom lip, it just fell

house's keeper, would later come take these items. They would be washed and ready again by day's end. He walked to the closet wearing only white gloves. He opened it. There were 4 hangers. On each hung the vestments of his profession. Intricate in their heaviness. Understatedly ornate. No subtlety in what the robes conveyed. He began the slow ritual of dawning the heavy cloth. We are not allowed to describe the formal procedures here only to say there is more to it than just putting on a robe. In everything there is meaning. That is worth noting. He walked to the door. There were two jars. One full of pebbles. One full of nettles of

waking hours. The limits of his waking senses were becoming a weight.

Then one night, he fell into sleep and refused to wake up.

And that's how the rest of the world formally turned grey.

But there were more Stevens coming, more who would dream the same dream. But as the world of grey aged, the dreams of the Stevens grew further and further apart.

Until one day, they stopped. Then, on June 10, 1972, a little boy by the name of Steven was

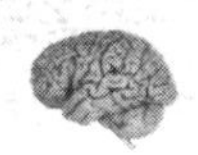

limp at the corner—one corner
animated, projecting a smile
that you literally felt, the other
corner dead, immobile. Sarah
was staring at the deadened,
half-frown section a bit too
intently and became conscious
of her rudeness just as Daniel's
grandmother's mouth opened,
and the pen/fork disappeared
into it with some white food
substance.

"She means *bed*."

"What?"

"She said *university*, but she
meant *bed*."

the common cocklebur variety. He took 4 pebbles from the jar of pebbles. And dropped them into the shoe on the right. He did the same for the shoe on the left. He stepped into them. He took 4 nettles from the nettle jar. And dropped them down the glove on his right hand. He flicked and jolted until all 4 came to rest against his palm inside the glove. He then did the same for the left. He clapped 4 times. And walked out. Into the daylight.

born in a tiny town, in the middle of the tall trees of eastern Texas.

The first thing he did when he got there was cry. This would not have been a problem and seemed quite an un-extraordinary thing at the time—seeing as this is how we all come here—(which should maybe tell us something about what we're in for), but when this particular Steven cried, birds fell from the sky.

It is the truth. When little Steven's cheeks were wet with tears, the ground echoed with the thuds of falling dead birds.

For each tear a bird.

HISTORY OF THE SOUL

— PART 2 —

THE CONTINUED PHILOSOPHICAL JOURNEY TO THE CENTER OF THE SOUL

or

The Weight Is a Gift, Part 2

THE ENLIGHTENMENT: René Descartes is sitting in a small room with a stove, doing some serious navel-gazing in the seventeenth century, when he comes up with this: "I think, therefore I am." For people who cared, this was apparently a very big deal. Frankly, we're surprised it took someone so long to come up with the phrase. In a delicious bit of irony, this same axiom would go on to be the butt of many a joke amongst students and Bugs Bunny cartoons. That said, Bugs Bunny was highly self-aware, so maybe it isn't that ironic.

In what Porter (yeah, he's still with us) calls a "subplot" during this era, the act of public confession became popular. He uses the example of Jean-Jacques Rousseau, a neurotic who would have been a handful for any therapist, whose autobiography is called *Confessions*. Because Rousseau "knew his heart" and therefore felt obligated to share it with everyone, he was the doorway to every other poet and artist who thought that their lives were interesting enough to bare all to the world. Porter describes this act as "a compulsion for self-exposure that has released, in a great act of homage, a never-ceasing confessional stream, from the poets, artists and geniuses of the Romantic era through to our latter-day drunks, drifters, drug-addicts, drop-outs, and depressives. Confession was thereby transformed from an office of the church into an affirmation of the 'will to truth' of the sacred sovereign self within."[1]

This may be an appropriate time to call old Porter into question. First off, while his use of vocabulary and his penchant for overly long sentence structure is admirable (truly it is), the further we get into this, the more it appears he may be writing words for the sake of seeing himself write words, and therefore producing a book that weighs (no kidding) a good couple of pounds. Normally this would be forgivable, but there is an item or two in that last quotation that really raises suspicion. How many crank-addicted, high-school dropout, train-hopping bipolar hobos do you see who are honestly paying homage to a Romantic era writer when they are asking you for spare change to buy a forty of malt liquor? Exactly. Roy Porter, consider yourself on the list. A big wag of the finger to you, sir.[2]

ROMANTICISM: The Romantic era gave us some of the best, most inspired, Western music there is. And by Western, we don't mean country. We aren't there yet. That comes a little later. This is the stuff you hear on the radio stations lower down the dial, the ones you flip past while in search of the latest single from Nickelback[3] or Kelly Clarkson.[4] We're talking Brahms and Mahler. Guys who wrote monster symphonies that take hours to perform, ones that marry great depth of emotion with superior technical ability. Incidentally, these guys were (nods to Porter) all doing some pretty heavy soul-searching. A good example is the Russian composer Tchaikovsky, who was so racked with intense guilt about his own homosexuality that he attempted to commit suicide via wading into a cold river after having

---

1. Porter.
2. Finger wagging inspired by Stephen Colbert.
3. If indeed you are searching for Nickelback, then a big wag of the finger to you, too.
4. We do, however, love us some Kelly Clarkson! Yes. We said it!

given marriage (to a woman) a go. His attempt was unsuccessful. But these inner conflicts were the springboard for some of the greatest music ever composed.

Tchaikovsky was in good company, as Frankenstein's monster was also roaming about town at this time, wading through some comparably weighty emotional baggage. Just a couple of bohemians looking for peace in an uncaring, unfeeling universe. It kind of pulls at the ol' heartstrings, huh?[5]

While Russian composers were crying themselves to sleep at night, those in the philosophical world were having a heyday with drugs and absinthe. Nietzsche came on the scene officially declaring, "God is dead." We guess this means that according to thinkers, so was the soul. Many years later, a friend of Hogan would wear a shirt to school that read "God is dead. —Nietzsche" and below that "Nietzsche is dead. —God." We may not have a soul anymore (and just to make sure of that, Dr. Faust went ahead and sold his to the devil[6]), but our sense of humor rages on unchecked.

In other news, we see the emergence of Sigmund Freud, which should bring a shared sigh of relief. He blew that whole "I think, therefore I am" thing out of the water by discovering the subconscious, finally relieving us all from the burden of responsibility for all the dumb crap we do—and want.

TWENTIETH CENTURY: Existentialism becomes very popular. Go ahead and look this one up for yourself. It's just too depressing to write about, and we need to save our strength for what's coming.

EARLY 1980s: Hogan is in first or second grade when his father dies. His memories are thus: A neighbor escorts him to the

---

5. If there isn't a B-movie out there about this odd-couple pairing, then there should be. In the unlikely case there is not, it is hereby claimed and documented that the idea was first seen here. Picture it now, the monster in his black suit with the bolts in his neck, speaking in broken phrases; Tchaikovsky in a grey tweed suit, pen and parchment at the ready in case a melody came to him—both roaming the European countryside encountering lively adventure while trying to come to terms with their inner selves. Themes of self-discovery and friendship, of overcoming political and social adversity would abound, giving the movie not only action, but also poignant layers of meaning. It has summer blockbuster written all over it.

6. It is the authors' assumption that he figured he didn't need it anymore.

open house at his elementary school. Some relatives come and stay at his house. At the funeral he rides in a limo for the first time and, honestly, thinks it's pretty cool. His mother's church friends come by to visit him and make sure that he's doing all right. One of them gives him a book titled *Heaven Has a Floor* by Evelyn Roberts, which has illustrations and tells the reader that heaven's gates are made of pearls and that the streets are made of gold. His own personal theology is shaped by this for years to come, and he assumes that all souls will eventually live in a mansion and walk around in sandals on golden tiles. He's not sure if he ever cries.

MID-1990s: One of Hogan's childhood best friends is sitting at his desk at home, making one of those annoying mums that guys give to girls for homecoming. He drops dead, the victim of a rare virus of the heart—one in which the odds of contracting and dying from it are like one in a million. Hogan is told this news while in his German class by a guy who sits next to him, a kid he never even liked. The disliked kid gives the news in the flippant tone of all teenage boys, "Hey, did you hear about that guy who just keeled over last night? He went to ______ High. Name was _____ something or other." At the funeral Hogan cries for the first time that he can remember. Not for the loss of a friend, but for the injustice of the whole thing.

AUGUST 1999: The worst week of Hogan's life thus far goes down like this: The girl he is dating gives him the heave-ho right before he leaves for college after summer break. The mother of one of his good friends loses an epic battle with breast cancer. He gets a phone call asking if he can transport his friend's black suit from Dallas to San Antonio for the funeral. Hogan leaves the next day. He stops in Waco, the halfway point, at his apartment to spend the night. He is sitting in his living room talking to his roommate when the phone rings. His roommate picks it up and shortly thereafter collapses to the floor upon hearing news that one of their best friends, along with two other acquaintances, has died in a car accident. The next day he continues on to San Antonio to deliver a suit and attend a funeral. He doesn't shed a single tear. This is the way life goes, *right???*

EARLY PART OF THE MILLENNIUM: On *The Simpsons*, Bart sells his soul to best friend Milhouse for five dollars. Homer sells his soul to the devil for a doughnut.

JANUARY 2005: Hogan and his wife eat Mexican food for lunch, and later that night find themselves in the hospital because his wife has kidney stones. Not only will she be wary of Mexican food from here on out, she is in the worst pain of her life, doubled over and vomiting because it hurts so badly. While the doctor takes her in to get X-rayed, her father calls to tell Hogan that his wife's grandmother has just had a stroke and died. He has no idea what to do.

SEPTEMBER 2005: The band that the authors of this book play in record and release a record about death. They tell death that they are not scared. It just seems appropriate. They hit the road to go on tour.

OCTOBER 30, 2005: On a Sunday morning at a club in Orlando, Florida, Hogan receives a call from his wife, who is so hysterical that she cannot talk. She hands the phone to a guy Hogan does not know, who tells him what has happened. Again, he has no idea what to do.

The band flies home for the funeral of their friend, where for the first time Hogan cries. And it's not just for this death, but it's for his father, for his friends, for his friend's mother, for his wife's grandmother. He tries to hold on to the composure that he has perfected and nourished his entire life. He tries really, really hard. But it is too much. All he can do is bury his head in his wife's shoulder and completely fall apart.

MAY 2006: Hogan is sitting at his kitchen table with a pile of books. Writing all of this down, he can't seem to get the sound of his wife's voice out of his head, the sound of her telling him not a week ago on the way home from church that Sundays give her the blues. Not because work is coming the next day, but because something about Sundays just isn't right anymore. As they exited the highway, she turned to him and said, "I just don't think I ever grieved properly."

She's right. We don't. None of us do. Maybe part of the reason is that we missed the soul's quiet exit. It died while we were away in Orlando or some other far-off land. And of course, that makes it uncomfortable and awkward for us while we are standing next to the spot of ground that will soon hold the one we love. We need the details. We need someone to tell us how it happened. We need it recounted. All of it.

IM CONVERSATION 2

so what do you remember about your dad? **:DAVID**

HOGAN: Not a lot. He had dark hair, a mustache.

how old were you? **:DAVID**

HOGAN: First or second grade. Second, I think. That would have made me like 7, maybe 8 years old.

huh. there's a lot that is really vivid for me in the second grade **:DAVID**

HOGAN: Weird. I can hardly remember anything from second grade. I try to think of what my classroom looked like, but then it just becomes a mix of first and third grade. Like the entire year at school vanished.

yeah that's weird **:DAVID**

actually i guess i don't remember a ton, but what i do is really vivid. **:DAVID**

that was the year of the dewey decimal system and multiplication tables. and the balloon launch! i tied with this girl for the most balloons. we got t-shirts. **:DAVID**

and i can remember exactly where i was sitting. **:DAVID**

Some details you never forget. Other things remain forever elusive and un-retainable. Like—what was the last conversation I had with Kyle? I can't remember.

HOGAN: Wow. The only thing school-related I've got is the night of open house. Our neighbors, who had a son my age at the same school, went in place of my parents. She talked to all of my teachers because my mom was at the hospital.

I felt special that night. I felt I was getting a lot of attention ... it was just pity from teachers hearing the news ...

HOGAN: Everything else is completely gone.

how did your dad die? **:DAVID**

HOGAN: Double pneumonia, I think.

what!? **:DAVID**

what is double pneumonia? **:DAVID**

and what do you mean, you think!? **:DAVID**

you don't know how your dad died!!? **:DAVID**

That is so weird. My head would never allow for that. I would have read everything ever published about double pneumonia. How can you not know!?

"Electrocuted." I still can't believe it. Who gets electrocuted? And dies?

HOGAN: Well, I would guess it's like regular pneumonia, but worse, maybe. I don't have a clue how you would get it.

HOGAN: I say "I think" because I have this fuzzy memory of someone talking to me about it, but I don't know if I just made that up or if it actually happened.

memory is so freaking scary. it can't be trusted. **:DAVID**

so when you read a question like "how did he die?" do you feel anything similar to sadness? **:DAVID**

When the phone rang for the first time, it was Toni, my wife. She had sounded flustered. Confused. Not scared or sad. Just like she didn't know what was going on.

"I just got a call from Tracey. She said Kyle was electrocuted." :Toni
"What? What do you mean electrocuted?" :Me
"I don't know really. She said she'd call back. She just wanted us to know as soon as it happened." :Toni
"Should we be worried? Is he ok?" :Me
"She said they were working on him." :Toni
"What?? What do you mean working on him?!" :Me

HOGAN: I don't know. I'm really not sure what I feel. It's been so long.

HOGAN: I think that any sadness I would feel would be from not knowing about anything.

HOGAN: It's like that whole thing was a chapter in a book that got closed and sold in a garage sale. You know the book couldn't have gotten too far, that it's somewhere nearby, but you can't really say where.

do you remember if you were scared of dying or of other people dying? you know, since you were so young and probably didn't know what to think about the concept of death in general at that point. **:DAVID**

After the first phone call I didn't know whether I should keep hitting balls. I remember standing with a club in my hand. Completely indecisive. The sun was still warm. The sky's blue was still perfect. The grass still had dew on it in the shadows of the pine trees where I was standing. It was still so green. I've been electrocuted before. People don't die from getting electrocuted? Really? I called Ben. I wanted to know if I was going to be able to play golf or not. How in the world was I thinking about golf then!? Why hadn't we been there?! I should not have been thinking of golf while ...

HOGAN: I don't think I was scared. I think it was more just confusion. It seemed like everyone at the church we went to was always clamoring around me and telling me things. Advice. The normal crap that people say in times like that, but as a kid it doesn't really mean anything, you know? I probably just wanted to be left alone for a minute.

i remember my second grade open house! **:DAVID**

hilarious. **:DAVID**

sorry for the burst of excitement. but i just remembered. memory is so strange. how a thing leads to another to another. **:DAVID**

our class had done one of those tissue paper projects where you take pieces of tissue paper and twist them on the end of your pencil eraser. then you put a dab of glue on it and stick it to some construction paper. **:DAVID**

we made american flags out of red, white and blue tissue paper. **:DAVID**

i didn't finish my flag. it had like three stripes left incomplete because i was apparently a "little slow." **:DAVID**

i still prefer to look at it as me being overly concerned with exactness. **:DAVID**

regardless of why, it wasn't finished, and i was terrified my parents would see it and conclude they had raised a failure in the creative arts department. **:DAVID**

wait. actually that is toni's memory. yeah! i know it is! She had the same teacher and told me that story, about her unfinished tissue paper flag. **:DAVID**

but it feels like it happened to me! i would almost swear to it! wow. that is too, too weird. **:DAVID**

HOGAN: They still do that project in school!

do you remember your mom being sad? **:DAVID**

Ben had answered. He was crying. I had never heard Ben cry. He sounded panicked. I could hear lots of commotion. Lots of people in the background. More crying. It sounded like children. Little children. All of the noises were

full of urgency. The club dropped from my hand ...

HOGAN: She's pretty stoic most of the time. There was a wake at our church, and a lot of people were crying there. I don't remember specifically how she reacted, but I'm sure that it was appropriate. I remember going to it, but there is just all this bustle around it. People everywhere. I was really hungry.

HOGAN: I think that that was the only time I cried ... but I can't say one way or the other if it was from the actual sadness, the hunger, the influence of everybody else in the room, or what.

I remember the crying ... everyone crying ... It seemed foreign. Uncomfortable.

HOGAN: I remember that somebody gave my mom one of those books on the stages of grief. I remember her sitting with me on our front porch with the cat on a leash tied to a post. I'm pretty sure she told me that it was very important to grieve properly, and that the book was supposed to help with that.

The cat's name was Shan. I never understood that. He was a big, cranky Siamese. My grandmother always called him "Pit," which only confused me more. She called every cat "Pit."

HOGAN: But again, that could be made up. I think it would be a little weird to remember that but to lose an entire year of elementary school.

kyle's kids are way younger than you were. **:DAVID**

it makes me sad to think

they won't know him. **:DAVID**

but then i sort of feel better thinking they won't carry this weight for long. **:DAVID**

Ben's voice was wobbly. It sounded like he was laughing hysterically while trying to talk. Crying and laughing are so close sometimes. It was terrifying to hear him like this.

"They're getting him in the ambulance. David, it's bad. It's really bad." :Ben
"I'm so sorry we're not there." :David
"They had a pulse again and then lost it. I'll call you back in a second." :Ben

I never want to hear his voice sound that way again.

HOGAN: I know what you mean.

I hope they won't ... but I hope they will ... there's no good way to hope.

i copied a deal from a children's website. it's what to say to kids when there's been a death in the family. **:DAVID**

i'm sending it to you. **:DAVID**

think of it as, you know, what i'd have said to you if i were sitting next to you in second grade or something. **:DAVID**

HOGAN: OK

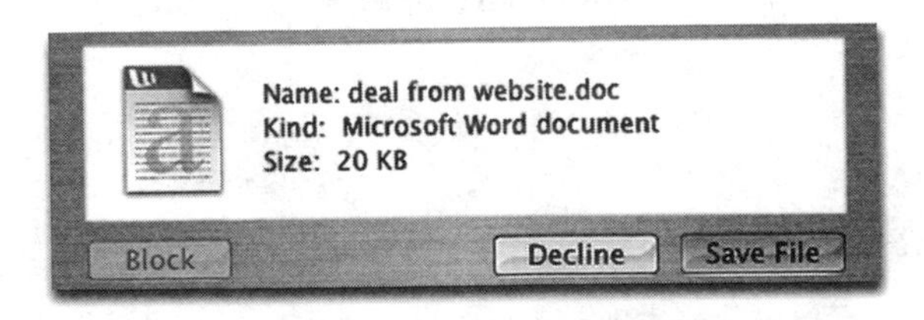

did you get it? **:DAVID**

HOGAN: Yeah. Thanks. I'll check it out.

you know toni's aunt? sandra? the one who died of breast cancer—you know the mom of the three little girls we took to disney world? **:DAVID**

HOGAN: Right

one of the girls this past christmas, or thanksgiving, said she couldn't remember their mom's voice. **:DAVID**

she sounded scared. **:DAVID**

like that shouldn't be something you could forget. **:DAVID**

Memory. I keep trying not to misplace his face. Kyle was prettier than the rest of us. Standing next to me, the stark contrast between the two of us was unsettling. And yet he stood there. Next to me. Always. His smile was the best. There have never been teeth so white! You could feel, literally feel, as fierce as electricity (such a shocking word choice), the vivacity behind the white glow. It was something tangible and present, something that set a room alive, and it was all coming from those teeth! I have tried Crest Whitening Strips and whitening toothpastes and some unknown gel substance that required a poorly fitted mouthpiece, but none of it works for me. His glow was coming from someplace deeper, less a surface shine; there were foundational elements that I am missing.

Wow. It is still hard and strange to use the past tense when talking about him.

I keep playing conversations from the day of his death over and over in my head, to make sure I don't lose the details. It's so hard to pay attention when you're crumbling. I'm afraid I won't retain what was said. Ben told me that he thought there was a fire. He saw Kyle falling backward, I think, I think he said that he saw Kyle falling backward but I can't remember, then he saw the candles that sit on the ledge of the baptistery strewn everywhere, and he thought that it must be a fire and that Kyle had been burned. Did he say he thought Kyle was burned or am I just assuming because he said the thing about the candles? I can't remember. But Ben said he immediately started trying to recall where the fire extinguisher was. So Kyle is electrocuted, and Ben is looking for a fire extinguisher. That's sort of funny. I should not be smiling. Picturing Ben spraying Kyle with a fire extinguisher. I am so wrong. What is wrong with me?

I don't know where the fire extinguisher is. I should know where the fire extinguisher is.

HOGAN: But it's surprising how easy some things vanish.

Or refuse to.

they watch home videos. she said she was always surprised when they'd be watching and her mom would talk for the first time. **:DAVID**

when she heard her voice she'd relax a little. like there would be this "oh yeah" moment and she'd feel better. **:DAVID**

like her voice was still in their head, it just needed to be prodded. **:DAVID**

I can't remember Kyle's voice. I can picture him talking, his mouth moving, saying stuff to me. I can even remember specific things he would say, and I can put those things with the memory of his face, and his mouth will be moving along with the words, but I can't hear him. Like the sound is turned off. I listened to one of his sermons the other day, and I understood what she was talking about. I felt this sad relief. I've already forgotten again.

HOGAN: Part of me envies that. I don't have anything from my dad. But a larger part is glad that things happened the way that they did.

HOGAN: I just can't help but wonder how things would have turned out if I did remember.

HOGAN: Deaths that are more recent, those I feel severely. I bear them every day. They are ever persistent because my memory is so vivid.

I wish I could take a strainer and dump my brain into it, sift through my collected thoughts, and just keep the things I wanted. Hmm. I wonder ... what would I keep?

HOGAN: The other seems like a completely different life. Not a bad life, but not the one I was supposed to lead.

nice **:DAVID**

toni just got back from baskin robbins **:DAVID**

she has bubble gum ice cream **:DAVID**

which means it's officially

summertime **:DAVID**

HOGAN: So good

they only carry it in the
summer. **:DAVID**

last summer they didn't have
it in town **:DAVID**

must mean this summer is
going to be a good one. **:DAVID**

HOGAN: Like when you buy one of
those ice cream cones from the gas station
and it has a big clump of frozen chocolate at
the bottom of the cone. You know your day is
picking up when that happens.

exactly **:DAVID**

anyway, i'm going to go eat pink ice cream
with frozen bits of gum. **:DAVID**

see ya **:DAVID**

In Orlando the phone had rung one final time. It was Toni. I have known my wife since she was in the tenth grade. It is crazy what emotions can do to a voice. I've never heard that category of panicked sorrow before. I can't rid my memory of that tone and those two words. They keep quivering with finality in my head ... "He died."

HOGAN: Late

My hands are trembling. I can't make them stop.

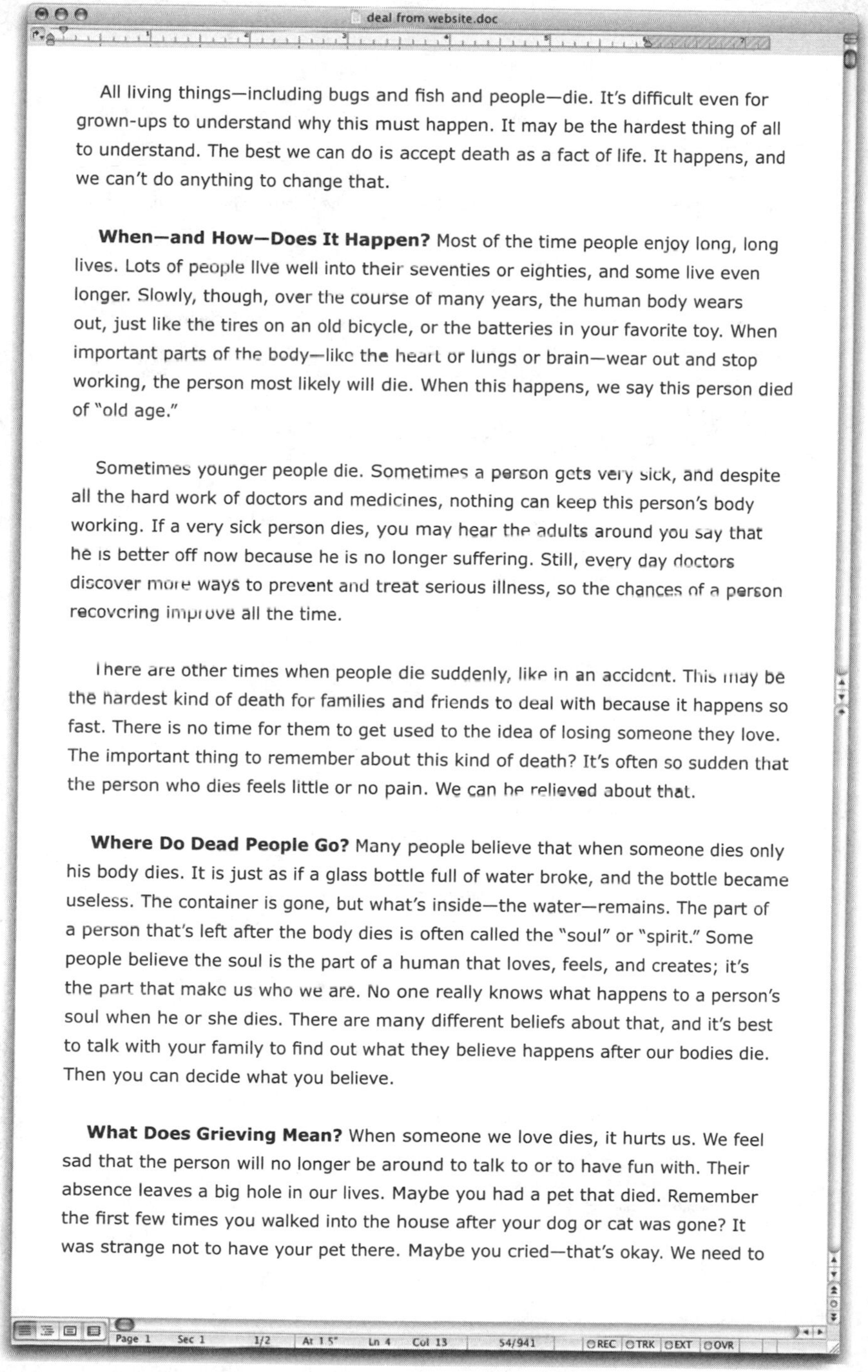

deal from website.doc

All living things—including bugs and fish and people—die. It's difficult even for grown-ups to understand why this must happen. It may be the hardest thing of all to understand. The best we can do is accept death as a fact of life. It happens, and we can't do anything to change that.

When—and How—Does It Happen? Most of the time people enjoy long, long lives. Lots of people live well into their seventies or eighties, and some live even longer. Slowly, though, over the course of many years, the human body wears out, just like the tires on an old bicycle, or the batteries in your favorite toy. When important parts of the body—like the heart or lungs or brain—wear out and stop working, the person most likely will die. When this happens, we say this person died of "old age."

Sometimes younger people die. Sometimes a person gets very sick, and despite all the hard work of doctors and medicines, nothing can keep this person's body working. If a very sick person dies, you may hear the adults around you say that he is better off now because he is no longer suffering. Still, every day doctors discover more ways to prevent and treat serious illness, so the chances of a person recovering improve all the time.

There are other times when people die suddenly, like in an accident. This may be the hardest kind of death for families and friends to deal with because it happens so fast. There is no time for them to get used to the idea of losing someone they love. The important thing to remember about this kind of death? It's often so sudden that the person who dies feels little or no pain. We can be relieved about that.

Where Do Dead People Go? Many people believe that when someone dies only his body dies. It is just as if a glass bottle full of water broke, and the bottle became useless. The container is gone, but what's inside—the water—remains. The part of a person that's left after the body dies is often called the "soul" or "spirit." Some people believe the soul is the part of a human that loves, feels, and creates; it's the part that make us who we are. No one really knows what happens to a person's soul when he or she dies. There are many different beliefs about that, and it's best to talk with your family to find out what they believe happens after our bodies die. Then you can decide what you believe.

What Does Grieving Mean? When someone we love dies, it hurts us. We feel sad that the person will no longer be around to talk to or to have fun with. Their absence leaves a big hole in our lives. Maybe you had a pet that died. Remember the first few times you walked into the house after your dog or cat was gone? It was strange not to have your pet there. Maybe you cried—that's okay. We need to

Page 1 Sec 1 1/2 At 1.5" Ln 4 Col 13 54/941 REC TRK EXT OVR

deal from website.doc

mourn, or grieve, over losing people and animals and other things we love. But just like when you skin your knee, the first intense pain will go away after a while. It takes time for your knee to heal, but it hurts less and less each day. It's the same when somebody dies. That doesn't mean you forget the person who died, or that you stop missing them. After a while, we can go back to our lives, still loving them and remembering them always.

Remembering people we love who have died is one way to keep them a part of us. Pictures help us do this. Looking at a photo album can help us remember fun times we had together. Lots of families bury the bodies of loved ones in a cemetery. Then they can go and visit the person's grave. It's not that they think of the dead person as really being there, but it is a special place to go and think about how much that person meant to them.

What About Me? When someone dies, you may start to wonder if the other people in your life will also die soon. You may ask yourself, "Will my mom or dad die?" or "Will I die?" The best thing you can do is share these thoughts with your family. It may be difficult—maybe even a little painful—to talk about these things, but it can feel good to share your feelings. It's important to talk about any fears you may have, instead of hiding them or pretending you aren't scared. The people who love you want to know you are having these feelings so they can help.

Did you know you can also help the grown-ups around you when they are sad that someone has died? Can you remember a funny story about the person who died? Or something nice that person did for you? Tell the good stories you remember out loud. They will make everyone feel a little better.

If I'm Going to Die Someday, What Should I Do Now? There are many things about death we do not know and may never know. We do know that it will happen, someday, to all of us. But you should not worry or wonder about it for very long. There are too many wonderful things to experience in the many, many years ahead.

This information was provided by KidsHealth, one of the largest resources online for medically reviewed health information written for parents, kids, and teens. For more articles like this one, visit www.KidsHealth.org or www.TeensHealth.org.

Page 2 Sec 1 2/2 At 1" Ln 1 Col 17 939/941 REC TRK EXT OVR

HISTORY OF BLUEGRASS

— PART 2 —

MIGRATIONS AND THE BEAUTY OF SHEEP

or

"Freeeeedooomm!!!"

Rock 'n' roll began with Elvis, true or false?

Now, the uncomplicated response is, *yes, this is true.* America didn't know what hit it until he swaggered on to *The Ed Sullivan Show*, shook his pelvis to and fro, and made the girls scream and pass out. He gave us a blueprint, detailing elements of the rock star lifestyle that included hair gel, pork chops, buying Caddies[1] for "momma," building mansions with jungle rooms, introducing the world to culinary delights like fried peanut butter and "nanner"[2] sandwiches, and dying early on the toilet all bloated and fat. In a way you could say that yes, rock 'n' roll did start with Elvis.

But you would be wrong. The fact is what Elvis did was nothing outside of the great American tradition of taking a thing that is already in existence, something with years upon years of history and evolution, and making the world *think* that you invented it.

Bluegrass has suffered a similar fate. In just about any book you pick

---

1. Cadillacs

2. Banana

up on the subject, you'll find a statement indicating that this genre of music began with a guy named Bill Monroe. And it did. Sorta. He was like the Elvis of the bluegrass world without the prescription pills. The truth, however, is a lot more convoluted than that.

To arrive at the source of this music with any amount of precision, we must go through Scotland, where the initial seeds of bluegrass were sown.

If you drive around the Scottish countryside long enough, you'll notice a couple of things: Grass, and a lot of it. You'll also notice rolling hills that seem to stretch off infinitely. (If you happen to make it over at the right time of year, the hills will be smothered in purple and red flowers. It's offensively beautiful.) And on these hills do in fact roam lots of huge fluffy sheep that munch on these same flowers and abundant grass, which as mentioned, are everywhere. These are the same sheep, perhaps, that give us scarves and woolen golf pants with patterns that are synonymous with roaming about while hitting a little ball at a hole, simultaneously ruining any chance of personal happiness in the process.

The particular group of Scots that concern us lived in the lowlands (as opposed to the highlands, where "there can be only one!"[3]) and border country. (The border country contains the aforementioned city of Edinburgh as well as the river Tweed, which at least in name furthers our little trouser motif that keeps popping up. Incidentally, the supposed birthplace of golf, Saint Andrews, is near Edinburgh. This is brought to your attention because the book is, after all, about loss and grief, two things golfers seem very much in tune with.)

The folks who lived in this region were a far cry from the peaceful, low-key farmer sorts that populated nearby England. Though they were loyal to the British monarchy, they had their fair share of issues with English rule, going back to the Wars of Scottish Independence, which not only gave Scotland its freedom, but also the movie *Braveheart* and the much maligned Australian-in-a-kilt statue. If you go to Wikipedia and look up Scotch-Irish,[4] you'll find them nonchalantly described as "warlike herdsmen." That is quite possibly one of the

---

3. *Highlander* tagline from IMDB (*www.imdb.com*): "He fought his first battle on the Scottish Highlands in 1536. He will fight his greatest battle on the streets of New York City in 1986. His name is Connor MacLeod. He is immortal."

4. Not to be confused with Irish-Scots who were Irish immigrants to Scotland.

greatest descriptions of all time. It's the sort of thing you would put on your resumé. Think about it. You go into a job interview, and the interviewer looks at your previous experience and qualifications when he comes across the words *warlike herdsman*. Most likely, he will hire you on the spot. Whether it's because of your genuine competency or just the fear that you could snap him in two is beside the point.

So there they were, hanging out in the lowlands, and they decided to move to Ireland. In all honesty, it's not completely clear why. It seems the real issue was the onset of hard times economically, some vague references to the *seven-year ills*, and English protectionism surrounding trade, but the authors have read nothing that gives a good, clear, obvious explanation. So they decided to make one up that is less troublesome than fuzzy suggestions of depopulation and famine: the beer in Ireland is traditionally better than that in Scotland.

Nevertheless, there was a large migration of Scots during the seventeenth and eighteenth centuries to Northern Ireland for what was most likely the hope of a little repose and improved conditions for the living of life; but if they were looking for an easier go at things, they were, so to speak, up a creek (or at least across the Irish sea) without a paddle. If they thought their troubles with the English were bad, the Irish folks were no better.

For one, Ireland has a lot of Catholics, and the Scots are fiercely Protestant. Specifically, they were Presbyterians.[5] This, in and of itself, is not a bad thing. But the Irish Catholics didn't approve, so they decided to give their new migrant neighbors some good old-fashioned persecution. You know, egging their horse-drawn carts, enacting harsh penal laws, normal stuff. Sure there were positives, such as the cultural exchange of traditional music (fiddle tunes, dances, and ballads), but who wants to spend your days scraping dried egg out of your work horse's tail or worrying when you're going to be thrown in the pokey next *because you democratically elect your lay officials*?[6] It was time to move on. Again.

---

5. Incidentally, Presbyterians happens to be an anagram for Britney Spears. It's true! We're uncertain what unsettling significance could be drawn here, but any good Presbyterian will advise you that this seemingly bizarre coincidence has been foreknown by God since the dawn of time.

6. Read: for being Presbyterian.

But this was to be the final move and, perhaps, the most important. The New World was calling and, along with it, the opportunity to change the face of the musical landscape.

COLUMNS, PART 2

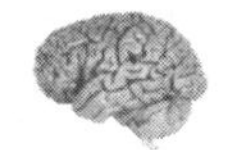
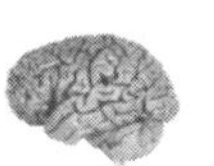

WHEN SHE SAID *Kentucky*, she meant *linoleum*. When she said *telephone*, she meant *overcoat*. When she said *Franze Kafka*, she meant *morning coffee*. Of course, the Kafka reference happened on only one occasion.

She hated the word *aphasia*. That particular word had not yet been misplaced. No, she knew exactly where it was. Every time she went to its drawer, it was there. She had wished and wished it would become one of

IT WAS A 7-BLOCK WALK to the church. He watched carefully. For the flickering of porch lights still burning from the previous night. When he passed the 4th street lamp, he touched the pole. He looked up to see if it went out. It did not. When he reached the church doors, he tapped the door on the right 4 times. Then disappeared inside. The smell was always a surprise. *Damp* is the word that would strike him. Though he knew *damp* certainly was not a proper word for the description of a smell. He

IT WOULD BE WEEKS before anyone pieced things together.

Not until the top avian scientists, (along with the *Great Avifauna Governmental Agency*) had unloaded all of their specialized equipment (with specialized dials, wands, and levers) and converged on the woods of eastern Texas in search of the source of the foul plight did Steven's mother first put the tears and deaths together.

the words that moved, that she'd go to retrieve it and instead find *dandelion* or *grapefruit* or *Please-God-help-me-somebody-please-help-me.*

Anything but that, "God-awful word *aphasia*," as she'd refer to it.

One of the things that brought her the most melancholy was the robbery of numbers. Oh how she used to love numbers. The way they fit together. The way they brought order and meaning to things previously untidy and chaotic, giving spaces and people value, letting you know where you stood. Now they could not be trusted. No, now, when she

searched his head but could not find a better one. He tapped his forehead 4 times. Things always on the tip of the tongue. Unable to fall out. He became nervous and agitated when his memory would not cooperate. It was all he had of her. If it failed him, she would be gone. He touched the 3rd stone from the right as he entered the corridor that leads to the courtyard. The corridor was dark and damp. *Damp* was exactly the word for the corridor. Here you could actually feel a measurable amount of moisture surrounding you. It was 43 steps and then a right turn. 3 steps and another door. He clapped 4 times. Reached out with his gloved

It was early morning. She was sitting in a chair, rocking the little boy with the bluest eyes you have ever seen and singing to him, when her eyes landed on a tiny red bird bathing in the rather scum-covered water of the concrete birdbath located just outside the sliding glass door.

Steven began to cry.

Immediately the tiny red bird fell beak first into the dark water and did not move.

She caught the boy's tears in the palm of her hand. She stared at the little boy resting in her arms, and she felt a great weight

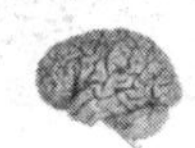

said *twenty-five*, she meant *sixteen*. When she said *twenty-one*, she meant *three*. When she said it had been *sixty-one* days since the stroke, she meant *737*. When she said *1.6180339887*, she meant, of course, *The Collective Weight of Human Existence*.

Since the stroke, quite a lot had had to change. For one, she had gotten really good at reading people and their various nonverbal reactions to her. For instance, if she were to say, "Could you please pass me the carpet" while pointing to the saltshaker, she would notice the slightest of muscular contractions in the forehead of

right hand. Pressed his palm hard against the knob. Squeezed. And turned. Ever since he had entered the priesthood he had become interested in gardening. *Interested* was not the proper word for it. The tending of things living had become a compulsion. She had loved gardening. The courtyard was surrounded by covered walkways on all sides. It was picturesque in the way that all nineteenth-century gothic churches could be. Old dark stone. Spires. A feeling that you should be quiet. But in the middle of all the stone and mortar was a garden. To call it a *garden* is not the use of proper terminology. For many people have seen a garden

begin to settle on the span of her shoulders. From that moment on she walked with the posture of someone carrying a heaviness.

The avian scientists soon packed up their specialized gear, left the woods of east Texas, and announced incorrectly that the world was getting colder. They had detected a global trend that things were cooling, a global frost was imminent that would be the end of everything that flew in the air. Anything that was not firmly attached to the ground was destined for demise. There was nothing to be done. No hope to be shared, but certainly nothing to panic her grandson as he attempted to meet her inquiry with a blank stare. She would then cackle out a laugh, exclaiming, "Oh, my! I'm getting so old. Just never you mind. Now, be quiet and hand it over!"—cackle, cackle, cackle. Laughing always made it better. It eased the nerves, both in her and whomever happened to be in the proximity of her misplacements.

Soon, she misplaced the laughter, and when she meant to laugh, she cried.

It became obvious to everyone that something must be done. Doctors were consulted. Retirement centers visited.

before. People journeyed from far-away places to visit here. And when the visitors would ask him how such things could grow all in one place. He would respond. "I'm sorry. I can't quite find the word for it." The courtyard was where he spent his waking hours. He walked along the southern side of the garden. 77 steps to the closet. He tapped 4 times before opening it. He pulled down on the string hanging from the light. It turned on and burned out at the same time. He took a breath and held it for 4 seconds. This always happened. At least since she had died. He was certain he had been electrically affected. He knew this. He pulled a new bulb

about. It was just a drop in the temperature, and everyone should merely go about their business and watch for things falling from the sky.

Steven's mother wept at the news.

She poured all of her energies into keeping him cheerful, but despite her best efforts, every day that the little boy lived, he shed tears. They would roll down his cheeks, and she would catch them in the palm of her hand. She began collecting them, storing each of them in jars that were kept in the back yard. She wasn't sure why she did this, but

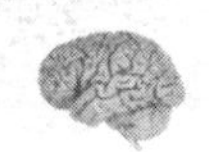

Eventually she had moved in with her son's family. They had insisted, assuring her she was not a burden. She did not know how to depend on anyone else. Even after her husband had died six years ago (when she said *six*, she meant *nine*), she had coped alone. Of course she missed him. When Frank was alive though, she had been quite independent. Now, now is when she needed him. Here. These people didn't understand her. Literally. He would have understood. He would have known what she meant when she said *carpet*.

Dignity is a thing hard to reclaim once it is lost—just one more item

from the row of bulbs on the shelf. Unscrewed the burned-out bulb. Stepped on the silver pedal of the silver can by the shelves. And gently dropped it in on top of the rest. He liked the hollow sound of the glass hitting. The pile of bulbs looked like a pile of bubbles. The silver can was almost full. He screwed the new bulb in and the light flickered on. He tapped it 4 times. He looked down at his feet. His shoes were already soaking through. And he thought. "Better get to work." The dirt of the garden would soon cake to them. When his shoes left prints it was assumed by the other priests that he had simply encountered a little mud while

she couldn't keep herself from it. Why? Why did the little boy cry so much? The weight spanning her shoulders seemed to take on the heaviness of water. The more jars that gathered in the back yard, the more difficult it became for her to stand. If you have ever attempted to pour from a large pitcher and have felt your arm begin to shake under the strain of it, you are acquainted with this heaviness. To walk from the bedroom to the kitchen was soon a task taking the better part of a day for her.

As the little boy grew in size, the tears began to take on a density that was immeasurable.

the stroke had misplaced for her. It is impossible to present yourself as stately when you are drooling out of the right side of your mouth.

She didn't complain. She wasn't a complainer. But Frank would have known what this did to her. What it would do to a person, any person. To have been watched by a bunch of stupid birds, with death so close, to think those stupid, stupid birds could have been the ones who sent her out, her last and only companions, sitting there, pecking around her feet, pecking at the seeds in her right palm, while she helplessly sat there unable to move.

laboring. He pulled out a spade. A trash bag. And two half-empty jars. One labeled "Pebbles." One "Nettles."

In time his mother could not rise from bed, and it was becoming obvious that the bed could not hold up under the labor of her support much longer. Soon things would collapse.

HISTORY OF THE SOUL

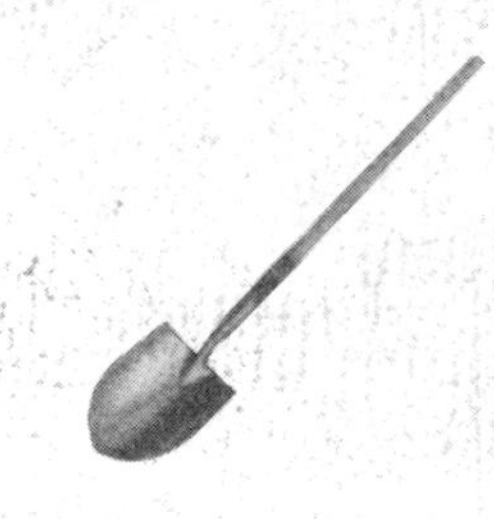

— PART 3 —

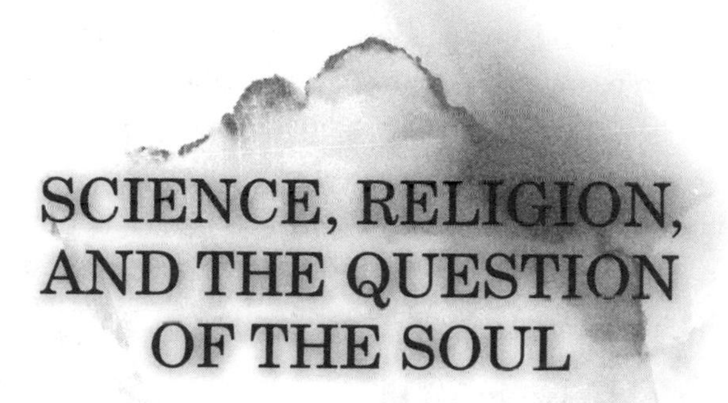

SCIENCE, RELIGION, AND THE QUESTION OF THE SOUL

or

The Big Empty, Part 1

Did you know that the most important man in the history of the brain was described by one of his neighbors as having hair like that of a "dark red pigge"?[1] There are a staggering number of questions that come to mind when considering this: 1) What is the deal with that particular spelling of the word *pig*? 2) Have you ever seen a dark red pig? 3) what would this hair actually look like? It's intriguing.

As important as those questions may be, the significance of our red-headed pig-man is not to be underplayed. He went by the name of Thomas Willis, and he is considered to be sort of the grandpappy of neuroscience. In the year 1662, the best place to find him (if you were looking for him, that is), would have been a little house in Oxford, England, where he and his buddies were busy cutting open the heads of the recently deceased and holding aloft the brains previously enclosed therein for all the world to see.[2] No doubt the neighbors were pleased.

Now obviously the brain has been around a lot longer than Mr.

---

1. Carl Zimmer, *Soul Made Flesh*, p. 10.
2. Ibid.

Willis or his red hair, and he certainly wasn't the first scientist to take a crack at unraveling the mysteries of it, not least of which was whether the brain had anything to do with the soul. Science and the soul have been tripping the light fantastic together for some time now. The dance has been at times beautifully in step, and at others the two have been incredibly adept at stomping on one another's toes. Throw in some good ol' church history and some major institutional influence, and we have ourselves a party. So without fear, without trembling, let us jump headlong into ...

ANCIENT EGYPT: These guys were the original gangstas (OGs) of messing with the brain. Of course, the brain appears to have been little more than dead weight to them, but it is interesting to note nonetheless. When someone died (read: someone with money), the priests would take a hook, stick it up the nose, pull out the brain, and properly dispose of it. Perhaps it was because the brain is not too unlike a bowl of porridge, and unless you are an orphan in Dickensian London, porridge does not hold a great deal of significance for you. The heart, however, was a different matter entirely. (You'll notice that this is a trend that will last for, oh, centuries.) When the heart was pulled from the mummified body, it was placed in an urn that befitted the organ in which the person's "being" resided. The Egyptians believed that upon entering the afterlife, the god Anubis would take the heart and place it on a scale to weigh against a feather. Then the god Thoth would have a sit-down with the heart and ask it forty questions regarding its owner. If the heart ended up feeling guilty, it would be eaten by some creature; if it didn't, it would go to heaven. The OGs played no games.

500 BC: In a stroke of genius that predates, well, almost everybody, the Greek philosopher Alcmaeon throws the hammer down and claims, "All the senses are connected to the brain."[3] This is a big "BOOYAH" to everyone else; they just don't know it yet.

---

3. Ibid.

ARISTOTLE: Take note, as this guy would spit out the philosophy that has more or less dominated all of Western thought up until the seventeenth century. This is saying something, considering that he was born in 384 BC.

Not only that, but it could be argued that he established himself as the very first biologist. Sure, this statement is up for debate, but trust us when we say this guy sliced and diced just about everything he could get his hands on. Everything from sea urchins to elephants got the sharp edge of his scalpel. It seems the only sentient beings safe were you and me. Cutting up a human being in ancient Greece was a big-time taboo, thanks in part to Aristotle's cunningly executed maneuver of placing all life forms on a ladder of sorts, with human folk sitting pretty at the top and plant life scrounging around at the bottom. He obviously had never spent much time with super-sweet plants like the Venus Flytrap, which would have, no doubt, vaulted the species up a rung or two. Aristotle or not, it's impossible to find a plant chomping down on some horseflies anything less than impressive.

Much like the Egyptians, he believed the soul resided in the heart. To him it made sense; speech comes from the chest, the heart *sits* in the chest, so there you go. Plus, the human brain looks like pudding. Not to mention that when a heart is removed from a living body, it will continue beating for a given amount of time before finally petering out, which would serve to suggest that something inhabited it. It is imagined that the observance of such a living, beating object continuing in its overly animated throbbing state upon separation from the body would provoke nothing short of this conclusion. How he knew the human heart behaved in such a way is, of course, a mystery, considering he wasn't supposed to be cutting people open.

Here is something funny ... if the brain looked like pudding (which it sort of does) and the soul didn't live there, then what would you suppose was its purpose? At that time, it was believed its function was to keep the heart cool. Sort of a biological air conditioner.[4]

---

4. Ibid., p. 12.

322 BC: Two Greek physicians named Herophilus and Erasistratus[5] went where Aristotle dared not go, at least not publicly. They decided that taboos did not concern them and started poking around fresh corpses. In and of itself, this is not all that remarkable. However, the fact that they discovered the nervous system is.[6]

AD 150: A doctor named Galen (who, like Madonna, Sting, Cher, Fabio, and a guy named "Pearl" who works at a Starbucks in the DFW airport, went by a single name) pops up in the Roman Empire. The Romans felt even more strongly about tinkering with human remains than the Greeks did. With it out of the question for him to go running around cutting folks open, he had the cleverness of working as a doc to the gladiators—a sort of doctor to the stars for ancient times.[7] He would make it a habit to peek inside the gaping wounds left by swords, tridents, and the occasional tiger to check out the inner workings of the body. He became known for his "philosophy of the soul," which again denied the brain the honor of being home to the soul, and instead gave it the esteemed label of "spirit pump"—a title that gets the award for best name ever. While the brain was busy pumping spirits around the body, a person's intelligence sat in the "empty space" inside the head. This theory either said a lot about Galen's knowledge (or rather, lack thereof) or the gladiators he was checking out. To put things in perspective, this same "intelligence" that occupied the head's empty space could also be found in the sun and moon and stars, and not only that, but they (yes, the sun and moon and stars) were believed to be much smarter than any of us poor humans could ever hope to be. Oh well.[8]

THE EARLY CHRISTIANS: It is finally time to initiate a small portion of the wonderfully weird relationship between Christianity and all this, umm, stuff we have floating around here. By the time the early Christians arrived on the scene, the most popular

---

5. Not to be confused with Erik Estrada, the actor from *CHiPs*. He rode a motorcycle and his hair was abundant, though he discovered nothing but a way into our hearts.
6. Ibid., p. 13.
7. *Gladiator 90210*, if you will.
8. Zimmer, p. 14.

guy around, medically speaking, was Galen. His theories had made quite an impact and managed to spread throughout the Roman Empire. So if you take a pinch of his teachings and a dash of the rest of the Greek philosophers, you'll have a good idea of the general take on things at this point. Basically, the brain was still functioning as a spirit pump (which, yes, is still a cool name), while pretty much everything else important made a home in the heart. Carl Zimmer makes an interesting note in his book *Soul Made Flesh* that it is no coincidence that pictures of Jesus depict Him with a Sacred Heart and not, say, a Sacred Brain.[9]

Not a brain

EPICURUS GOES TO HELL: Epicurus—not to be confused with the word *epicurious*, which is a cleverly and purposely misspelled word referencing the desire to seek out new and sensual foods, as well as a show on basic cable—was a Greek philosopher who lived three hundred or so years before the birth of Christ. He decided that the universe, including the soul, was made up of tiny little particles that are impossible to see. He called these particles atoms. This is amazing because, well, have *you* ever seen an atom? Not unless you happen to have access to a highly powered electron microscope. The closest view of atomic particles most of us have ever had is the cover of the first Strokes album. Epicurus obviously had superpowers or access to magnifications unknown to anyone else at the time. Or he was just a really good guesser.

Epicurus ended up hacking off a lot of people, mainly Christian theologians (when he was no longer around to feel the brunt of their disgust), because he claimed that the soul must die along with the body. For all of his effort, the poet Dante went ahead and placed him in the sixth circle of hell when he wrote *The Inferno*.[10] Dante, like the gods of ancient Egypt, was not a man to be messed with, apparently.

---

9. Ibid., p. 17.
10. Ibid., p. 17-18.

THE FOUNDING OF NATURAL PHILOSOPHY:

In the thirteenth century, theologian Thomas Aquinas[11] made a choice, and that choice was to blatantly reject the concept of atoms randomly bouncing around, rubbing against each other. Instead, he embraced the teachings of Aristotle, who stated that everything in the universe existed for a purpose. Thomas figured this was good form, and just tweaked stuff a little by pronouncing that everything in the universe came together for a purpose under God's plan. The nature of the soul factors in as well. Thomas agreed with Aristotle's idea that life is in the soul, be it plant, animal, human, whatever. But he took it a step further by dividing the soul into certain parts, giving these parts jobs and different places to live.[12] Imagination and memory, for instance, took up residence in the ever-popular empty spaces of the head.

The result? Both Thomas and the long-dead Aristotle enjoy the warm and fuzzy embrace of the masses. In fact, Thomas' theories were so popular that an entirely new tradition called natural philosophy was birthed. In modern times you could describe someone who doesn't bathe or shave and wears a lot of hemp clothing as subscribing to a natural philosophy. In the thirteenth century that probably applied to most people, so the term referred to the act of using reason to show that there was one sovereign God who made the world, therefore making Himself evident in all the workings within that world. Natural philosophy and its proponents steadily took the helm of the universities that had begun popping up around Europe, effectively setting the climate for higher learning across the land.[13]

Scientifically speaking, the teachers at many of these universities, in simultaneity with the rise of natural philosophy, revived the anatomy lessons of Galen (who, if you'll recall, never actually dissected any people), building large theaters where surgeons would

---

11. His name sounds like he should be the alter ego of a comic book character. Like Aquaman. Though a clue to his identity would be right there in his name, no one would ever suspect a thing, which is why the universe of comics is so neat.

12. Sort of like the suburbs.

13. ... and assigning many term papers.

slice and dice bodies of the recently executed in front of a live studio audience. These little shows were open to not only students, but anyone who was curious. And why not? To add a sense of drama to the dissections, professors would sit in elevated chairs during the procedures and read aloud from Galen's writings. Sounds like a hoot. Most likely the best show in town.

THE SOUL FINDS A HOME: In 1537, the head of the Italian University of Padua's surgery and anatomy department, a lecturer by the name of Andreas Vesalius, finally calls to question the gospel truth of Galen's anatomy. When a judge in town began to send him more cadavers than he could shake a stick at (hanged criminals, for the most part), he began to realize that things weren't quite adding up. (Side note—have you noticed what a rough racket it is to be a dead criminal around this time? No love, man, no love at all.) Remember us saying that it would be centuries before anyone figured this out? 1537 is a long way from the thirteenth century of Galen's time. For all of those bodies that were dissected in front of a live audience of students and onlookers, you would think someone would have figured out that the kidneys Galen had described were those belonging to a pig rather than a human being. Likewise with the womb (which according to Galen's description looked an awful lot like that of a dog) and the brain (goat or cow, depending on whom you ask). All in all, once Vesalius got down to business, he found two hundred pieces of animal anatomy inserted in place of the human variety.

So what does one do when faced with hard facts that contradict almost everything that is known regarding the makeup of the human body? Simple. You publish a multi-volume work titled *Seven Books on the Structure of the Human Body*. This book featured many detailed drawings of skinless humans and skeletons alike hanging out and relaxing in the Italian countryside.

While dissecting humans and composing his list of Galenian items to amend, our man Vesalius took on the considerable task of investigating the brain and made a significant find. At that time, according to the Church's official anatomy, the brain contained three spherical chambers that had something to do with a person's essential being. (Perhaps these were the empty spaces in which bits of the soul lived ...) These three chambers did not exist. So maybe, he thought, the soul resided in the brain's pudding/custard. He kept this thought quietly to himself, chiefly due to fear that the Church might hang him for heresy.[14] Regardless of the reason, this particular notion did not make it on his amended list.

THE SPLIT BEGINS: One of the most colorful and entertaining characters we will meet in this little journey is a British doctor/minister named Richard Napier. He was a perfect example of the oddly anomalous relationship between Christianity and the sciences. During his career he kept detailed records that documented more than 60,000 patients. Much of the time, he would attempt a diagnosis by checking a person's horoscope to see how the planets and stars were doing. He wouldn't hesitate to diagnose demon possession as an ailment.[15] He fed his patients tobacco and laxatives, made use of leeches, and instructed them to wear amulets and pendants depicting planetary signs; all the while sermonizing with them and taking part in rigorous prayer that they be cured. Surprisingly, folks traveled for hundreds of miles to seek his advice.[16]

As fun as all of this sounds, Napier was something of a dying breed. In the century preceding him, academics had been translating the works of philosophers like Plato and Aristotle from the original Greek, and they were finding some things that disturbed them. It was the beginning of the split between Christian thought and Greek philosophy, which had been pretty buddy-buddy up until this point. One of the main problem areas was Plato. These new translations revealed that though humans had a spirit, so did everything else. Apparently, the Earth spirit influenced the spirits of humans by

---

14. Zimmer, p. 19-20.

15. One such possessed individual was a guy named Edward Cleaver. He told the doctor that after thanking God for his dinner, a voice came into his head that said, "Kiss my arse." Zimmer, p. 22.

16. Zimmer, p. 22.

a method called cosmic sympathy, which operated on the same principle as a plucked string on a lute (the lute was BIG back then), making the strings next to them vibrate. The Church decided this was bad thinking, a little too pagan, too natural magic. They placed the works of Plato on the banned books list.

Not even Aristotle was safe. Arguments were made that if the soul was part of the body, as Aristotle claimed, then when the body died, the soul did too. The big dogs in Rome found this about as comforting as they did the readings of Plato and ordered a cessation of questions regarding the immortality of the soul. They insisted upon its immortal position by use of natural reasoning, and a century-long scuffle of the intellect ensued, eventually reaching explosive heights when attention turned toward the heavens and major advances in astronomy.[17]

17. Ibid., p. 23.

IM CONVERSATION 3

HOGAN: Opiuwer

? **:DAVID**

HOGAN: Seeing if you were there.

right **:DAVID**

HOGAN: I'm starting to wonder about this.

wonder about what?
the media stuff? **:DAVID**

Ah! Why do these things surface in my head most when we're doing these IMs? And why in the world would I assume he was thinking about the same stuff I was?

HOGAN: Uh. No. What media stuff?

nothing. doesn't matter.
what were you wondering? **:DAVID**

They kept saying "was electrocuted" in the same exact tone on every single channel as they dipped their heads and peered empathetically toward the camera. I hated the way they said that word. Why did it have so many syllables? I think it would have been less damaging to hear if it had fewer syllables. It took too long to hear it. The whole scene had time to play out in my head before the final consonant hit. It should be a shorter word. And they should take less joy uttering it. They feign concern with their furrowed foreheads and falsely raised sympathetic eyebrows.

I hate the news anyway. They have nothing to say that they haven't already said. I wonder if this is the first time they have gotten to say all of these words together and that's why they're taking such pleasure pretending not to take such pleasure. They should have to be standing up to their chests in water when they say it. Now that would be empathy. I can't believe I just thought that. If they wouldn't take so long to pronounce all of those syllables, I wouldn't have time to think such thoughts, enunciating so plainly, with such complete clarity in their little newscaster cadence. Died is a shorter word. Dead. There. One syllable. Fast. Easy. Comes and goes before you have time to brace or think or act or curse or hate the person saying it. And why does it have to be on every channel? And why do they all articulate it exactly the same? Always with the furrowed brow. Sympathy is power. If you are able to offer it, you are in a position above the ones who are suffering. You are not feeling the same things banging brutally around your insides, or you'd be unable to offer your so thoughtfully extended hand. And the images they were trying to stir up weren't at all reality. It was most definitely not a spectacular event. At least it wasn't according to my friend Pete, who was there! Traumatic sure, but

spectacular no. There were no sparks or flames or violent cartoonish shaking, while people were screaming and running chaotically. It was not a spectacle! He just sort of sank back into the water. So just move along. Nothing to see here. Nothing at all to pronounce in five overly exaggerated syllables.

HOGAN: Well, we have been working on this science and brain stuff for a good while.

HOGAN: I think I'm getting confused.

and? **:DAVID**

HOGAN: Why are we talking about all this science and chronology crap?

HOGAN: What does it have to do with what we're trying to say?

... **:DAVID**

Everything.

well the study of the brain and biology have always related to the study of the soul. **:DAVID**

I had resolved not to look at Kyle's body at the funeral. By then I had read too much about electricity. I knew what signs to look for to conclude whether he had been in pain or not. I came through the doors, near the back of the sanctuary, and there he was. I was 100 feet away from him. He was dead. From 100 feet away he looked so, so dead. How is the deficiency of life visible from that distance? How is it so obvious despite all the makeup and flowers? Everybody kept saying he looked great. He didn't. He looked dead. His cheeks were sunk in. He was wearing blush.

and to understand the soul, we need to understand the historical and chronological framework **:DAVID**

which means looking at the history of the soul as it relates to science and specifically the brain **:DAVID**

I guess it does seem tedious ...

it seems tedious. **:DAVID**

later it will pay off. **:DAVID**

HOGAN: But I know how this is going to end up.

It's going to be bad.

we don't have a choice. **:DAVID**

I have to know.

it's going to be ok. **:DAVID**

HOGAN: It doesn't end in a happy place.

It's going to work against us.

trust me. **:DAVID**

i think this is going to be really great. like the ims. awesome. **:DAVID**

HOGAN: You think?

yup. in the least we'll have shown how different it was not all that long ago. **:DAVID**

we'll have shown that in our not-too-distant past we didn't have the concept, or room for the possibility even for the soul's inexistence. it was a given! science just needed to figure out where it was. **:DAVID**

like locating the thorax **:DAVID**

way different climate now **:DAVID**

HOGAN: No kidding.

HOGAN: Hey. Isn't the thorax part of
an insect?

no. no. it's the part of the body between the
neck and abdomen. **:DAVID**

HOGAN: So wait. You're telling me that it
took science years to locate basically the—
chest!?

dude, i don't know.
thorax just came to mind. **:DAVID**

For weeks after the funeral there was a maliciously concentrated beam aimed at the center-most portion of my chest, directly between my breasts, just at the top of my sternum. It followed me. In the beginning it had the diameter of a fifty-cent piece and penetrated to the depth of two and a half inches. And then it pulled. Or it pushed. I couldn't discern the difference. It's like when water is so cold it burns. With this category of intensity it becomes impossible to distinguish such differences. Its malicious power folded on top of itself, it grew. And for weeks it pushed and pulled with the expanding heaviness of a collapsing galaxy inside my chest cavity. With such terrific weight, the weight of stars folding in on themselves, it felt like an entire universe pushed and pulled to the depth of two and a half inches in the middle of my chest. The beam penetrated without resistance. I could plainly feel the skin melting and falling away, the bones splintering, splitting, breaking apart to let it in, and the malicious beam did not even notice. It was unaffected and distant, oblivious to the damage that was being done

here inside of me. Why wouldn't it notice? Why would it not relent? Why could it not feel what its detonations sent through me? It was unaffected by the burning chest. The fuel-air that disparaged me fed it. Why was it so hungry? Why would such toxicity exact itself upon the growing void two and half inches beneath my protective coverings? A human chest was not made for the accommodation of such a mass of sadness.

actually, it may be part of a bug. do bugs have chests? **:DAVID**

HOGAN: I've never thought about it.

hmmm. **:DAVID**

hey, guess who decided when we officially die? **:DAVID**

HOGAN: What!?

well, you know how for a long while it was believed that the soul was in the heart? **:DAVID**

it seemed obvious. when the heart stopped—you were dead. **:DAVID**

but then sometime in the '70s lawyers declared that we are alive until brain impulses stop. **:DAVID**

lawyers!!! **:DAVID**

HOGAN: Yeah that's funny. We should insert a lawyer joke.[1]

---

1. A man went to a brain store to get some brain to complete a study. He sees a sign remarking on the quality of professional brain offered at this particular brain store. He begins to question the butcher about the cost of these brains.

"How much for engineer brain?"
"Three dollars an ounce."
"How much for programmer brain?"
"Four dollars an ounce."
"How much for lawyer brain?"
"$1,000 an ounce."
"Wow. Why is lawyer brain so much more?"
"Do you know how many lawyers we had to butcher to get one ounce of brain?"

see, that's all we're exerting effort toward with this brain/science matter. just following our collective human train of thought is all. we don't think about this stuff much, and it might do us good. **:DAVID**

Two things we do in an attempt to prevent mortal contemplation:
Make Plans (1
Procrastinate (2

dude, don't even worry. **:DAVID**

We will die. All of us. Everyone. We know this. But it will always feel like a surprise.

HOGAN: Yeah, OK.

HOGAN: I thought the Elvis jokes earlier were good.

HOGAN: What'd you think?

LOL, please say LOL.

LOL!! **:DAVID**

I'll give it to him.

YES!

but you're cool now? feel alright? get it? **:DAVID**

HOGAN: I get that we are using a silly literary device to air out our fears. I get that writing a medical history of the brain or soul or whatever this is will somehow benefit us. Maybe ...

Or bring even heavier sadness.

yeah. think of it like watching a bad horror film. everyone watching knows the protagonist shouldn't go in that door. he should stay with the group. there are just common sense rules. but sure enough, there he goes—he's going to open that door, and you're yelling at the screen begging him to stop but he won't. he just has to go in. yeah, that's us right now. **:DAVID**

But This, My Heaviness of Heart:
My heart is heavier today than yesterday. It is taking on mass. My shoulders are being pulled toward the ground. There is an emptiness in my chest. It is a vacant cavern, and something is pulling and pushing at my heart, and it is sinking with a momentum that I cannot impede. It is tugging at the things it hangs from. I read in a book somewhere that the number-one cause of death in car accidents is from the heart being torn from where it hangs in the chest by the sudden impact of the collision. Apparently the heart hangs from vessels too weak to stand the momentum of such a heavy organ. It tears from the vessels holding it because they are too weak to stand the weight of it, the organ's momentum producing such heaviness, and the vessels so small that it swings forward and pulls free. I have come to a stop, and my heart is still being pulled by its own impetus, and I fear it will be torn away soon. The physics of tensile strength will not allow it to hold. What happens when the heart pulls loose? When a body falls and hits a surface, the heart swings on these fragile vessels, and it cannot hold against the force.

HOGAN: Right.

this is going well. just keep at it. **:DAVID**

HOGAN: Right.

I know where this is going to end up.

HISTORY
OF
BLUEGRASS

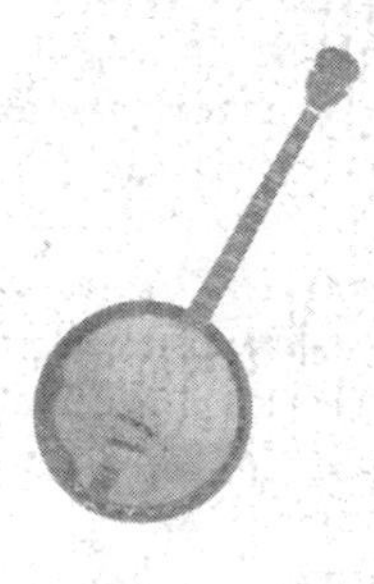

— PART 3 —

COMING TO AMERICA

or

Just Let Your Soul Glow

or

Back Woods and Black Holes

or

The Fear of Jaws in an Indoor Pool

The thing about traveling by boat is, it really, really sucks. This statement is based solely upon a traditional family vacation taken to Florida by Hogan near the age of ten—just the proper stage of life for the display of a very large amount of joy at the news his folks had booked a day excursion on a cruise ship to break up their time. He was helplessly delighted for no other reason than huge machines manufacture an unavoidable fascination in small children, and a larger-than-life boat fit the bill perfectly.

The ship turned out to be a ratty claptrap. It was, however, quite sizable, which meant it could spread its dilapidation over a larger area of water. It was dirty and old, and he is unconvinced, to this day, that it could have made a voyage of any great length without things ending *Titanic*-style, iceberg or no. Which is why—it is assumed—that it departed from the dock, sailed until the coast was barely out of sight, and dropped anchor for the rest of the day. This was to be fun, he was told: to go out upon the sea just far enough to escape the familiarity and comfort of land in a large, floating self-inflicted imprisonment of broken deck chairs and a smoke-filled casino.

Here is his most vivid memory of the experience: After eating bad food, wandering the boat for a bit, concluding the boat not worthy of wandering, and then sitting around completely bored, Hogan decided to have a go at some "exciting deep sea fishing." He and his family proceeded to the back of the boat, rented fishing rods, and cast their lines into the deep blue water. And for a time, there existed a feeling that you could truly quantify as "fun." Even though it boiled down to him still basically just sitting there watching the water, at least he felt he was doing *something*. There is no recollection of him actually catching anything, but if he had, it would have been overshadowed by what happened next. Someone acquired a colossal hit on their line, and with a terrific amount of pugnacious fighting (and some aggressive help from a number of the deck hands) they reeled in what appeared to be a baby shark. And WOW was that thing pissed. Thrashing fins and teeth were everywhere, an amazing show of nature's power and possibility in a small three-foot-long package. That is, until the overly aggressive deck hands produced a baseball bat and proceeded to beat the creature to death right there in front of everyone, leaving the unambiguous, telltale signs of blood and saltwater all over the deck long after the pulpy remains had been thrown overboard. Hogan observed as the whole drama played out in front of him, then promptly turned around, threw up, and cried.[1]

Ships are simply an oppressive means of transportation (our collective apologies to the shipping industry). And it is certain young Hogan's maiden passage was a cakewalk compared to the hardships our band of immigrants faced when they set out from Ireland to

---

1. And here is his second most vivid memory: trying out the indoor pool. Imagine a steel, windowless room with a pool of water in the middle, and not another human in sight. For a grown adult this could prove nerve racking and scary. For a young only child with an overactive imagination, it proved utterly horrifying. What if Jaws were in the water? Where could you run?

the New World. They would have neither the luxury of a smoke-filled casino nor the delights of third-rate seafood and E-glass fishing rods,[2] though surely there were plenty of opportunities to throw up over the side of the ship and beat a fair number of wharf rats into submission. Perhaps to pass the time of mind-numbing sea travel they made a game out of it, a primitive Whack-a-Mole of sorts. It is unsure. We weren't there. But rest assured, the amount of time it took to cross the pond most likely sucked infinitely more than the daylong-slice-of-perdition Hogan experienced as a kid.

The majority of perdition aside, there's a documentary that aired on PBS called *The Appalachians*, which is an in-depth cultural and historical study of the Appalachian mountain region. In a moment of providence, one of the authors happened to be flipping through channels one evening when he landed on it. The interviews—with such icons as the awfully revered Johnny Cash, bluegrass musician Ricky Skaggs, and the legendary Marty Stuart (more on this guy a little later)—sucked him in. Normally he would have passed by without much thought, landing on some lamentable pseudo-reality MTV program or a show featuring immense, hairy men modifying vehicles, but it was as if the Lord Himself had landed in his living room and proclaimed, "Thou shalt not watch *Laguna Beach*, but rather this dry PBS documentary instead, for you shall coauthor a book about this very subject, and it shall be good." (That last part, about the book being good in the Lord's eyes, may be a bit presumptuous.)

In the film there is a section where the word-of-mouth transfer of traditional songs from the Old World to the New is being discussed, how these songs soon became a deeply rooted part of the culture in the Appalachian region. Among the artists and historians, the consensus was that 1) boat travel did in fact suck, and that 2) there wasn't any room to bring along your creature comforts, save for a fiddle and a brain full of songs. Our heroic immigrants possessed an entire oral history set to the music in their heads, as well as a cultural identity of mirthful community gatherings fostered by this music,

---

2. This is a rod of fiberglass construction apparently able to withstand enormous amounts of oceanic distress, such as baby shark thrashing.

with the hopes of creating a tiny reprieve from the hardships of day-to-day life. Don't you love the image this conjures—a boat filled with starving, seasick families, nothing but the clothes on their backs, gathering on deck to sing and dance together to the fiddle songs of the one guy who managed to sneak an instrument on board, all with the expectation that they would be transported, at least temporarily, from the horrors of oceanic travel and seventeenth-century Whack-a-Mole to a place where their souls might soar, where they could find the freedom they were so perilously in search of.

Of course, this might never have happened. As stated previously, we weren't there.

The important thing is that they eventually made it to America, where they came face to face with a bunch of people who got there before them and who already had a nice little racket going and were none too pleased to see them. Safe to say, being a staunch Presbyterian isn't all it's cracked up to be when the descendants of the Church of England, who had settled all over the Northeast and East Coast, are once again surrounding you. Nothing is ever easy, you know?

But instead of climbing back on the boat, the Scotch-Irish gave everyone a hearty "later, suckers" and headed inland, to the wild and untamed mountains of Appalachia, a place, even then, considered to be backwoods. The way they saw it, they could set up camp in relative seclusion and not be bothered, possibly for the first time ever, by those who acted and worshiped in a different manner. And sure enough, if seclusion was what they wanted, it was exactly what they got. In fact, their separation from the rest of the world proved vital to the endearing legacy of their culture, both in terms of their music as well as the importance they placed on family and community. In this isolation, the seeds were planted for a musical style to grow and flourish with little regard to the passing trends of the day, even though in time it would become an amalgam of nearly every musical inclination it had come across. Or, to use a black hole analogy, it was as if in the hills of Appalachia time had stopped and all the various articles of faith and reason, music and hope, heartache and suffering that these people had collected inside themselves on their perilous journey were being squashed into an indefinable mass that would soon hold the heaviness of all of us—without, of course, the volume.[3] The volume, however, was soon about to increase.[4]

---

3. In this instance, we intend to evoke ideas of size or cubic measurement. Geeky science humor. Yet watch how quickly we turn a phrase; it is word wizardry that follows.

4. In this instance, we intend to evoke a measure of loudness. Sheer wizardry, we tell ya.

COLUMNS, PART 3

IT HAPPENED IN THE PARK.

She began the late afternoon routine of going soon after Frank had died. As many years as she had lived in the city, this was the first she'd ever spent any real amount of time there. She had regretful thoughts, wishing she had come more often. Now that she had all the time in the world for relaxation, she had no sincere need of it.

She would buy seeds at a shop called 33rd and Bird between

HE HADN'T ALWAYS BEEN like this. He used to not need to touch every 4th light post he passed. He used to not have to explain red-tinted gloves and muddy shoes and glass jars carried to and from his house. He used to not count constantly. Now he counted everything. It was like a thing did not exist until it was counted. He did not want to forget. He did not count when she was alive. He could not remember how many times she had washed her hair in the sink. He could not remember

BIRDS OF NORTH AMERICA

blackbird

~~bluebird~~

blue jay

bobolink

bobwhite

bunting

cardinal

catbird

Park and Madison. Routine was
good. She had just sat down on
her bench; the birds were already
gathering as she tried to unfold the
top of the bag. The fingers of her
right hand would not cooperate.
She stubbornly managed a small
handful of seeds when the bag
dropped. Her vision went blurry.
She tried to stand but couldn't.
The birds were oblivious, their
beaks stabbing about everywhere.

A young couple stopped to help,
as apparently it is impossible to
miss an old woman having a
stroke while covered in pecking
pigeons—even in New York City.

She hadn't really thought

how many times she had placed the mail on the corner of the kitchen counter. He could not remember how many times he had called her. Saying he was just finishing up at the office and would be there soon. He could not remember how many steps it was from the hospital's elevator door to the door of her room. He could not remember the exact number of hours spent listening to the sounds of the machines that sat beside her bed. He could not remember how many bites of food he had taken alone in the cafeteria. Her. Just a few floors above. Fed through tubes. But now he was counting. The bites he had taken alone had

chat

~~chickadee~~

chuck-will's-widow

cowbird

creeper

crossbill

crow

cuckoo

~~dickcissel~~

dove

finch

~~flicker~~

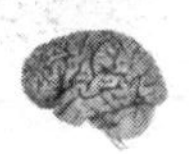

much about death before the
stroke. Not even when Frank
left. And more recently, when
her sister Emily had died, she
had still been fairly unaffected.
A long drawn-out illness gave
everyone plenty of time to brace.
The phone call was expected. At
the time she hadn't given much
thought to how lucky Emily
would be. To have had someone.

been exactly 3. He no longer ate
solid food. He could remember
the exact number of syllables
uttered into the phone. As he
announced her death for the
first time. 14. It never felt more
final than those 11 words. He
called her sister. She too lived
in New York. She had never
visited. Not once. He had
counted. He remembers her

She remembers his breath on the other end staccato
and shallow. He spoke. "She died this morning with me holding
her hand." At least she had passed peacefully. At least you could see
it coming from a long way off. At least it could be said that she
did not go alone. Someone was with her at the end. Touching her.
Telling her it would be okay. Telling her she would be missed.
A day wouldn't go by that she wouldn't

be remembered. He began
counting as soon as the words

think about how lucky Emily
was. To have had him there.

flycatcher

gnatcatcher

goldfinch

grackle

grosbeak

~~hummingbird~~

junco

kingbird

~~kingfisher~~

kinglet

lark

began falling from his lips into the phone. He had known. For a very long time. That she would be gone. That this day would arrive and he would be left with only the memory of her. Yet he was angry. Angry at himself. That he was still here and she was not. That already he couldn't remember. What was the last sentence she had said? Or more precisely. What was the last one that had made any sense. He clapped his hands 4 times hard. He felt the stiff points of the nettles enter the skin. He clapped again. 4 times. He was crying now. Then he saw the bird lying in the clean mulch. Next to the

To have anyone,
besides a bunch of pigeons.

She still went to the park. Every other afternoon. She felt like she owed them that. They had been there for her; she had the scars from a few of their pecks as a reminder.

She would watch their tiny dark eyes, and she was convinced they were getting brighter and more sympathetic with each visit, that there was genuine concern coming from some of them. It seemed like they understood what it took for her to come here now. Occasionally one of them would

~~longspur~~

magpie

martin

meadowlark

~~mockingbird~~

nighthawk

~~nightingale~~

nightjar

nuthatch

oriole

~~ovenbird~~

~~phoebe~~

patch of lavender hyssops. He knew for certain that the birds were his fault. He bent over. Took the spade. And gently lifted it out of the soft dirt. He opened the bag and let it slide in on top of the other two he had found that morning. The birds and the flickering lights. He was sure that both of these had begun after he had started counting. He wasn't going to stop though. He would not forget. He would not forget. He would not forget. He would not forget. He pushed all of his weight down to the ends of his shoes. At times he could make himself heavier than he really was. His jaw clenched.

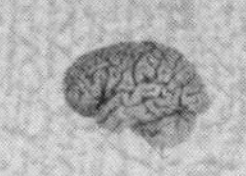

stop pecking, lift his head from
the sidewalk, and stare back
at her. Maybe they did know.
How heavy a thing this was to
carry. How nervous she was all
the time. How every time she
entered a new space she would
look around. Watch the faces
of the people. Thinking these
might be the ones. The last ones
to see her alive. Wondering if
someone would hold her hand.

Dying alone had become her
greatest fear.

pigeon

pipit

raven

robin

sapsucker

skylark

~~sparrow~~

starling

swallow

swift

tanager

thrasher

~~thrush~~

warbler

waterthrush

waxwing

wheatear

~~whippoorwill~~

woodpecker

wood thrush

wren

~~yellowthroat~~

THE ART OF CONDOLENCE

What to Write, What to Say,
What to Do at a Time of Loss

LETTERS: THE SEVEN COMPONENTS[1]

1. Acknowledge the loss. Note how you heard the news.
2. Express your sympathy. Do not hesitate to use the word *death* or note the actual cause of death.
3. Note special qualities about the deceased. They may be personal characteristics, for example, courage, leadership, or decisiveness.
4. Recount a memory about the deceased. Early in bereavement, memories of the deceased are often temporarily dimmed. This can be frightening for those in grief. Relate a brief anecdote or two.
5. Note special qualities of the bereaved. The bereaved will typically experience a transitory impairment in their usual capacity for self-appreciation. It can be helpful to recall a loving remark about the survivor that was once made by the deceased.
6. Offer assistance. Make a specific offer (doing the grocery shopping, running errands, answering the phone, taking care of the children, helping with correspondence.)
7. Close with a thoughtful word or phrase.

---

1. From *The Art of Condolence: What to Write, What to Say, What to Do at a Time of Loss* by Leonard M. Zunin, MD, and Hilary Stanton Zunin (New York: HarperCollins, 1991).

Dear Justin,

It was awful hearing your voice on the phone announcing Emily had passed. I am so sorry for your loss.

Her death is truly that - a loss. I remember when Emily lost her ring at the beach. I'm certain we would have endlessly dug in the sand had you not found it lying on her beach towel.

She was always so sensitive. You were her strength. If I can help in any way, whether it is getting groceries or returning correspondence, please don't hesitate to call. It is in moments like these that we are able to remember the beauty of life.

Sincerely,

Virginia

HISTORY
OF THE
SOUL

— PART 4 —

SCIENCE, RELIGION, AND THE CONTINUING QUESTION OF THE SOUL

or

The Big Empty, Part 2

The year 1543 was a landmark of sorts. That was the year Vesalius published his book with the pictures of skinless people lounging around. While he was busy changing the way everybody thought about anatomy and the human body, a guy named Copernicus was doing the same for the world of astronomy. He published a book that claimed the Earth was not the center of the universe, but rather a planet that revolved around the sun. Not only that, but all the other planets revolved around the sun as well.

This was not in line with what Aristotle had laid out, which had, as mentioned earlier, become church doctrine. Aristotle's teachings did not take into account any sort of math—a non-proclivity that he and the two authors share ... we warn you, very little math was incorporated in the assembly of this book. Copernicus, on the other hand, was quite fond of math and used it to predict the motions of the planets. He believed that his model of the universe was one of order and beauty. The Church cared not for his version of order or beauty and, for the most part, ignored him. They too couldn't be bothered with math.[1]

GALILEO: Other than being the namesake of one of the only good songs by the Indigo Girls, Galileo was the type of guy who didn't take kindly to bad science. That is, science without the proper physics to back it up. He decided to be the one to go head-to-head with Aristotle. In one corner, we have Aristotle, bolstered by his generally accepted theories (church doctrine, no less) that the Earth is the center of everything. In the other corner, the young upstart challenger, Galileo, armed with ... mathematics. Awesome. (Somewhere Copernicus was crying because no one paid him any mind.)

To make his case, Galileo developed a new theory of physics (inertia!) and built himself a telescope.[2] It was with this telescope that he noticed a number of things. Such as moons orbiting Jupiter and how our own moon had craters and mountains aplenty. Oh yeah, and that the Milky Way was actually made up of stars. Basically, at the end of the day, he was able to confirm all the theories laid out by Copernicus, who rolled over in his grave to celebrate. The Earth was, in fact, not the center of the Universe. And he had proven it.

The Church took notice of this one and responded with a collective sigh of "Oh, crap." For good measure, in 1616 they went ahead and placed the works of Copernicus alongside some of his esteemed colleagues on the list of banned literature.[3]

MONKS FIGHT BACK: Not everyone within the Church agreed with the head honchos. A small number of priests and monks saw the need to break from the philosophy of Aristotle (yeah, he's still around), which, again, by now had become doctrine. In light of the recent translations of his works, these mutineers began to notice that his notions allowed no room for the spiritual belief of angels, demons, and miracles or, perhaps most significant to our discussion here, the immortal soul. A young monk in Paris named Marin Mersenne

---

1. Zimmer, p. 25-27.
2. All in a day's work, really. What, you don't just go around discovering laws of physics and building devices to study the expanses of the universe?
3. Zimmer, p. 28.

decided to officially part with tradition.[4] The way he saw it was, if the Church continued its relationship with Aristotle, it would no longer be relevant and eventually die out. He was extremely concerned with this "soul as part of the body" thing that no one wanted to talk about. But how would the Church accomplish such a severing from its previous thought and still remain intact? Simple, by taking "the soul out of nature."[5] A soulless mechanistic world was the only route visible to Marin. The universe must be made up of passive matter subject to laws laid out by God at the dawn of time. Plus, Marin was enamored with the way Galileo had used math to make sense of the cosmos, so being the killjoy that he was, he applied the same methods to music, basically stripping it of all its more magical qualities.[6] It became nothing more than just a series of vibrations in the air, rather than sympathy between souls causing all of the influence.[7]

Marin was not alone in his thinking. He had a buddy, a priest named Gassendi, who claimed that the world was made of invisible particles called atoms,[8] which got together to form molecules, and that this did not conflict with Christian beliefs and therefore was not a threat. God Himself had created the atoms at the dawn of time, setting them on a course to play out in accordance with His grand designs. These atoms were also the composition of the soul, which was passed on through sex, through the generations, making new souls whenever an embryo was formed.[9] He called this the "sensitive soul." He also believed that since humans were able to think in the abstract, they must also have a second soul, an immaterial rational soul. This one lived in the brain (no mention of "empty spaces") where it hung around and thought about all of the sights and sounds brought to it by the sensitive soul. They

---

4. Leave it to the French ...

5. Zimmer, p. 28.

6. Again, leave it to the French ... Okay, okay, just kidding. The French are lovely, as is their country. We, the authors, really enjoy the delights of pastries and bicycle racing.

7. Zimmer, p. 28.

8. Either Gassendi was just buying into ideas that were around already, or he had the same incredible superpowers that Epicurus had.

9. A Salesian Catholic priest and moral philosopher named Norman Ford gives a clever argument that an embryo cannot become infused with the soul until fourteen days past conception, which is the recognized length of time before identical twinning is no longer possible. If the zygote were to split in two after being infused, each embryo would be using only half a soul. This could quickly become awkward and create unnecessary insecurity issues. However, it *would* allow for the half souls to play numerous look-alike jokes on their friends. Mary Roach, *Spook*, (New York: W.W. Norton & Company Ltd., 2005), p. 65.

were BFF.

This theory seemed to work for him, because it fit in nicely with the "oh so popular" (and previously mentioned) natural philosophy of the day. The sensitive soul was bound to the body, while the rational soul was immortal, unbothered by the physical laws of the world.[10]

THE SECOND COMING OF DESCARTES: Sure, Descartes was a philosopher (some would say that he was the father of modern philosophy), but did you know that he was also a scientist? He wore many hats. (Specifically, he liked hats with plumes. He also fancied wearing a sword.) He was a devout Catholic, but wasn't really sure about much else.

Descartes moved to Paris, where he fell in with Marin the monk and his gang of free-thinking ministers, and proceeded to happily go about replacing the soul of nature with mechanics and patterns,[11] under the rationale that he was giving the Catholic Church something firm and absolute to stand on.

Soon after he had explained the mystery of rainbows and sufficiently made them less fun, he turned his attention to the human body, calling it an "earthen machine," having about as much use for a soul as a clock.[12] Every move of the body could be explained as the tugging of nerves reacting to stimuli around them. He did, however, recognize a fundamental difference between animals and humans. Here, once again, comes the rational soul. But how could he explain it?

He figured that this soul lived somewhere in the head. So he studied calf brains and decided that it must reside in a diminutively modest ball called the pineal gland. Unfortunately, the human pineal gland is nowhere close to where he thought it was, but hey, he was only human (albeit a human with a sword and a feathered hat). Not to be deterred, he continued his efforts at proving the body was more mechanical and less spiritual in operation.[13]

Descartes began compiling all of his work. But as his claims mounted and conclusions loomed, his fear grew that the Church he was so

---

10. Zimmer, p. 29-30.

11. He studied matters such as light and figured that the color of light was due to physics. He took apart a rainbow, long seen as the covenant of God, showing it to be light bouncing around between drops of rain.

12. Zimmer, p. 34-35.

13. Ibid., p. 37.

devoted to would declare him a heretic. After all, Galileo had just been blasted for his support of Copernicus, and Descartes deduced he was in no way any safer. So, ever the inventive one, he reworked things. It's at this point that it hits him: "I think, therefore I am." This was his big eureka moment! The way he saw it, this proved all of the science he had worked on and, in the process, proved that God existed. In his head it all made sense. He wrote about these ideas in the modern vernacular of the day, and his books were a big hit among the populace.[14] But much to his chagrin, he wound up on the blacklist of not only the Catholic Church, but the Protestant Church as well. The current theologians saw his philosophy as still doing away with the soul, and teachers at the universities taught his material, just without the metaphysical stuff, which for Descartes was the foundation the rest of his philosophy sat upon. He caught it from all sides.[15]

So just as anyone might do when coming under fire from all he holds dear, Descartes went to Sweden.[16] Even here he was unlucky. He caught pneumonia and, in a nod to our friend Richard Napier, tried to cure himself with a regimen of wine and tobacco mixed together in hopes that he would induce vomiting and rid himself of the crud in his system. Needless to say, it didn't work. On his deathbed, he had a true moment of clarity, apparently saying to his own soul, "My soul, you have been a captive for a long time. Now the hour has come when you must leave your prison, this body; you must bear this separation with joy and courage."[17]

Despite the deathbed confession to his essential being, he had done his part in killing much of what the soul was thought to be. He had used science to explain the mechanics of the body, in movement and the senses and even in memory, and despite having acknowledged another variety of soul, he had set science on a whole new irreversible path.

---

14. Rather than other philosophy books, which were traditionally written in Latin, furthering the cause of snooty university types all the way. Zimmer, p. 38.

15. "I think, therefore I can't win ..." Sorry. That was a really, *really* bad joke. We are embarrassed by it, yet decided to keep it simply because of its remarkable lack of humor.

16. Sweden is generally considered to be prosperous, clean, and socially liberal. Its countrymen are thought to have a very high standard of living, a notion put forth by every single Volvo on the road today. It is funny to note that Sweden is primarily Lutheran and historically was at odds with Catholicism—Descartes' faith of choice. Taking all of this into account, it seems to be something of a paradox that he would have ended up there. Perhaps we have underestimated the powerful lure of the meatball.

17. Zimmer, p. 40.

IM CONVERSATION 4

Plane flight from Dallas to San Diego

HOGAN: Yo

yep **:DAVID**

HOGAN: Dude, I'm in such hot water.

HOGAN: You know when you try to do something, and you have the best intent, but you get completely hosed in the end?

uh, yes **:DAVID**

HOGAN: So I was trying to take Robin out for some ice cream today to celebrate the last day of the school year, but we never even made it.

HOGAN: Mostly because I'm stupid.

HOGAN: There was all this construction going on, so I figured I would take this side street to avoid it.

HOGAN: We ended up going like 5 minutes out of our way, only to wind up at a dead end.

HOGAN: By the time we got to the ice cream place, she was so hacked at me that she didn't want the treat anymore. I had to turn the car around and go right back home.

HOGAN: Lame.

:DAVID

3.7 minutes later—What the crap? Did he freaking fall asleep?!

HOGAN: Dude, you still there?

2.5 minutes later—This sucks.

sorry **:DAVID**

i was pulling up something to listen to. **:DAVID**

i missed all that. **:DAVID**

hang on. let me catch up ... **:DAVID**

HOGAN: OK

oh man. that's lame. **:DAVID**

HOGAN: Yeah ...

Like I said.

HOGAN: Story of my life.

i picked bright eyes. **:DAVID**

HOGAN: What?

i'm listening to bright eyes **:DAVID**

perfect for such a sad story
of ice cream unprocured **:DAVID**

HOGAN: Tell me about it. It's just that it's
warm outside, and with the newfound freedom
of school being out and all, I thought it would
be a really good idea.

no. it sounded sweet. **:DAVID**

HOGAN: Yeah, just another example
of best intentions gone foul.

ahhh ... descartes **:DAVID**

? **:DAVID**

Where is he? Come on.

right? **:DAVID**

HOGAN: Uh sure

HOGAN: If you want to look at it that way.

no. i thought that's what you
were talking about. **:DAVID**

this im is supposed to appear just
after the chapter ending
with descartes. **:DAVID**

HOGAN: Ah.

HOGAN: He got messed over too.

i think it's pretty funny. well in a very sad
bright eyes sort of way. i mean he gets all this
flack and blame thrown on him, and the whole
time he was trying to give the
church a foothold. **:DAVID**

sad really **:DAVID**

but funny **:DAVID**

HOGAN: Yeah

HOGAN: At least he wasn't trying for ice cream.

ha, the death of ice cream **:DAVID**

and cotton candy **:DAVID**

and other fluffy things **:DAVID**

HOGAN: Nice

it's all very santa claus. **:DAVID**

this best intentions stuff, that is. **:DAVID**

HOGAN: How do you mean?

santa started out as a pretty good idea. **:DAVID**

then it turned into something a little more vicious i think. **:DAVID**

all teenage rebellion comes from santa. **:DAVID**

HOGAN: Yeah.

What in the world?

parents lie **:DAVID**

great intentions **:DAVID**

i'm sure they're just eager to provide some enjoyment to their children, you know, bestowing dreams of reindeer and candy canes upon them. maybe hoping to provoke some small amounts of affection from them. **:DAVID**

i don't own any kids,
so what do i know? **:DAVID**

but seriously a fib this grand can only
bring injury in the end. **:DAVID**

i mean, how better to annihilate trust in a
young impressionable child than to have
the people they trust most tell them such a
profound lie as the existence
of this fat jovial man **:DAVID**

HOGAN: But lots of big folks are jovial.

HOGAN: Granted they don't sneak into
your house in the dead of winter.

HOGAN: At least most of them don't ...

see, great idea **:DAVID**

but then it all
goes to no place good. **:DAVID**

HOGAN: Sort of like this IM
exchange.

HOGAN: I always wanted to be on the
naughty list but still get all the presents.

HOGAN: The naughty list just seemed
to have more fun.

HOGAN: I just never got around to
doing anything bad.

ha! procrastination! **:DAVID**

HOGAN: Truth be told, I'm actually
just trying to put off work right now.

see? procrastination. **:DAVID**

HOGAN: Yeah, amazing how you can get excited about things like Descartes and Santa when you have impending deadlines hanging over your head.

procrastination is just one more symptom and verification that we do not consider our mortal state in the planning of our day-to-day activities. **:DAVID**

HOGAN: Wow. You just got really serious really fast.

sorry **:DAVID**

i'm listening to bright eyes. **:DAVID**

Man. Conor Oberst [Bright Eyes] is such a nihilist! Is anyone more dismal? Wow. Cheer up, Charlie. I love how something as simple as a song can color reality. It can change a moment.

HOGAN: Oh yeah.

HOGAN: It's remarkable how music can paint a moment.

yeah. i love that. **:DAVID**

No, actually, after thinking about it for a second, I hate it. How music now invades our experiences without permission. How it has become unavoidable. There is always music playing. When did this happen? When did we decide that we must always have music? Who did this? Didn't we realize what impact this would have? Arbitrarily shaping what we feel and what we will forever associate this or that experience with. Right now a girl is in a Wal-Mart somewhere buying a pregnancy test and "Like a Virgin" is playing over the Wal-Mart PA. Did we not see this coming? We are now helpless. There is no control to be exerted.

HOGAN: Right. What song are you listening to right now?

:DAVID

The evening of Kyle's funeral my wife and I, along with four close friends, walked into Chili's for milkshakes. (Milkshakes!) Death Cab for Cutie was playing over the speakers. (Death Cab!) I heard the chorus as we stepped through the doors, "... bop bah this is the sound of settling ..." A guy was sitting by himself at a table, happily singing along as I walked by, "Bop bah ...!" Why was his voice so sad? Not the guy who was sitting at the table, but Ben Gibbard—the Death Cab guy. I could not believe Death Cab was coming through the Chili's speakers. Then. Why then? Death Cab never used to get played in places like that. We used to be safe from this at least. Safe from Death Cab in our public spaces!?! Death Cab! That moment was too volatile. It is reckless to have this kind of music playing in such a freely available space. And it was not the sound of "settling." Ben was getting this moment all wrong. Settling is a quiet and floating thing. This was the sound of something too terrifically loud and damaged and crumpled, and it was rolling over me, and I could not believe flipping Death Cab was coming from the speakers. In that Chili's. On that night. After carrying my friend in his coffin. After putting him in the back of a hearse. A hearse! I put my friend in a hearse!! After taking him back out and setting him over his grave, Ben freaking Gibbard was singing in his whiny little voice, and my heart was tugged from where it hung in my chest and was suddenly sitting in front of me on the table at Chili's. And it was not at all settling! No, Ben, settling is when tiny grains of dirt have been stirred, and they stop rising and spinning and start floating to the bottom of a fluid, drifting this way and that, back and forth toward the

bottom, slow, to the right and the left and the
right and always moving down,
but incrementally.

HOGAN: Hello?

Come on!? Again?

:DAVID

No. There was nothing settling in that moment, and the music played on, and Ben kept singing and singing, and there I was, forced to sit in that unrestricted Cab of Death (Ha! Public transportation! That's what it was!) with that Ben freaking Gibbard. But I loved him. I loved his whiny little voice. Even though he was not playing fair. Why was his voice pulling my heart out of my chest and setting it in front of me? I loved him. I loved his voice. Why would he do this to me? I wanted to cry. I wanted to cry a cry that wouldn't contort my face and scare everyone. I didn't believe what Ben was singing. If it was "settling," I could've cried a cry that was less fierce and horrific. The thing that came in waves left me hunched and caused my body to shake and my mouth to stretch out and out to the point it looked almost like I was smiling, and you would think that except for the ridiculous wail coming from my gut out my throat with such velocity and force to throw my mouth so wide. It was unquestioningly not a smile. I understand now the word guttural. I was tired of this crying. And Ben freaking Gibbard was doing this on purpose. He was taking advantage of the situation. I didn't want this kind of crying. I wanted to cry a quiet settling cry.

HOGAN: Hey!

This sucks.

:DAVID

I wanted to sit there, quietly, with my heart sitting in front of me on the table (Ben Gibbard set it there! In front of me!) and let the tears just leak, without noise, across my cheeks and let them follow the surface of my jaw and let them cling to my neck and let them run down my chest into this hole, this cavity that sits vacant, let these quiet tears fill the void. I am taking my heart from the table and shoving it back into my chest, and it is beating hard in the water of my tears, my chest still cracked open, still exposed, and the heart's beating splashing my tears out onto the table where it used to sit. Beating and splashing and the need for napkins and beating and splashing and napkins soaked through. Bring me more! Beating and splashing, and the tears are running off the table and taking the napkins that were just brought, and beating and splashing, and they run wet to the floor and float, and I move my feet, and I hear them splash, and I pick my feet up and stomp them down, and there is splashing and beating, and it is running off the table, and I feel the tears running down my cheeks holding to my face, following the curve of my jaw, holding to my neck, and running down my chest into this hole, and there is beating and splashing, and there is water up to my calves, my knees, my waist, and I yell, "Everyone out! Everyone out! I'm going to drown us all! I can't stop it! I can't stop it! Forget Ben Gibbard, save yourselves!!!" And this water that is composed of my sadness is now up to my chest, and there it finally covers the hole, and there is no more splashing, and I put my hands to the hole, and I can feel the beating and the force pushed through the liquid to my palms, and my eyes stop the flow, and I sit there, up to my neck, and as things settle the guy with a red Chili's shirt brings my milkshake. I notice that I don't know the song that is currently playing.

HOGAN: Yo? Are you gone?

no. sorry. i was scrolling
through my ipod. sorry. **:DAVID**

I can't believe he's gone. I can't believe he's gone. I can't believe he's gone. believe he's gone. i can't belevehe's gone. i can't believe he's ogne I an't blinev hs' gone. Is he gone? i cna' blive. i just can't believe. i just can't. i just can't. i just.i just. i just. believe ...

HOGAN: No

HOGAN: It's fine.

no really. i'm really sorry. **:DAVID**

HOGAN: Really it's fine. I don't feel
like working, remember?

hey **:DAVID**

HOGAN: Uh, yeah?

you know the flood? **:DAVID**

HOGAN: What? You mean like
the 40 days and 40 nights?

yeah. i know it sounds completely childish, but
i think that might have been when god was at
his saddest. he knew what was coming. what
would be necessary later. i know it's like a
child's notion, but i've felt that sad
sometimes. **:DAVID**

HOGAN: Huh?

nothing **:DAVID**

HOGAN: So anyways, I did see your point
earlier.

what point? **:DAVID**

HOGAN: About procrastination!

Come on?! Pay attention!

oh yeah. seriously. **:DAVID**

we put stuff off because, of course, we'll have time to get to it. **:DAVID**

or it just helps assure us that we'll still be around. maybe we need to put stuff off to help promote the lie. i should start using that. "no. i'm not lazy, thank you very much. i am simply making an attempt at providing myself assurance that i will be here tomorrow." **:DAVID**

HOGAN: Honestly, it's easier to put off thinking about all of this stuff rather than considering it now.

HOGAN: Of course, like with most things, the longer you put it off the harder it is to deal with later. Maybe.

seriously **:DAVID**

planes remind me of melancholy things **:DAVID**

is it ok to be networking on a plane? **:DAVID**

HOGAN: No

HOGAN: I think we run the risk of making the plane crash by having this conversation.

that's not at all humorous **:DAVID**

well in a cartesian way of sorts, i guess it is. **:DAVID**

HOGAN: Maybe so. But think about it ...

HOGAN: We are having a conversation about putting off thoughts of death, right?

HOGAN: And by doing so, we could make the plane's systems malfunction and send us all into a deadly freefall, making death a very real imminent problem.

why am i practically laughing right now? **:DAVID**

i am sick **:DAVID**

i have an incredibly stupid grin on my face. **:DAVID**

what row are you in? you have to see this ridiculous grin. **:DAVID**

HOGAN: Errr. 19. Right next to the kid who crapped himself a little bit ago.

no! i can smell that! **:DAVID**

we're row 7. **:DAVID**

always makes me nervous sitting in this row. **:DAVID**

hey, so by us continuing to type we're rebelling. **:DAVID**

i would like to again blame the jovial little man. **:DAVID**

HOGAN: I like Santa taking the brunt of things here.

and of course i don't believe networking dorks with a plane at all. liars. **:DAVID**

which is also why i secretly

listen to my ipod at
both takeoff and landing. **:DAVID**

HOGAN: Same here!

i will say that while i'm covertly dialing up
listening material, i always consider that this
could be the last thing i hear. **:DAVID**

i am intensely aware
that i could be choosing the
soundtrack of my death. **:DAVID**

what do you want to be listening to when
you die? **:DAVID**

HOGAN: Depends.

HOGAN: It's always different.

yeah! **:DAVID**

HOGAN: Yeah, on whether or not I just
hacked my wife off before leaving on a plane
by having good intentions but then being
colossally stupid.

HOGAN: That would determine if I were to,
say, listen to something angry, so then I'd go
out with fury and clenched fists.

HOGAN: But then sometimes I'm wistful, and
I would like to go on a quiet note.

HOGAN: But most of the time I feel
epic and sad, so I just end up listening to
Death Cab.

yeah **:DAVID**

conor [bright eyes] just sang the following ... **:DAVID**

"now i don't know when
but a day's gonna come

that there won't be a moon
and there won't be a sun **:DAVID**

it will all go black **:DAVID**

it will all go back **:DAVID**

to the way it's supposed to be" **:DAVID**

HOGAN: Well played, hipster elite.

i'm like 7 times more indie than you. **:DAVID**

HOGAN: Maybe we should crash this plane.

dude. so not cool. they could be listening/
watching. and that, my friend, would have
just been a threat. **:DAVID**

that kid who smells could be an air marshal
or something. **:DAVID**

they're crazy good at disguise. **:DAVID**

i'm done here. **:DAVID**

HOGAN: Now I'm scared.

HOGAN: I'm out too!

cool. get to work! **:DAVID**

HISTORY OF BLUEGRASS

— PART 4 —

DEFINITIONS AND TRANSITIONS

or

Gettin' All Academic on Y'all

So this is the point where, if you could, you, the reader, would grab me, your charming bluegrass narrator, by the collar and shake me around a bit and ask, "What is the point of all this, anyhow? You have spent a lot of time talking nonsense about how crappy it is to travel long distances, and how there were a bunch of angry nomadic types who ended up in the backwoods hills of North America for reasons which even you yourself aren't completely sure! What do these people have to do with me? I don't even like bluegrass music, much less care about where it came from! I don't even know what it is to be honest with you!" (Commence to animatedly slapping me, classic *Ren & Stimpy* style, while calling me an "eediot.")[1]

Upon recovery, I would calmly smile, assert that everything is okay, that the real morsels of this little venture are still on their way, and then direct you to this lovely definition of bluegrass by author and

1. Consider this your fair warning. This will not be the only time you wish to confront your brave and fearless narrators with the threat of violence for leading you down the path of mystification.

historian Neil V. Rosenberg:

> Bluegrass is part of country music; it originated with Bill Monroe and his band, the Blue Grass Boys, during the 1940s. During the fifties, it was named and recognized as a unique form—a music in which singers accompany themselves with acoustic rather than electric instruments, using the fiddle, mandolin, guitar, five-string banjo, Dobro, and bass. Its performance demands mastery of virtuoso instrumental techniques (such as Earl Scruggs' banjo style), often executed at rapid tempos. This emphasis on individual virtuosic self-expression led some to call bluegrass the jazz of country music. Bluegrass singing is high-pitched, lonesome sounding; it often involves tightly arranged harmonies. The form and content of its songs and vocal styles, reminiscent of mountain folk singing traditions, have prompted some observers to define it as modern folk music. As important as any defining characteristics of this contemporary hillbilly music is the way it has spread far from the original culture and class in which it emerged. Bluegrass bands and their followers exist all over North America, Japan, Australia, New Zealand, and Europe. Like jazz and blues, bluegrass is an American cultural export.[2]

There you go. That is a sterile, academic, and wholly accurate definition of bluegrass music. It is almost everything you need packed into one paragraph. If you were to memorize it, you could spout off bits and pieces at dinner parties, genuinely annoying those in attendance, prompting them to tag you a know-it-all, yet at the same time undeniably respecting you for committing such a bizarre piece of information to memory.[3] (This modus operandi got Hogan all the

---

2. Neil V. Rosenberg, *Bluegrass, A History*, p. 3.

3. Example: **Snooty dinner party guest:** "Through our mass consumerism, there is no longer a true folk tradition left in our country, only kitschy artifacts produced for tourists by actors playing a part. Our national identity, like the soul of man, is all but dead!"

You: "I beg to differ. The form and content of bluegrass songs and vocal styles, reminiscent of mountain folk singing traditions, have prompted some observers to define it as modern folk music. As important as any defining characteristic of this contemporary music is the way it has spread far from the original culture and class in which it emerged. Like jazz and blues, bluegrass is an American cultural export."

Snooty dinner party guest: "Harrumph! Touché!"

You: "That's right! Now hand over that shrimp cocktail shooter, yo!"

way through college, amazingly enough.)

The thing about the paragraph though, is that while it gives a very informative, clinical working definition, it doesn't, on the surface, get you much further than you were already. You're still left wondering, "Okay, but now what?" The language is scholarly and a little confusing, not to mention that it operates on the assumption that you know what a "Dobro" is and what the "Earl Scruggs banjo style" refers to. (In turn, the authors of this book operate on the assumption that the only reason they know about the Dobro is because they're both rather un-hip individuals who've spent more time learning about just this sort of nonsense than actually having a life. If ever they get the call, they will most certainly be ready for the snooty dinner bash. Incidentally, they know who Earl Scruggs is because he was one bad mother. He also wore a cowboy hat, and that is cool.)

To really get under the skin of bluegrass, to really *get it*, we will need to systematically sort through some of the specifics in Mr. Rosenberg's definition. We have at this point spent quite a bit of time on the history of the immigrants who were instrumental in forming the genre. Those people give us a cultural context and a foundation of traditional songs to build on. What they don't give us, at least by themselves, is the reason that we are even talking about bluegrass, the reason that all of this fits together. What does all of this have to do with death? How does it help us understand grief and personal hurt? Who the heck are Bill Monroe and Earl Scruggs anyway?

All in time. We know now where bluegrass came from (at least the region) and the ethnic background of its primary developers (warlike herdsmen!), but it is necessary at this point for us to dig a little deeper, to pick at some of the individual elements that make up the whole and explore some of the paradoxes held within—namely, how one of the most inherently emotive instruments on the planet can also be one of the most annoying, and how one of the most inherently annoying can at the same time be so freaking cool.

COLUMNS, PART 4

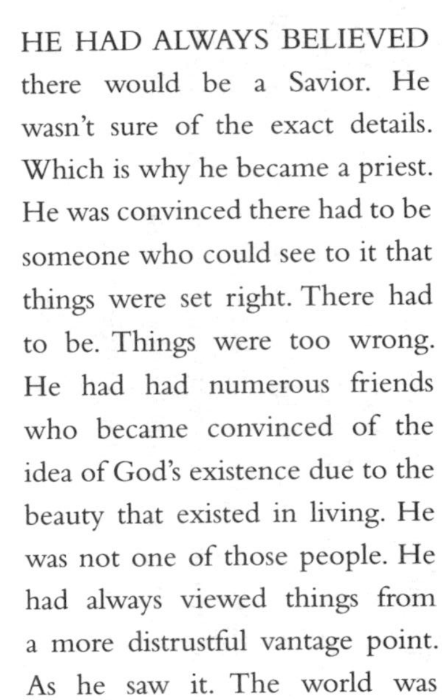

HE HAD ALWAYS BELIEVED there would be a Savior. He wasn't sure of the exact details. Which is why he became a priest. He was convinced there had to be someone who could see to it that things were set right. There had to be. Things were too wrong. He had had numerous friends who became convinced of the idea of God's existence due to the beauty that existed in living. He was not one of those people. He had always viewed things from a more distrustful vantage point. As he saw it. The world was

LIVING WITH HER SON'S family had not been too intolerable.

She had people near, even if some of them found her confusion more entertaining than she was fond of. Her grandson was young and could not possibly know the weight of things yet. She assumed, in all actuality, it must be reasonably comical. But to be the one excluded is difficult when a joke is occurring and there is laughter, even more so when you are the punch line.

HIS MOTHER HAD NOT left her room in seven years.

The bed had long ago collapsed, its four legs stretching out from all four corners as if pointing the weight in all four directions.

Steven had by now grown old enough to care for her, as well as handle most of the daily household responsibilities. He had always managed, functioning beyond his years and containing an understanding of things most obtain only in old age. This

crowded with innate ugliness. He could and would deliberate with anyone brave enough to engage him on the subject. They would talk of mountain ranges. And waterfalls. And sunsets. Or a full moon. Or a quiet lake. Or even the complexities of the human creature. The way the cells of the body fit together. The organs working in harmony. The complexities of the human mind. But he would in turn point to the moment when mountain ranges split apart. When heat would come up from the guts of earth to bury civilizations—talk to the inhabitants of Pompeii about the beauty of a mountain! He'd calmly make mention of

Sometimes she would misplace things on purpose, just to distinguish what it was the others were experiencing.

For instance, they all believed she referred to *forks* as *pens*. When she felt the need to exercise an amount of control, to feel a tiny bit of unhelplessness, she would implement the "pen/fork." They would laugh. She would disappear to her room. And cry.

She disliked that she constantly worried about another stroke. Once, last week, she was riding in a taxi and felt a quick throb to her head. She read the

detail was immediately visible in his eyes. His eyes held lifetimes.

The one thing his mother insisted upon was the continued collection of tears. He did this for her, for when your mother requests one thing of you—a thing she would gladly do herself if only she could lift her arms—and this thing also happens to be your doing, you too would oblige.

Soon, the collection of jars had outgrown the yard. Covering it entirely, both front and back. A path from the street to the front door is all that was afforded it. The jars had then taken

tsunamis. And earthquakes. And request that the individual not get him started on the ways the cells of human beings fit together—ask someone at the bottom of a mass grave how well the cells of the human brain fit together! They coalesce in just such a way as to allow for the worst kinds of injury to be both inflicted and justified. That's how they fit together. Talk to someone who has just cared for their wife 4 long years while the beautiful cells of her body turned on themselves. Robbing him of her. And when he said *someone*. He meant himself. No. He was unconvinced by the ideas of beauty. There was a God. But he was persuaded by the prevalence

driver's name: Luis Ogden. She remembers staring through the plastic window separating the two of them, wondering if he would reach through it and take her hand if she were to request it. She doubted she would have the bravery to ask this of Luis. No, she would sit, quietly, drooling, until he became aware of her unresponsiveness.

She wished for bravery.

The only time she felt any sense of peace was on her bench in the park. She assumed it was due in large part to the fact that she knew exactly what it would be like for the end to find her there.

over the house, being stacked in precarious piles around the kitchen and living areas, allowing little more than space to walk from room to room.

Watching television required it to be viewed through a pile of clear jars containing the heaviest of tears, which obviously distorted the image, causing the people's faces to stretch and augment, and when they talked their mouths would move in unnatural directions. It was hardly worth the trouble anymore.

It was really the lack of space that precipitated Steven picking of all that was ugly and wrong with this place. There had to be a Savior. The gloom required it. And it would take a God. A real God of gods to fix this place. She had been one of those who always found the beauty. She had been good for him. She had been hope. With her death the hope had died. And so he became a priest. It had been difficult to hide the real thoughts living in his head while studying to reach priesthood. His tongue had the teeth marks as proof. Once. He thought he had bitten through it entirely. He had felt his mouth filling with the warmth of his own blood. He swallowed. And swallowed. It is difficult to hear

It was peaceful knowing. The only thoughts that would enter her head would pertain to the birds or Emily.

She thought of Emily a lot.

How she hadn't visited her sister. How she hadn't been there for her. Why hadn't she visited? She had been busy. She was sure she would have time. Emily wouldn't have known the difference.

Then she noticed him. Initially it was because of the eyes. They were haunting. Piercing. It was only after being stunned to a

up the phone. He had tried to keep the jars out of his mother's room, but now there was no choice. The number he dialed was that of a hospital in New York City, one which specialized in heaviness. He would transport his mother there, along with a suitcase full of empty jars.

"Yes. My mother is in great need of assistance, and if you cannot aid us, we will all perish in a flood."

They traveled by train, as it was the only means that would support her weight. It still took seven weeks to get there. Special engineers had been called in to

of the generosity of God when you have stood at the open grave. Of your father. And your mother. And your child. And your wife. When you are the last one above the ground. She was the last to leave him. He wanted to know where Emily was. He wanted to know how this could have all been allowed. He wanted to know what God might be thinking and feeling. At the seminary he had been instructed that God did not feel. That these were simply traits of human finiteness that should not be assigned to the infinite. To grieve and feel were conditions of humanity. They were portions of the earthly. Bound to the husk we leave behind.

stop, mid-stride, by the unnatural blueness of them, that she noticed it to be her bench he was occupying.

He was crying. Had he not been, she would have shooed him along. The fact of the matter was that this was her bench and her pigeons, and there were plenty of other benches to rest his posterior on.

He looked incredibly sad. No, *sad* was not the word. It wasn't that it had been misplaced, just that it was too weak a word for his countenance. A tear rolled from his cheek and fell. She must officially be going crazy because she could have sworn she felt a

try to ascertain why so much fuel had been consumed. Never for one instant was it suspected to be the little lady in cabin thirty-four.

He had made it a point to go to the park every day, just to get out of the sterile hallways and fluorescent lighting and circular conversations. On every floor they were the same.

It was so incongruent to have this park in the middle of all the concrete and steel and noise. It made you want to be quiet. At first it had helped to come here. Then he noticed this was where all of the birds

He acquired large words such as *anthropomorphism*—the attribution of human characteristics to a being that was not human. He did not find this beautiful. He found the thought ugly that God could breathe "inspired" words that were a lie. That He might lead us on through the Scriptures in such a pitiless way. Why would God assign attributes to Himself again and again that He did not have? If God did not have the capacity to feel such a severing as the ones that had come to us mere mortals. Then it follows that He could not possibly know any real relationship within the community of the trinity. Maybe "relationship" was just another

tremor through the ground when it
hit the dirt.

She had never beheld
such sadness. The look on
his face was as if
he felt the collective weight
spanning the width of his
shoulders. She felt the weight of
the bag of seeds in her hand. She
thought of the birds.

"Excuse me?"

"Oh, no. Oh my, no. That's
quite okay."

"Oh, no. My goodness, I don't

came. He heard them singing. Each day he came, it grew more quiet.

Soon it would be done. It would not be much longer before of human existence settling to rest solely upon his shoulders. He prayed the jars would hold until then.

"Sorry."

"I said, 'sorry'. I'm on your bench."

"Well it seems your birds are a little disappointed."

finite concept. Maybe He was lying again. And this is exactly why he had become a priest. The compelling that had overcome him to enter the priesthood would be similar to someone suddenly becoming obsessed with say—food preparation. To the point that they simply *had* to become a chef. *Obsessed* seems too tame a word. There was no relief from it. Well. Actually. The only occasions he felt any peace from this obsession were here in the garden. Now of course. Neither *obsession* nor *garden* were exactly the right words. He could never find exactly the right words.

think they know the difference between one lamp shade and another."

"I don't mean to be so very cushion, but may I inquire why you are weaving?"

"Oh my, yes. You feel it too, do you? You look too terribly blonde for such a thing."

"Oh that I understand most definitely. You see, I drop these pebbles here every other afternoon. It feels like exactly what is required. But it is for the birds that I drop them."

"I'm so tired though."

"You're absolutely right."

"It's because of the heaviness."

"It is what is required of me."

"Yes. Exactly."

"What is that in the palm of your right hand?"

"Soon it will be lifted."

"It is to be a message."

"Who is it for?"

"Everyone."

"It sounds very important."

"It is the most important. It is the heaviest thing to ever be sent."

"What will carry such a message?"

"A bird. The only bird that can bear such weight."

CONVERSATION KEY

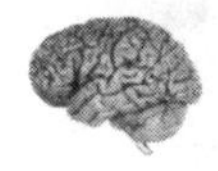

WHEN SHE SAID ...

lamp shade = person
cushion = forward
weaving = crying
drop = carry
blonde = young
pebbles = seeds
birds = love

HISTORY
OF THE
SOUL

— PART 5 —

SCIENCE, RELIGION, AND THE STILL CONTINUING QUESTION OF THE SOUL

or

The Big Empty, Part 3

1662, OXFORD, ENGLAND: The man with the hair of a dark red pig cuts open the skull of some poor, recently deceased sap and holds it aloft in the air for all of his buddies to see. Thomas Willis, a brain in hand, begins the age of neurology.[1] He also grossed out his friends, which goes without saying because he was holding *a fresh brain*.

If you look up Thomas Willis in an encyclopedia, you'll notice that there is much more written about his accomplishments than his life. This is due to the fact that he studied the brain in more detail and with more accuracy than anyone before him.

Over the course of his career, Willis became quite famous as a doctor. For the most part, the brains he literally got his hands on were those belonging to the ruling class of England. This alone speaks to his standing in society and the level of respect shown to him by the

1. Zimmer, p. 5.

upper class. In no small way did this success and notoriety help him continue research sans the fear of being called a heretic, a luxury his predecessors never knew.

Willis, despite such great achievements in mapping the layout of the brain,[2] was ever consumed with the same question everyone else we have discussed so far has been consumed with; namely, *what is the deal with the human soul?* He became confident that through his research he could map out the soul just as he had done with the brain. He believed that animals had a material soul that was mortal and that resided in the brain and nerves. Humans were a slight exception, having both the material soul, like that of an animal, as well as the more mystical immaterial soul. In order to further understand the material soul, he dissected the brain of every creature he could get his hot little hands on. No animal or man was safe from his blades and boundless curiosity.

Creatures as diverse as lobsters, worms, and dogs came under his scrutiny, eventually leaving him to conclude that since they all had different brains and nervous systems, then they must all have slightly different types of souls. However, when he finally got around to monkey brains, he was thrown for a loop, finding them eerily close in design to those of humans.[3] He concluded that animal souls and human souls were very alike, with one major exception. The rational soul of the human being was what set us apart, evidenced by the human's ability to conceive of the abstract and think of matters far outside of ourselves.[4] He deduced that if this rational soul were a material thing, he would have found it. Our brains and animal brains were materially *way* too alike. Therefore, the rational soul is not anything material. When a baby was in the womb, he decided, God would endow it with the rational soul.[5] Because it was of God, it had

---

2. He had help in his drawings from a friend named Christopher Wren, who went on to design cathedrals. It is the authors' personal opinion that this is equally impressive yet in a manner of speaking, not a too-distant task. What is the brain but a cathedral for the mind? Talk about *that* in your reading group!

3. Zimmer, p. 217-219.

4. Well, *some* of us, that is.

5. One more shout-out to Salesian Catholic priest and moral philosopher Norman Ford. Come on, zygote.

no tangible substance and was immortal.[6]

Willis died believing in the immortal, rational soul. That said, he is now remembered more for his medical and anatomical discoveries than anything else he did involving the essential being of the human race, further testament to the notion that the "soul" has died in public consciousness.

MODERN TIMES: Have you ever observed one of those shows on the Discovery Channel or PBS where scientists are shown all bunched around a computer screen while some poor sap is lying in the next room, his head crammed in an MRI machine? The computer screen that is receiving all of the attention is generally busy displaying a digital image of the poor fellow's brain, and if you are lucky, it's depicted as a three-dimensional object, revolving around in space with little sections of it lit up in an incredibly pleasing array of colors. This would be the modern equivalent to Willis' work. It is perceptibly more high-tech and certainly less bloody. Technological developments such as the MRI have allowed current neurologists to discover some really fantastic things in relation to the human brain and how it works. At the same time, these advances have caused questions concerning the soul to become more complex than ever before.

One way of understanding this would be by dissecting the four pillars of neuroscience and how they relate compared to the beliefs of Thomas Willis.[7]

1) Willis believed that the animal spirits of the material soul traveled through the brain and governed nearly everything in our day-to-day lives. We now commonly refer to these "spirits" as little electrical impulses. This is no less cool, but it is a lot less mystical.

2) Willis claimed that as the spirits moved to different parts of the brain, they performed different functions for the soul. Modern science has shown us that the brain is indeed divided up into

---

6. Zimmer, p. 221-222.

7. Bet you can't wait for this? Once again, stick with us. This should all pay off in the end.

sections, with different networks of cells (called neurons) designed for very specific jobs. Again, no mention of *spirits* in modern terminology.

3) Willis remarked that human brains and animal brains are remarkably similar, and for him this posed a problem. Neurologists now purport that the human brain is unmistakably something of a very complex "theme and variation" on the animal brain. For modern science, no real problem is presented by noting this.

4) Willis was on a mission, as a doctor, to find the diseases of the *soul* and cure them. Today this is seen as exploration of the human *brain*, seeking out the disorders within and curing them. One needs to look no further than the enormous business of brain drugs, both legal ("It makes me feel like me again, with a low risk of sexual side effects!") and illegal.[8]

We have been reduced to electricity and chemicals. Science has been able, through the use of ever-impressive technology, to explain away notions that we once thought exclusive to the human spirit; this spirit that was once mysteriously moving through our bodies and heads has suddenly become the same thing as the lightning we see during a thunderstorm, albeit on a much smaller scale. Carl Zimmer writes, "Everything that neuroscientists have learned in recent years goes against the notion of the self."[9] We scrutinize a scan of someone's brain from an MRI machine and are able to distinguish an individual's thoughts and feelings; we are able to now hold in our hands a colorful picture of electrical impulses, the ebb and flow of blood to particular regions, the complexities of our emotions explained by variances of color.

These advances are simultaneously amazing and depressing, but still nothing conclusive has been found to explain that certain essence, that "self" that makes every person so unique. If in fact the soul

8. Zimmer, p. 264-265.
9. Ibid., p. 265.

were immaterial, wouldn't it seem to follow that no material means of discovery would permit scientists to find it? Zimmer says, "That which does not obey the laws of nature is beyond science's scope."[10] But don't think that just because the soul is no longer on the radar of mainstream scientific exploration, researchers will stop looking.

The field of psychiatry, for example, is all about discovering the "self."[11] The self, however, is not to be referred to as the "soul." Dr. M. Scott Peck, in his book *Denial of the Soul*, explains the reason:

> One [reason] is that the concept of God is inherent in the concept of the soul, and "God-talk" is virtually off-limits within these relatively secular professions. Religious as individuals in these professions might be personally, they would not want to offend their secular colleagues. Nor, for that matter, would they care to lose their jobs. The fact is that to speak of God or the soul in their professional gatherings would be politically incorrect. The other reason is that these professionals properly have a taste for intellectual rigor, and the soul is something that cannot be completely defined. We can only fully define those things that are smaller than we are.[12]

God-talk and issues of political correctness aside, there are other fields of research besides psychiatry and neurology that are in the soul business (the wackier side of the biz, that is). One particularly interesting guy is Bruce Greyson, a professor in Virginia who has been studying near-death experiences for almost thirty years. His methods, while strange at first glance, are subtly brilliant. In a particular operating room, one in which doctors perform regular heart surgery—actually, the specific procedure performed in this room on a regular basis requires the patients to be killed for a minute or two and then brought back ... (!)—Greyson places an open laptop computer in the room with the screen displaying a sequence of easy-to-recognize images that are brightly colored enough to catch the eye of any wayward spirit in the room. The computer screen is situated atop a

---

10. Ibid., p. 287.
11. And, apparently, having Doctor Phil yell at you.
12. M. Scott Peck, MD, *Denial of the Soul*, p. 129.

high bookshelf in such a way that the patients are not afforded a view of it unless they die for a moment, float out of their bodies, and gaze back down upon their earthen home. Once the patients are revived, he interviews them to determine whether or not they can recall the brightly colored images. While it may sound a little crazy, consider this: there are many documented cases of individuals who have near-death experiences and are able to recall things in incredibly vivid detail upon being brought back, often staggering details regarding the procedures which were performed on their bodies or the observance of a discarded sneaker on the roof of a nearby building. Remarkable as this is, and as brilliant as Greyson's idea, he has yet to have any success. But one can imagine that this sort of research would take time.[13]

What is this work but another attempt to figure out if there is an immaterial soul? Greyson, who comes across in interviews as optimistic yet completely even keel to the point of dryness, explains his aspirations this way:

> I see part of my role as educating doctors, and that's kind of a small role to play. I think the larger thing that needs to be done within the field is to look at the connection between NDEs [near-death experiences] and other types of spiritually transformative experiences. Obviously, an NDE is only one of many ways of changing your life and turning it around.
>
> One other area that may be fruitful to explore is what these tell us about whether we survive death of the body. This is a much more difficult area in which to do research. A lot of people will say that it's pointless to research; you can never prove anything scientifically in this area. I'm not that hopeless about it. I think it may be possible to learn some things about that from NDEs. I think we're a long way from getting an answer, but I think NDEs can help us move in that direction. That's something I'll be working on for the next twenty years or so.[14]

---

13. Mary Roach, *Spook*, p. 263-291.
14. *www.newsun.com/greyson.html*

We, the authors, wish him nothing but the best of luck. As well, we generously concur with Professor Bruce, that a brush with death is in fact transformative, as is a Chipotle burrito.

One of the more interesting stories of science's attempts at proving the existence of the soul includes the theory that when we die we all lose twenty-one grams of weight, which, in turn, would lead you to infer that the soul must have a weight of twenty-one grams. It is a fascinating idea, as well as a depressing movie about loss starring Sean Penn and Naomi Watts. The theory is considered silly by most scientists today, but the movie garnered two Oscar nominations.

The theory was set forth by a doctor in the early 1900s named Duncan MacDougall who placed dying patients on a scale in order to weigh them at the exact moment of death. All in all, he weighed six patients, and only observed the twenty-one-gram thing with the first patient.[15] Sure, it's a far cry from anything conclusive, but fast-forward to the present day, and you will find a guy named Gerry Nahum. This fellow has a pedigree that would make MacDougall spin in his grave. He is a professor at the Duke University School of Medicine, and he has devised a theory that will put this whole soul question to rest once and for all. He basically wants to build a box that is devoid of all outside influence—this box is where the living (or dying) thing will be placed to study—that is capable of weighing whatever is inside it to a degree that is incomprehensible to your authors' feeble minds. Suffice to say, you could probably sit inside of this box, think about a doughnut, and it would register the weight gain.[16]

But a simple scale is not good enough. No, this box would also be outfitted with all manner of energy sensors and scientific gadgetry that could scan for whatever it is complex and scientific gadgets scan for. Basically any change, any change at all, would register in some manner somewhere in the box. How is this possible? Glad you asked. The answer is the first law of thermodynamics, which, for those of you just coming back from an out-of-body experience right now,

---

15. Roach, p. 80-89.

16. Unless you are David Crowder, in which case the thought of a doughnut would actually cause you to lose weight. Perhaps Dr. Nahum needs to study this mystery instead.

states that energy can neither be created nor destroyed—it has to go somewhere. Therefore, whenever the living creature unfortunate enough to be on the inside of the box finally bites it, the box will register how much energy (or weight, or whatever) leaves said creature. Genius.

There are only two hitches in Dr. Nahum's plan. The first is funding. This super box does not come on the cheap, and he speculates that he would need a minimum of one hundred grand to build it. One would think that there are plenty of curiosity seekers out there with deep enough pockets who would be more than happy to give him the scratch he needs. But one would be wrong. Which leads us to the second hitch—the Church. Dr. Nahum approached the Catholic Church thinking they would be on board, but was shot down. Not only that, but they implored him to stop his quest altogether. Historically speaking, this sounds familiar. But seeing as how the possibility of scientifically proving the nonexistence of the soul would be detrimental to, oh, millions of Catholics the world over, you can't really blame them. The good doctor continues his search nonetheless. Again, the authors wish him nothing but the best of luck. It just seems like the nice thing to do.

Not to be outdone, even folks in the world of engineering are getting in on the soul racket. A little poking about on the Internet will reveal one of the most entertaining and mind-bogglingly weird websites around. The author of the site is unknown, probably because his theories are, scientifically speaking, crazy. The purpose of the site is to validate and advertise an institution called the "Soul Science Institute." The origin of the institute, according to its mystery author, lies in his application of engineering equations to prove the existence of the human soul. The site sells books, contains a link for all of us common folk, or as the author calls us, "lay people," allows you to donate to the institute, and even more delightful, shows diagrams such as this one:

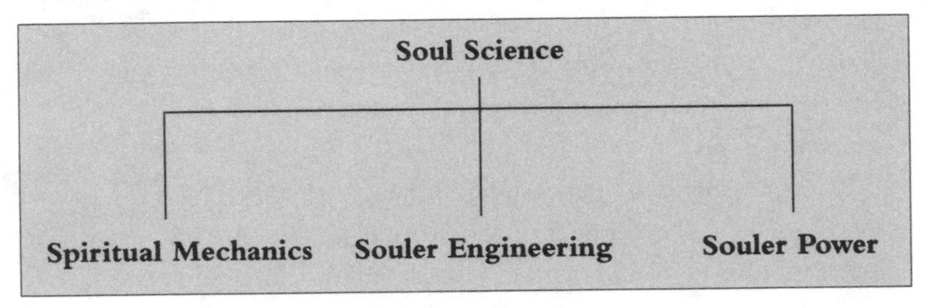

Not only are we offered such explanatory tools as that simple chart, he also gives us a list of 103 differential equations that apparently prove the soul's existence once and for all.

Granted, the only way these equations can be seen is if you click on the link designated "Scientist/Engineer," of which your two authors are neither. But they have friends who are,[17] and like any good students they contacted these friends who confirmed their original suspicions. In other words, as far as the Soul Science Institute is concerned, a swing and a miss.

Which brings us where, exactly?

The soul has never been the exclusive property of religion, and despite its apparent exit from mainstream research, it doesn't look like it ever really will be, no matter how clinical and politically correct science decides to be.

Human beings have spent ages, as detailed in this book, exerting attempts to figure out the self. Attempting to figure out where the soul resides. Is it in the brain or the heart? Is it material or immaterial? If every thought and emotion can be mapped out on a computer screen as electrical impulses, where is the soul? Is it in the realm of science? Does it necessitate sitting inside the most advanced scale on the planet to measure what, if anything, is inside of us? Or is it truly in the realm of the spiritual, left to theologians to figure out?

Frankly, all of this leaves us a little uneasy.

---

17. To be less vague, one of the individuals contacted was J.D., Hogan's old roommate from Part 1 of the bluegrass story. It turns out J.D. is not at all German, but Scotch-Irish. You'd think the red hair, pale skin, and biting wit would have tipped us off. Oh well. The email was enlightening and enjoyable. You should read it sometime.

RAUL'S EMAILS

Subject: RE: Hey man (a small request)
Date: May 6, 2006 12:52:54 AM CDT

Hogan,
Great to hear from you! Yes, indeed, the crank[1] does continue to turn, though not as quickly as I'd like. I'm hoping that the PhD saga will finally wrap up around this time next year, but that largely depends on me, and given my penchant for online crossword puzzles and reruns of *The People's Court*, it could be a while.

Anyway, your book with Dave sounds especially interesting ... death and bluegrass do seem to have a connection that, while not readily evident, is intuitively satisfying nevertheless, much like that between Paris Hilton and Carl's Jr.

Regarding the findings of the so-called "Soul Science Institute," after a brief review I find them to be what we in the business refer to as "a heapin' helpin' of horse poo." Not to say that scientific credibility and mathematical complexity are directly related, but when the underlying theory is contingent on undefined cryptic quantities like "Planetary Ghost" (as opposed, I'd assume, to "Space Ghost," or perhaps the even more elusive "Zorak"), any person capable of critical thinking, whether formally trained in the sciences or not, should definitely hear their

---

1. Inside joke referencing a professor Raul had during his undergrad work. "Turn the crank on it" was one of his professor's favorite expressions, and it is still unsure exactly what is meant by its frequent use.

[unprintable] detector pinging loudly. All that's to say that you're right on in your first instinct: this dude's a fruit loop.

Well, sorry to ramble so much, but pseudoscience does crack me up, so it was nice to see such a sterling example. I'm very flattered that you'd seek my opinion ... I'd certainly agree with the "off his rocker" assessment of the author. Take care, and give my best to everyone.

Cheers,
Raul

The following is an addendum email, and is placed here for the mere purpose of showing the thoughts of a modern-day enlightened thinker.

Subject: Addendum - RE: Hey man (a small request)
Date: May 6, 2006 1:52:43 AM CDT

Hogan,
I was just thinking some more about the issue of science and spirituality. Personally, I'm of two minds on the whole issue. On one hand, the scientific-minded side of me finds it intuitively pleasing that capturing the entirety of someone's being should be possible via physical means, e.g., by somehow identifying the entire quantum state of a person. I'm also curious as to the possibility that there are yet-undiscovered facets of our physical world that may affect our being. For instance, as you may have read, string theory in physics suggests that there are nine or ten dimensions, rather than just the four we perceive in everyday life. Could there possibly be some information about our reality tucked away in these (yet unproved, might I add) "extra" dimensions? On the other hand, as a Christian, I believe that there's a certain *je ne sais quois* that eludes physical description. After all, if we as Christians believe that this body is just a wrapper of sorts and that we'll be reborn into new, glorified bodies ... then the soul really conveys all the relevant information about "me," however one defines that. If I lose a limb (God forbid), my quantum state has drastically

changed, even so far as to affect how my brain processes information, but I'd still say I'm the same person at my core, so there has to be some limit to which our physical incarnation defines us.

Whew ... well, sorry for the ramble-fest, but after thinking a little more about your topic, I figured I'd share a few random thoughts. It's a very interesting subject to me, and I'm always fascinated by it. Again, best of luck, and keep in touch!

Cheers,
Raul

The following is a follow-up email from Raul concerning the matter of privacy and legality.

Subject: RE: THANK YOU! and another question
Date: May 9, 2006 3:47.43 PM CDT

Hogan,
Thanks so much for your kind words ... I'm always glad to help out an old friend (especially one who put up with my alarm for the better part of a year's worth of Saturdays)! Also, please feel free to use any of our exchanges on the matter, past, present, and future, edited for content as you (and the editors) see fit. I don't at all mind keeping it "on the real" (as I generally try not to write anything which I wouldn't own up to in public), but if we do go the pseudonym route, I'm definitely on board with "Raul" ... it makes me sound like a suave pool boy, and that's always good. As always, keep in touch, whether in pondering these and other interesting questions of the universe or just to chat.

All the best to you and the crew, and I'll talk to you again soon!

Cheers,
Raul

HISTORY
OF
BLUEGRASS

— PART 5 —

THE DIFFERENCE BETWEEN A VIOLIN AND A FIDDLE

or

"B" Is for Banjo; This Is the Longest Chapter Yet

or

Seriously, Go Get a Beverage, This Is the Longest Chapter Yet

The violin is a remarkable instrument. For one thing, there is the sheer look of it. It would be a lie to say that it doesn't resemble the sensual curves of a lady, especially a lady fitting the cultural ideal of beauty in the Renaissance. It is most assuredly possible that part of the instrument's popularity rests on this fact. Antonio Stradivarius (the famed instrument maker who perfected the art form and who has no equal) knew what he was doing when he developed the molds and sketches that, to this day, have never been improved upon.

And speaking of old Antonio, there is the everlasting mystery of his instrument-building techniques. Namely, why in the world does his stuff sound so flippin' good? Scientists have studied his instruments under electron microscopes, analyzed the varnishes he created down to the molecule, copied his measurements exactly, and still only come up with close approximations of his final product. It's like one of the great philosophical debates of our time: how many licks *does* it take to get to the center of a Tootsie Roll pop? The world may never know.[1]

It is attested here, that the privilege of hearing a Strad in the hands of a master truly is a life-changing experience. It sounds as pure as a church bell, filling every last nook and cranny with the most amazing tone ever to grace the air around it. It leaves an indelible impression and has to be the single closest sound to angels singing this side of heaven.

And in contrast, to hear a beginner scratching out the remains of "Twinkle, Twinkle, Little Star" on a cigar box of an instrument is also a sound you will be unable to rid from your head. Its only possible equal would be the mating call of feral alley cats or perhaps fingernails scraped down a very dry chalkboard. It is confounding that one of the loveliest reverberations known to mankind can, in less capable hands, literally raise the hair on the back of your neck and send goose bumps down your arms.[2]

Which brings us to the fiddle.

The number-one question Hogan gets from people is "What is the difference between a violin and a fiddle?"[3] And the honest answer is, not much. They are really one and the same. The distinction lies in the attitude of the person playing it and the context in which it is played. For instance: If you are wearing a tuxedo and the patrons listening to you are dressed in suits and ties and elegant gowns, odds are you are playing a violin. If you are wearing either overalls or a plaid shirt (or both, or neither) and the patrons listening to you are standing on a floor covered in sawdust and look just like you do, you're probably playing a fiddle. It's sort of like one of those "you

1. Professor Owl says "three."

2. The wife of one of Hogan's violin professors in college was a British lady who consistently referred to "goose bumps" as "goose flesh," a distinction that always managed to make the stomach churn a little bit.

3. The number-two question asked is "How do you keep it fresh?" This query comes in an astonishing variety of flavors. The answer is returned in equal variations, but our personal favorite to the how-do-you-keep-it-fresh disease is "Gold Bond Powder." "Deodorant" or "chewing gum" will work equally as well.

might be a redneck" jokes by the comedian Jeff Foxworthy.[4] If learning "The Devil Went Down to Georgia" and never wearing shoes are your only goals in life, you might be a fiddler. Here is another one, a little subtler this time. If you are totally at ease and having the time of your life, you are most likely playing a fiddle. If you are plagued by feelings of inadequacy and can't sleep at night because you will never be good enough—violin.

We realize that certainly some stereotypes are being played up here, but let's be honest—it's true. The violin is snootier and more self-conscious than the fiddle. So are the people who prefer to listen to it. Very rarely do you see someone who crosses the boundary between the two worlds, but they do exist. One example is a guy named Mark O'Connor, who has the alien ability to seamlessly cross from one genre to the other and make his compeers look stupid in the process. He sometimes does this on a skateboard because he can and because gimmicks are fun. Another guy, Will, went to college with Hogan. Will was a great classical player but had some crazy fiddle chops. He was normally right-handed but could play left as well, which is infinitely more comical and astounding in person than it is on paper. It seems if you are serious about fiddling, you have to be able to do tricks of some kind.[5]

All of this begs the question, why is bluegrass dominated by the fiddle rather than the violin, especially when you take into account the fact that the classical style of playing has been around for hundreds of years and is considered one of the highest of the fine arts, while bluegrass as we know it has been on the scene since, oh, the 1940s? The simple answer is this: Bluegrass folk aren't violin folk. They are

---

4. Foxworthy's superior mustache has its own buzz on the Internet, which your narrators appreciate and envy, as the mustache is a symbol of vitality and class. For even more facial hair fun, check out *www.worldbeardchampionships.com*. It will blow your mind, and you will thank us for it.

5. The same goes for the banjo, which you will be learning about shortly. During the initial research stages, your two authors had an early dinner one night with the legendary Marty Stuart. He told them a story about the best banjo player he has ever known, but the authors left unsure about whether this gentleman in question was the best because of his playing ability or because he "had tricks." As Marty told it, this guy would be playing, and he would look you dead-on, his eyes would get wide and buggy, and he would proceed to "do tricks. The guy was a wizard!" Incidentally, your authors both had a sandwich for dinner. Marty had a piece of a pie and a cup of coffee.

fiddle people by nature. If your ancestors were warlike herdsmen who moved countries twice so they could be left to do as they please, who cared about the farm, the church, and the family and not much else, they honestly probably couldn't give a flying rip about the latest violin concerto taking Western Europe by storm. No! These people went into town once, maybe twice a week, and that was for worship and supplies. Symphony halls and violin masterpieces just did not factor into their daily lives. If, however, you were to say to one of them, "Hey, all of us neighbors are getting together on Friday night at Uncle Joe's barn, and Jethro is going to throw down on some fiddle and lead us in some dancin'," you might just have a riot on your hands.

The fiddle played an intrinsic role in these folks' cultural existence long before they ever contemplated departure from the British Isles. It was the primary apparatus used to lead their dances and traditional folk songs, and it was pretty much the only musical instrument they brought with them to the New World. The fiddle fit 'em. There was a rawness and grit to it that echoed their struggle. In contrast, the violin represented, to them, a world of English protectionism, high tariffs, and a monarchy that brought with it all manner of tools used for their oppression. No, these people wanted the world of the fiddle, the world of freedom. And if you could go back and watch as one of those barnburners of a dance fired up, the dirt kicking up under their kilts, their voices and glasses rising together, you'd think they fiddled themselves right into that freedom.

This brings us to the following: if a Stradivarius violin is the be-all and end-all as far as good tone goes, if the instrument is virtually the same no matter what, and if it's all in the way you play it, then doesn't it stand to reason that the better the quality of the instrument being fiddled upon, the better the sound of said fiddling?

Maybe.

Allow me to throw this at you: the technical difference between the two styles is solely technique, yet the two techniques *could not sound more different*. The tool is the same. The approach is antonymic. Classical players spend years perfecting the exact method of holding the bow, positioning the arms for precise ease and flexibility up and down the neck of the instrument, and properly drawing it across the strings in such a manner as to incite the highest quality of tone.

In contrast, the fiddle player just seems to be hanging out, with dreadful posture and excessively casual technique on display for the entire world to behold, the bow never residing in one place for more than a second, fingers flying around willy-nilly. If you have ever seen Charlie Daniels play (the "Devil Went Down to Georgia" guy), you know exactly what is being suggested here. He is an immense man and the instrument so small; it looks as though he is slapping the fingerboard with sausages rather than human digits. It boggles the mind that he is hitting notes at all. But the dude can flat *throw down*. To do this, he is most decidedly defying numerous laws of Newtonian physics; it will therefore be chalked up to good ol' quantum mechanics. And why not? It currently takes the blame for every other item exceeding explanation.

Truth be told, the intended tonal qualities of the two approaches are as different as the methods used in achieving them, and when it comes to fiddling, tone gets the back seat. More crucial is whether or not you know all of the old standard tunes, can rip up a solo, and, most importantly, do it all with heart. If those things fall into place but you scritch-scratch around, who really cares? If it isn't precisely in tune but it dazzles an audience and moves them in some fashion, does it really matter? No, it does not. It is this very looseness, messiness, and authenticity that make the fiddle so cool. (And for trained "violin" guys, so darned annoying.)

Likewise, if you have ever observed someone playing the banjo who really knows what they're doing, it can be pretty impressive, due to the solid fact that there are somewhere in the vicinity of one million notes coming your way at the speed of light in a single file line. Conversely, this is *exactly* why the banjo is, at its core, so annoying. (How's that for paradox?)

But seriously, you may ask, what is the deal with the banjo? If its import is of such significance as to grace the cover of this book, shouldn't we make some sort of case for its necessity? To that question we give you an unequivocal "suppose so."

Some history: The banjo is a modern version of an African American instrument (read: slave instrument) that consisted of a gourd with some skin stretched over it, a neck, and some strings. Unlike today, the old versions did not have frets—a fact that we would guess made the instrument even more likely to annoy the pants off you (as something without frets is exponentially more difficult to play in tune). As far as where the name came from, we have a couple of different options. One is that we derived the word *banjo* from the word *mbanza*, a term meaning "a plucked string instrument" from the Kimbundu language (which was widely spoken around Central Africa in the pre-colonial days). Another option is that it came from the term *bandore*, a word whose meaning the authors could not uncover but one they think sounds a little closer to where we want to end up. A third option is that the name was derived from, and we're not kidding here, a Senegambian[6] word for the stick used to make the neck of the instrument.[7] Apparently, among those who care about such things, this debate is something of a hot-button item. But since care for etymology was not a characteristic written into the narrative, let's say that aside from a predilection toward sticks, we don't really care.

The modern banjo comes in a variety of forms, ranging from four to six strings, from open-back designs to closed-back designs, from acoustic to electric. For our purposes we need only concentrate on the five-string acoustic variety and can assume that all other species are abominations of nature and that God will punish them accordingly. The playing style has already been discussed, but to re-enforce the idea: Breakneck speed.[8]

Okay, brace yourself here, because this may start to get a little bleak. The banjo came to America with the slaves, and not surprisingly it took quite a while for it to catch on with the white public. The slaves used it to lead dances and to provide music for observing holidays and special occasions. (Sound familiar?) Check out this painting, which is

---

6. All that business about where the word *banjo* came from? Wikipedia.

7. We're drawn to this option because we're boys, and boys think sticks are neat.

8. Or "fast as the infernal regions," whichever you prefer.

one of the earliest records of the banjo. While at first it may seem a little stagnant and flat, pay close attention to the person dancing with the stick. That guy is obviously working it. Which only leads to one conclusion: the banjo player, while appearing calm, has to be just *throwing down*. Have a look.

Figure 1: *America's Musical Life*, Richard Crawford, p. 114.

Eventually, the banjo was destined for a wider audience than this. Hogan serendipitously discovered that, according to scholars, the first-ever white guy to learn the banjo was a dude named Joel Sweeney from Virginia. Before all of you Virginians get too excited, know this: Joel was taught the instrument by his father's slaves.[9] Regardless of where he picked it up, he decided that one good turn deserves another and taught his skills to another white guy named William "Billy" Whitlock from New York. Billy, however, was unaware of the "one good turn ..." rule, and rather than teaching others how to play, toured around for fun and profit with a group called the Virginia Minstrels.

Here is where you might say, "Wait, what's so terribly bleak about that?" To which we respond: The Virginia Minstrels were what was

9. For those keeping track, this would have been around the late 1820s.

known as a "minstrel show," or rather a bunch of white guys made up to look like caricatures of black people who performed songs and skits aping the African American culture. To be fair, scholars argue that the minstrel shows were so widely popular that troupes were invited to perform for at least four different presidents and were a vital contribution in the history of traditional American theater and music. And who are we to disagree? They also argue that while the performances might be seen as horribly racist now, at the time these shows elicited a level of respect for black people on behalf of the performers in terms of their musical sensibility, cunning, and dance. Not to mention that it offered a platform for social commentary that would never have been tolerated in polite white society. Okay. We'll give them that. But then we'll show everybody this:

Figure 2: Richard Crawford, p. 200.

seriously?

No matter where you fall in this debate, you cannot deny that the minstrel shows increased the banjo's popularity as well as suggested, along with the fiddle, that it was okay to be a traveling, performing musician without the Western European pedigree of classical traditions. The skills one needed to perform in a minstrel troupe (fiddle, banjo, tambourine, bones, and comic timing) required no precedent of formal study. Please observe the following quote, whose purpose is to both back up what has just been stated and further drive home the point made regarding the violin versus the fiddle: "Only the violin was a European instrument with established methods of instruction and repertory of composed music. Yet the violin led a double life in the British Isles and North America. As the fiddle, this bowed string instrument stood at the heart of Anglo-American dance music, with its jigs, reels, and hornpipes and its characteristic ways of playing them."[10]

Booyah![11] So, there you have it. That's how we got the banjo. But there is still one huge gaping hole, and that hole is shaped like Earl Scruggs (with a cowboy hat, which is still cool).

---

10. Richard Crawford, *America's Musical Life*, p. 205.

11. The authors offer their deepest apologies for their use of the term *booyah* and assure you it will be used henceforth in moderation, if at all.

COLUMNS, PART 5

HE KNEW THERE WAS a word for what made the garden grow. He tapped the ground 4 times with the spade before shoving it into the loose dirt. He couldn't find it though—the right word, that is. People asked. All the time. How? How could all of these things grow in such a place? There was a word for it. He couldn't find it. He sifted through the dirt. He extracted from it 4 pebbles. He placed them 1 at a time in 1 of the open jars beside him. That

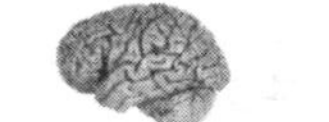
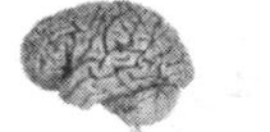

SUCH A NICE BOY. SHE hated to witness that depth of sadness in such concentratedly beautiful blue eyes. The sadness was of a different kind than that felt by most. It had a broader profundity and intensity to it. Like it had worked its way into all the nooks and crannies. Filling all of the radiant spaces with its graveness.

She had seen this mass of sadness before. In Justin.

It seemed the world was growing

BIRDS OF NORTH AMERICA

~~blackbird~~

~~bluebird~~

~~blue jay~~

~~bobolink~~

~~bobwhite~~

~~bunting~~

~~cardinal~~

~~catbird~~

made 34 so far today. The white gloves had become black. Blood and fluids mixing with dirt now gave the white the appearance of black. He touched things and his hands turned black. He thought this meant something. He didn't intend it to mean anything but it most definitely did. To some. There were few things that he could definitively announce as bringing him pleasure. But unintended meaning was for certain one of them. He was in search of meaning. And when or if he stumbled onto it he was most definitely pleased. No. *Pleased* was too tame a word. Abruptly

full of sadness.

The first moment she had seen it in Justin was at the graveside of his and Emily's little boy. Eventually a lightness had returned. Emily had helped bring it. The second time was after Emily. After Emily died, everything went dark. She wished, oh how she wished, that she would have known back then that he could sink to such gloom.

Maybe some of us are more predisposed to it. At this age she had seen grief take many forms. She used to think that everyone just came at it differently. But the more people she had outlived,

~~chat~~

~~chickadee~~

~~chuck-will's-widow~~

~~cowbird~~

~~creeper~~

~~crossbill~~

~~crow~~

~~cuckoo~~

~~dickcissel~~

~~dove~~

~~finch~~

~~flicker~~

Father Briscoe was calling him. "Justin." He called. Justin looked up from his digging. "Justin. You are needed inside." He said. "Please come now." Justin let his spade drop. He looked at his dark gloves. He followed Father Briscoe. They walked back along the southern side. He matched Father Briscoe's stride. Only 70 steps were taken. They entered the dark damp hallway. Only 41 steps. Crossing through the sanctuary. Candles burning. 1,156 prayers ascending. He clapped 4 times. 34 steps across. A right turn. 14 steps. And then they were in Father Briscoe's study. He clapped 4 more

the more she had seen of it;
and the more she had seen of
it, the more she was becoming
convinced that it was the grief
that was the assailant. That grief
was a living, breathing thing.
Vicious and selective. No, it
wasn't that different people came
at it in different ways—it was
that it came at people in different
ways. It brought down the ones
it could. That's what she thought
for the longest while.

But then this boy. This young
boy with the bluest eyes she'd
ever seen.

He had said something.

~~flycatcher~~

~~gnatcatcher~~

~~goldfinch~~

~~grackle~~

~~grosbeak~~

~~hummingbird~~

~~junco~~

~~kingbird~~

~~kingfisher~~

~~kinglet~~

lark

times. His damp black gloves made a heavy wet noise when they collided with one another. The nettles digging in. Adding more fluids. Father Briscoe sat down behind his very large oak desk. Justin loved Father Briscoe. But Father Briscoe had never loved anyone like Emily. So he could not know. Father Briscoe pulled out a large white envelope and handed it to him. "This arrived moments ago for you." Justin took it from him. And opened it. The envelope now smeared with bits of black, brave and stark against the white, the words began falling from her, out into his open spaces ...

This is what I meant to say. I am not sure if I am writing this for you or

Something about grief. About it coming to the ones who could bear it for the rest of us. That we bear it for one another. That we do our part.

We do our part.

She had not done hers.

She needed to. She needed do this. She needed to do this before she could not.

She took out a piece of paper and a pen, and in

Dearest Justin,

~~longspur~~

~~magpie~~

~~martin~~

~~meadowlark~~

~~mockingbird~~

~~nighthawk~~

~~nightingale~~

~~nightjar~~

~~nuthatch~~

~~oriole~~

~~ovenbird~~

~~phoebe~~

me. It is so difficult to make sense of the things in my head these days. Regardless of my televisions, I want you to know I have birds for you. There is never enough sadness here with those whom you have birds for. I don't think it matters much when it comes, whether young or sad, whether quickly or slowly, painfully or peacefully, we are still left here with a severing. We are still left wondering what is next. For us and them. What could be out there? And will we remember them? Will our jars turn them into something they were not? I am so sorry I never came. I should have come. I should have dropped everything and sat with you, holding your hand while you held hers. Please forgive me. Emily was so lucky to have you there. I pray I don't die alone. I never thought that I would feel this way. But every time I am injured by someone, I think of all the birds. It doesn't matter how brief or unintentional the moment of contact, it is holy. I have the same dream every night. Dreaming, I enter the room and I lie on the bed, lying down like I am dead. People start entering the room. First my family. Frank comes through the door. Then my son, Donald, his wife Becky, their son Daniel. Emily. You. Your son, even your young son Isaac is there! He is smiling. Then people from my work. Robert Wright, Susan Woodrow, James Beckham, Gene Howe, Joseph Bell, Charlotte Carson, Carey Perkins, Margery Beck.

~~pigeon~~

~~pipit~~

~~raven~~

~~robin~~

~~sapsucker~~

~~skylark~~

~~sparrow~~

~~starling~~

~~swallow~~

~~swift~~

~~tanager~~

The room keeps filling. It is everyone I have ever known. All these years.
All these people. They take my hand. I'm not dead, but they think I am.
I'm just sleeping. I've just fallen asleep, and they don't know it. They
are weeping. There are faces that I barely recognize, that at first look
unfamiliar, and then for a moment their childhood features surface, and it
dawns on me that this is my childhood friend Elizabeth, and I remember
how she would tilt her head to the left when asking a question she
already knew the answer to. And they are holding my hand, and they are
weeping. You are there. You are there, and you hold my hand. I wake
up, and I'm alone. I wake up, and it is dark, and I am alone. The rest of
the family is in the house. We are divided by walls. Daniel's room is on
the other side of the wall that my headboard is touching. His headboard
touches it from the other side. The top of his head only seven inches
away from the top of my head. I awoke one night to another shooting
pain, and I thought, "The top of Daniel's head is less than a foot away
from the top of my head, and I will die here alone." How can such small
amounts of distance feel so vast? A shooting pain in my head here in the
dark with no one to hold me. A bird is falling from the sky
to peck the palm of my hand.

Sincerely,
Virginia

~~thrasher~~

~~thrush~~

~~warbler~~

~~waterthrush~~

~~waxwing~~

~~wheatear~~

~~whippoorwill~~

~~woodpecker~~

~~wood thrush~~

~~wren~~

~~yellowthroat~~

CONVERSATION KEY

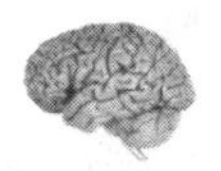

WHEN SHE SAID ...

televisions = motives
birds = love
time = sadness
sad = old
quickly = electricity
slowly = cancer
painfully = electricity
peacefully = no such thing
wondering = alone
jars = memories
dropped = carried
held = forgave
forgive = heal
I pray I don't die alone = Oh God, help me; someone please help me
I never thought that I would feel this way = You feel this way too
injured = touched
brief = 33 years

holy = the face of God
dream = hope
Donald = you
Becky = you
Daniel = you
Emily = you
Isaac = you
Robert Wright = you
Susan Woodrow = you
James Beckham = you
Gene Howe = you
Joseph Bell = you
Charlotte Carson = you
Carey Perkins = you
Margery Beck = you
The room keeps filling = Will there be another flood?
dead = here
weeping = singing
asking a question = "will you remember?"
walls = nothing
the top of his head = all the love in the world
the top of my head = all the love in the world
I will die here alone = He is holding you
How can such a small amount of distance feel so vast? = He is holding you
no one to hold me = He is holding you
bird = love
Sincerely = I am so sorry I was not there. Please forgive me.

HISTORY OF THE SOUL

— PART 6 —

OUR GOD-FEARING SOULS

or

It's About Dang Time

Carl Jung was a really, really smart guy. Like scary smart. After reading so much about philosophy, about science, about how for all intents and purposes the soul is dead, you get this weird, sinking feeling in the pit of your stomach. It's uncomfortable. Your mind starts putting the pieces together and running ahead of what you're reading. You know what's coming. But what's coming is unavoidable.

Then you come across a forty-dollar quote like this one from nothing less than one of the greatest minds of the twentieth century, which sums up everything we've covered thus far yet still manages to keep that sinking feeling firmly in place. It's just that now, not only do you realize that, according to mainstream thought, the soul has officially departed, you also know exactly why. Granted, this is blanketed in difficult language and grammar, but the gist of the whole thing is there, serving to only further solidify the pit in your gut.

> It was universally believed in the Middle Ages as well as in the Græco-Roman world that the soul is a substance. Indeed, mankind as a whole has held this belief from its earliest beginnings, and it was left for the second half of the nineteenth century to develop a "psychology without the soul." Under the influence of scientific materialism, everything that could not be seen with the eyes or touched with the hands was held in doubt; such things were even laughed at because of their supposed affinity with metaphysics. Nothing was considered "scientific" or admitted to be true unless it could be perceived by the senses or traced back to physical causes. This radical change of view did not begin with philosophical materialism; the way was being prepared long before. When the spiritual catastrophe of the Reformation put an end to the Gothic Age with its impetuous yearning for the heights, its geographical confinement, and its restricted view of the world, the vertical outlook of the European mind was forthwith intersected by the horizontal outlook of modern times. Consciousness ceased to grow upward and grew instead in breadth of view, as well as in knowledge of the terrestrial globe. This was the period of great voyages and of the widening of man's ideas of the world by empirical discoveries. Belief in the substantiality of the spirit yielded more and more to the obtrusive conviction that material things alone have substance, till at last, after nearly four hundred years, the leading European thinkers and investigators came to regard the mind as wholly dependent on matter and material causation.[1]

Jung had an interesting take on these things. He was born in Switzerland, and by all accounts was a very withdrawn and quiet child. Unlike a lot of these jokers who we have come across on our journey together, Jung had what appears to be a very twentieth-century upbringing: His dad was a vicar in the local church, but was plagued with doubt, something that did not go unnoticed by his young son. His parents were also financially unable to send him off to whatever prep school or college was popular at the moment in

---

1. Carl Jung, *Modern Man in Search of a Soul*, 1933. Published by Routledge & Kegan Paul, translated by Cary Baynes. Reproduced here, Chapter IX, "The Basic Postulates of Analytical Psychology."

Europe, which is a nice change from all of these other cats who only seem to congregate around exclusive academic communities. Sweet.

He went on to pursue psychiatric medicine, where he became a star of sorts. In fact, he fell in close with Freud, the brightest star in the psychiatric galaxy. The two of them were chummy for a while, even taking trips together to the United States to promote their brand of psychoanalysis. Their close relationship went on for about six years, until they began to disagree on one particular thing: Freud believed that the unconscious was a murky, ugly place where a person's darkest desires directed his or her daily life, while Jung believed that the unconscious was a place capable of creativity, that everyone had a collective unconscious that formed and shaped modern society and culture. To understand the nature of the soul, he believed, one need not look just at the depths of the mind and what mommy did to you as a kid, but at your dreams, art, and spiritual journeys.

Hold up! Did you see that last part?!?[2] Spiritual!!!!! Oh my gosh, we are now entering an entirely different realm here. Did Carl Jung become disappointed at the faith of his father? Yes. Did he later believe in UFOs? Apparently, yes, but that is for another book at another time. The point, right here and now, is that Carl Jung, a scientist and philosopher, acknowledged the "death" of the soul, but acknowledged its life as well. To understand a person, you had to probe the soul, whatever that is. In his book *Modern Man in Search of a Soul*, Jung said, "The spirit is the life of the body seen from within, and the body the outward manifestation of the life of the spirit—the two being really one."[3]

Okay. All of that is great, and we feel a little better about things. But we are still left with some burning questions. Questions that will hopefully address the still present pit in our collective gut: *What are modern enlightened Christians to do with the soul? What are we to do with contemplation of our eternal home?* There has been an obvious shift away from the "turn or burn" proselytizing that was so prevalent in the not-too-distant past, back when the soul was still alive and

---

2. Snap!

3. From "The Spiritual Problem of Modern Man," *www.usd.edu/~tgannon/txts/jungquot.txt.*

kicking. And it appears to be out of a genuine care for the emotional well-being of those outside the faith. In turn, we talk less and less of heaven and more and more about the here and now, how faith affects the present physical world. Which can only be helpful, right? Seeing as how in our not-too-distant past, the emphasis on the ever after led to many a head in the clouds and the neglect of social and environmental issues that concern the here and now.

But is this shift from future hope to present hope due to the fact that talk of heaven becomes emotionally awkward territory and winds up right back in the discussions of our eternal states (which we still don't have an answer for)? Or is this shift just a transitory attempt at getting the "turn or burn" taste out of everyone's mouth?

Or might it be that the soul has just been slowly dying the same death inside the walls of the Church that it has in the rest of the public consciousness? Has our theology slowly become just as materialistic as our science by having to adapt to whatever the changing scientific and philosophical climates may be?

Is the reason the Catholic Church denied funding to the researcher from Duke for the magic soul-weighing box because they didn't believe it was possible to construct, or out of fear that if he proved the soul was in fact an unquantifiable entity, it would require more intellectual maneuvering than they were currently up for?[4]

Yet while staring at a friend in a casket why is it so completely obvious that what we are looking at isn't a *person* at all anymore? How and when should we think of the nature of our souls outside of standing around an open grave?

Why is this all so hard?

In *Longing for Heaven*, Peter Toon writes:

> "To believe in, and to long for heaven are particularly difficult spiritual and moral exercises in our Western world. This is because we find it difficult to shake our human spirits free from the view that this material world (which modern science and technology are slowly

---

4. Of course, their verbalized stance was—why waste money proving something exists that is already known to exist. That, and they voiced concern that the magic box might open a black hole or a window to another dimension, bringing an end to us all. Which you'd think they'd want because of their souls' final destination. Right?

> mastering) is effectively the only real and true world, and thus from the further suspicion that heaven is, at best, secondary and, at worst, nonexistent or superfluous! To make matters worse, our normal way of viewing this world is dominated by scientific knowledge, and thus we have lost the art of seeing God revealed in and through his creation."[5]

A tension in the shoulders seems to lift a little after sitting with that quote for a bit. Now, we don't wish to suggest that science and technology are bad or evil or whatever other negative connotation may be taken from the writings herein. Far from it. Science and technology are beautiful and wonderful. Look at heart transplants. Also, the iPod. Remarkable.

But has all of this progress—whether in the field of portable audio, philosophy, psychiatry, or medicine—killed the soul? It has, in the least, muddied the water, and at most, obscured it completely. But if there is any field that should corner the market when it comes to the soul and its current standing within our society, it is religion and, most specific to our journey here, Christianity.

We performed a quick search of our new best friend (for those of you who have been asleep or away from your bodies up until this very moment, we are once again referring to Wikipedia,[6] which we have determined is not only a wonderful springboard for research, but also a bringer of warm cozy feelings during winter and milkshakes on a hot summer afternoon; it shall also be henceforth known as "W") yields the following definition:

> The soul, according to many religious and philosophical traditions, is a self-aware *ethereal substance* particular to a unique living being ... In Christianity, some believe that as soon as a person dies, their soul will be judged by God, who sees all the wrong and right that they

---

5. Peter Toon, *Longing for Heaven*, p. 5.

6. We continue to debate the dubiousness of this website as a source. Is it reputable? Are we going to get laughed at by those in the academic community? (The answer to that one is undoubtedly yes, but not because of our questionable resources; more for our global ignorance that shines like a beacon in the night.) We wondered about it until we looked up "UFOs" and found ourselves face to face with a big cartoon stop sign declaring that the information that was to follow had not been fact-checked and to basically take it all with a grain of salt. This made us feel marginally better, and we soldiered on unhindered. All hail the mighty Wikipedia. You make life easier.

> have done during their lives. If they have repented of (to turn away from) their sins and put their trust in Jesus Christ (the one who took the punishment for our sins) before death, they will inherit eternal life in "heaven" and enjoy eternal fellowship with God. If they have not repented of their sins, they will go to "hell" and suffer eternal separation from God.[7] [emphasis ours]

And there you have it. In one singular paragraph, our friend W has given us enough ammo to start a marginally sized war. There is no doubt that your head immediately instigated a highly graphic and demonstrably rousing internal debate over a myriad of statements made here, and it could continue this course for hours on end. If you were to do this in public, out loud to another person, say at a coffee shop perhaps, you would get promptly punched (by one of the authors), so for now let's just keep it to ourselves. We can split enormously large hairs later.

There is one phrase within the quote that needs immediate attention, and that is "*some* believe." Wait, *some*? Some?!? Right, so let's quickly discuss what those outside of the "some" believe.

No really, let's actually do this. And remember, this is all flying under the propitiously large and multicolored umbrella of Christianity.

NO SOUL: There are those who believe that there isn't a soul. According to W, these groups believe that the mind and the body are done, kaput, at the onset of death. This viewpoint could come across as a little "glass half-empty" depressing if it were not for the end of the world, at which time the minds and bodies of those who believed in Jesus will be brought back to the land of the living. Aristotle would be proud.

SOME SOUL: There are others who think that a soul is a soul is a soul. You die, the soul goes too. That is, unless you believe in

---

7. *http://en.wikipedia.org/wiki/Soul#Christian_beliefs.*

Christ, in which case your soul has become immortal. What about those who don't believe? What happens to them? They're screwed, that's what.

FULL-ON SOUL!: James Brown. He is the godfather ...[8]

THE MEDIEVAL SOUL: This is more of a reminder. Once upon a time, the belief was that the soul controlled thought, imagination, love, etc. Everything else was, well, controlled by something else. This gets back into the whole "rational soul" and "sensitive soul" thing. However, the medieval age was a long time ago, so there is really no point in talking about it right now. Except it does make the authors crave a leg of smoked turkey, for some reason. Mmmmmm ... giant turkey leg ...

JEHOVAH'S WITNESSES: Uhhhh ...

SOUL SLEEP THEORY: The title more or less sums it up. When you die your soul goes to sleep. You wake up when it's time for the last judgment. Sort of an Ambien for the afterlife. This one is appealing because naps feel good.

NO BODY, NO PROBLEM: Another theory is that the second your soul leaves the body (or, for the more bottom-line-oriented consumer, you kick the bucket) you are in the presence of God. No matter how much time has passed between the moment your little flame is snuffed out and the end of the world (or whenever the final judgment goes down), you will have not felt a thing. One moment you are alive, and the next you are standing before God Almighty at the end of the universe. The phrase *time flies* would take on a whole new meaning, unless of course you were living at the very

8. ... of soul. He is also a sex machine, and he has a brand-new bag. When Hogan was but a youngster, he had a birthday party at the Hard Rock Café in Dallas. On the way inside he noticed a star on the sidewalk for James Brown and proudly exclaimed, "Look! He's the godfather of soul!" This statement was met with blank stares by the rest of his ten-year-old friends, and proved that he was a music nerd even back then. Seriously, how many ten-year-old pasty white kids get excited about James Brown? Dork.

end of time to begin with. But you would never know this, primarily based on that whole "thief in the night"[9] business. Whatever. We're getting off course.

This one is commonly referred to as the "absent from the body, present with the Lord"[10] theory.

PURGATORY: This one says that an imperfect soul will spend some time in a place called, well, purgatory, cleansing itself before going on to the final judgment. Some think that this is where the soul pays the rest of its penance for sin before continuing on its journey to heaven. The good news is that if you made it to purgatory, then you will most certainly make it to heaven. It's just going to take a little longer. Incidentally, when the authors looked to see if there were references to purgatory in Scripture, they didn't find any. They did, however, find several references to a refining fire and silver and gold and prayer and stuff.[11] "The presupposition of the doctrine of purgatory is that there is a special judgment for each individual immediately after death. Hence, the logical conclusion is that purgatory ceases with the Last Judgment. The stay in purgatory can be shortened through intercession, alms, indulgences, and benefits of the sacrifice of the mass."[12] Feel free to debate amongst yourselves.

A TEN-GALLON NAME: "Swedenborgianism teaches that each person's soul is created by the Lord at the same time the physical body is developed, that the soul is the person himself or herself, and that the soul is eternal and has an eternal spiritual body that is substantial without being material. After the death of the body, the person becomes immediately conscious in the spiritual world."[13]

Swedenborgianism? According to W, it is a religious movement based on the writings of a guy by the name of Emanuel Swedenborg. Overall, his theories are fairly similar to others with less audacious

---

9. 1 Thessalonians 5:2. How about that? Scriptural references!

10. *http://en.wikipedia.org/wiki/Soul#Christian_beliefs.*

11. Zechariah 13:9, Malachi 3:2-3, Matthew 5:26, 1 Corinthians 3:13-15

12. Ernst Wilhelm Benz (d. 1978), "Christian Afterlife Beliefs," *www.widowwidowersupport.org/Christian%20Afterlife%20Beliefs.htm.*

13. *http://en.wikipedia.org/wiki/Soul#Christian_beliefs.*

names, but that's unimportant. No, the real reason to spend time here is for one simple fact: Johnny Appleseed was a Swedenborgian.[14] This surprises us because we always thought that Johnny Appleseed was nothing more than a character in a children's story. We were wrong, and we apologize.[15]

We assume that if you have made it this far, you've realized that there has been no one good way to think about this whole thing. There is no manual or guide to tell us, beyond a shadow of a doubt, whether there's a soul, and if so, what happens to it when we die. Of course, some wonderful folks will immediately respond, "Yes. Yes, we most certainly have a manual, and it has a black cover with gold-leafed pages, and the good parts are written in red!" While the authors agree wholeheartedly with this sentiment, they would like to kindly point to the aforementioned list of beliefs representing large portions of the community of believers adhering to a particular outlook, which in turn was derived from the same manual the other guys were looking at, and then we'd also offer a reminder that there has been an endless stream of exceedingly intelligent folks spending the whole of their professional careers debating the eternal statements contained in said manual, delving into the finer points of it, going much deeper than we would or could ever care to go here. Has it helped us? Has it really done any good? Has it served to only muddy the water more? Has any clarity come to the issue in the past two thousand years?

You would think Christians would be on the cutting edge of this whole debate. You would think that with the word *soul* popping up in the Bible in 425 verses (New American Standard translation) that we would be a little further along than we are. A large portion of the problem is the belief of the early Church fathers that the Last Judgment was imminent, that many of them would experience the kingdom of God prior to death. The interim between fatality and this future kingdom was, for them, of little concern. This expectation is therefore inherent in their writing and, in turn, creates much difficulty for our efforts in interpretation.

The hard truth of the matter is that we, as humans in the twenty-

---

14. *http://en.wikipedia.org/wiki/Swedenborgianism.*

15. He was not only real, but sort of a proto-ecologist. Good for him!

first century, rarely think about what happens to us when we die. We subscribe to a system of beliefs that revolves around life after death, but the moments we consider it seem to grow further and further apart. The twenty-first-century church has all but deserted instruction on the last things.

In his book *Life After Death*, Alan F. Segal states that, "For the majority of Americans, Heaven has become a virtual democratic entitlement."[16] He refers to a Gallup poll about what the American public thinks the afterlife will be like.

- It will be better.
- There will be no problems.
- There will be no sickness.
- It will be peaceful.
- We will be in the presence of God and/or Christ.
- The crippled will be healed.
- We will see friends and family that have died before us.
- We will be eternal.
- There will be humor.
- People in heaven will be recognizable as they were in life.
- There will be angels.

All in all, it sounds pretty good. Never mind that very little of this is in The Manual, save for the presence of the Lord. Segal claims that this vision of Heaven is a very uniquely American way of looking at it, that we have projected our own desires onto the mystery of the afterlife. We have given heaven somewhat of an outline that makes us feel cozy and then sort of forgotten about it. He says:

> The idea of the Last Judgment has often become incomprehensible to the modern world. At the most, people apparently are still open to the concept of judgment of the guilt and innocence of the individual. The idea decisive for the early church's expectation of the Judgment,

16. Alan F. Segal, *Life After Death*, p. 11.

> however, was that the Last Judgment will be a public one. This corresponds to the fundamental Christian idea that human beings—both the living and the dead—are bound together in an indissoluble communion; it presupposes the conception of the church as the body of Christ. All of humanity is as one person. Humans sin with one another, and their evil is connected together in the "realm of sin" in a manifold way, unrecognizable in the individual. Each person is responsible for the other and is guilty with the other. The judgment upon each person, therefore, concerns all. Judgment upon the individual is thus, at the same time, judgment upon the whole and vice versa. The Judgment is also public in regard to the positive side—the praise and reward of God for that which is done rightly and practiced in the common life, often without knowing it.[17]

In our day-to-day lives, the notion of a Last Judgment rarely comes up. It is only in moments of hardship that we feel the need to look toward the possibility of an eternal future, when we're faced with the notion that we are, in fact, mortal, we consider eternity.

Mortality is a very scary thought. Deep down, we know that no matter how strong our belief, death is still the big unknown. Segal puts it this way, "Death anxiety infects everything we do as humans, even when we are trying to be brave. It is part of the human condition; indeed it seems a consequence of self-consciousness itself. It is a price we pay for being aware of ourselves as beings."[18]

Why is it that the only time we contemplate the soul in an everlasting way is when somebody else dies, when we are standing at an open grave, wondering why we can't find the right words to speak to one another? Is it because all we can think of is our own impending doom? Is it *fear* that keeps our contemplative selves quiet? Is it fear of the question: when that little spark of energy leaves our bodies, does that little spark go to heaven? Or is it fear of the even simpler question: does it go anywhere?

---

17. Ernst Wilhelm Benz (d. 1978), "Christian Afterlife Beliefs," *www.widowwidowersupport.org/Christian%20Afterlife%20Beliefs.htm.*
18. Segal, p. 22.

IM CONVERSATION 6

man **:DAVID**

HOGAN: Yo

that is some heavy stuff. **:DAVID**

HOGAN: Soul, part 6?

yes **:DAVID**

HOGAN: Yeah, I was just reading it again.

sometimes i wish someone would just say something definitive to me. **:DAVID**

you know even if they don't know. **:DAVID**

just give me something to tell myself so i can move on. **:DAVID**

HOGAN: I know.

HOGAN: All of the indecision ...

the uncertainty. It makes me uncomfortable.

it's most unsettling. makes me nervous. **:DAVID**

i guess by not saying anything completely definitive, there's still room to be right. **:DAVID**

we can place the blame elsewhere. **:DAVID**

HOGAN: Right. Blame displacement—
the way of the human.

i feel a definitiveness to things when staring at someone in a casket though. **:DAVID**

there is without a doubt something very definite about that experience. **:DAVID**

HOGAN: I know.

HOGAN: There is that thing that's missing. What you are looking at is familiar, but it's not the person you knew. What you are looking at is only *like* the person you knew. That is definite.

HOGAN: You know?

yeah **:DAVID**

HOGAN: It's kind of, I don't know, a rubbery approximation of the person you loved.

Regardless, it's empty ... whatever it is ...

i didn't want to look at kyle **:DAVID**

mostly because i knew what to expect **:DAVID**

that to see him would
bring finality to it **:DAVID**

that to observe him would be proof that kyle,
his essence, was no longer
observable **:DAVID**

HOGAN: I couldn't do it.

Robin asked me if I wanted to get up ...

HOGAN: I couldn't get out of my seat.

But it was just enough to see the top of the face propped up in the casket. I could tell from the tip of the nose. That was all it took ...

the pastor doing the ceremony gave like four
or five depictions of the afterlife. **:DAVID**

none of them were compatible. **:DAVID**

HOGAN: I don't remember that.

toward the end of the ceremony he quoted
different apostles and church fathers **:DAVID**

just rattling off some nice sounding things.
it helped, i think. **:DAVID**

If my memory serves, Kyle was apparently, by the time of the funeral, holding a stone with his name on it, while walking down a road hand in hand with everyone in the room as well as the rest of the saints and Church fathers. How he was simultaneously holding our hands while holding the stone is one of those eternal mysteries. And of course, all this was transpiring outside of time, which sort of negates the linear idea of a journey. But maybe not.

his point was simple enough— **:DAVID**

we just don't know. **:DAVID**

"we see dimly." **:DAVID**

couldn't have felt more
true than at that moment.
i felt rather dim trying
to follow everything. **:DAVID**

HOGAN: No kidding.

but there was something that i hadn't felt with
any other death. **:DAVID**

it was like since i knew kyle and we were so
close, it made me less afraid. **:DAVID**

like if he went to, say, cancun. i felt like then
cancun became a real, visitable
locale. **:DAVID**

i sort of knew cancun. **:DAVID**

before he went to cancun it was sort of a
place of postcards and travel magazines. not
completely real. **:DAVID**

that doesn't make any sense. **:DAVID**

sorry **:DAVID**

HOGAN: No.

HOGAN: I know what you mean, though.

HOGAN: There are certain people that, when
they die, there is that level of comfort.

HOGAN: *Comfort* isn't the right word ...

Comfort goes with Cancun, not caskets ...

HOGAN: But it's something like that.

yeah **:DAVID**

part of the "comfort" with kyle's death—i'll stick with the word—was everything he left us. **:DAVID**

you know? **:DAVID**

HOGAN: Like a legacy ...

HOGAN: Which is an even lamer word than *comfort*, but the idea is right.

i was going to comment on that word. **:DAVID**

i don't know why i dislike it so much **:DAVID**

but i find it completely distasteful **:DAVID**

like it is simply what is supposed to be said or something **:DAVID**

HOGAN: Legacy, you mean?

yeah **:DAVID**

HOGAN: Sorry

comfort sucks too, but *legacy* is worse. **:DAVID**

you know what was sort of funny after he died ... **:DAVID**

is how often the word *shocked* was given in response to the news of his death. **:DAVID**

HOGAN: And irony is supposed to be dead! Ha!

i would see someone i hadn't seen and who i hadn't shared that "i'm so sorry" moment with yet, and they'd say, "i was just so shocked." **:DAVID**

it got really funny to me. **:DAVID**

i would brace for it **:DAVID**

try my hardest not to smile **:DAVID**

HOGAN: Yeah. He would have found that so hilarious.

oh he would have so egged it on. **:DAVID**

HOGAN: In a way, that's what was so great about him. The ability to take those really uncomfortable social norms and turn them around to find the humor in it.

HOGAN: Being around him made me take myself a lot less seriously.

you know what we're doing right now, don't you? **:DAVID**

HOGAN: What's that?

we are recalling for each other kyle's good attributes. **:DAVID**

we're *comforting* one another. **:DAVID**

this sucks. **:DAVID**

this im was supposed to be about other stuff. **:DAVID**

HOGAN: Weird. I guess it goes to show how strong that impulse is.

the mourning chapter is later. **:DAVID**

you know i'm getting nervous about
being done **:DAVID**

with the book, that is **:DAVID**

not the mourning **:DAVID**

well, ok ... both **:DAVID**

HOGAN: Yeah, kind of like postpartum depression, only we've given birth to this weird, strange mess of a book about something that we are, obviously, still in the middle of.

yeah **:DAVID**

the end of projects are always really
volatile times for me. **:DAVID**

the end of recording *a collision*[1]
was the worst. **:DAVID**

it's just you work really hard on something,
and then you have to let it go. **:DAVID**

and that's when people tear at it **:DAVID**

when you're most vulnerable **:DAVID**

HOGAN: You always wonder if there was one more thing you could put down or say or take back.

HOGAN: And then, all of a sudden, it's not yours anymore.

with *a collision* it was partially the
subject matter. **:DAVID**

HOGAN: That makes sense.

---

1. Vide *www.everybodywantstogotoheaven.com/themakingofacollision.*

Well, what do you think is going to happen when you taunt death? It's like that old SNL skit for "Happy Fun Ball ..." "Do not taunt Happy Fun Ball!"

to make a concept album for one ... **:DAVID**

that's just asking for it. something you definitely don't say out loud and hope no one notices. **:DAVID**

and then with the subject being death and mortality and the christian response to it, it was all just a tad daunting. **:DAVID**

it is nuts that we were the ones that would wind up needing it most!? **:DAVID**

there were so many moments i thought we should just bail and turn it into a nice tight little collection of songs. **:DAVID**

HOGAN: What kept us from it?

something would come along insisting we keep forging ahead. **:DAVID**

kyle happened to be that something on several occasions. **:DAVID**

it's so frightening to look back on the role he played in assembling such a thing that we would need in his absence. **:DAVID**

HOGAN: Yeah, I know.

and there was the sandy thing! **:DAVID**

HOGAN: Yeah

Oh, man ... Sandy ...

HOGAN: It was like they knew they had to be

strength for the rest of us. In order to leave
us with what we'd later need.

yeah. well, one of my lowest points was right after we had tracked the opening piece—the "everybody wants to go to heaven" bit. **:DAVID**

i was having doubts, and then toni and i were talking to sandy. **:DAVID**

this was when she was in remission. she looked great. **:DAVID**

she was talking about coping with death **:DAVID**

and out of her mouth comes, "it's not that i'm afraid. i mean i want to go to heaven. i just don't want to die." **:DAVID**

she had never heard of the song! **:DAVID**

here we were making an album, her battle with cancer a major provocation for its assembly, and just about the time i'm ready to pull the plug, wondering if it is all just too much, out come those words from her mouth. **:DAVID**

crazy! **:DAVID**

HOGAN:

The last time I saw her, she looked amazing.

HOGAN: Wow.

a friend of mine, t.d. oakes, emailed me. remember him? he's from kentucky. always comes and hangs out when we're up that way. **:DAVID**

HOGAN: Yeah. Absolutely.

well, in this email he was talking about *hallel*
you familiar? **:DAVID**

HOGAN: I want to say yes.
It sounds really familiar ...

well, *hallel* consists of 6 psalms that are recited at the jewish celebration of passover. a group of songs really. you know the recitation of "his love endures forever ..." well that's part of it. so you get the tone. now this might be a little crazy, but follow me ... ok? **:DAVID**

HOGAN: Yeah.

so the night of the last supper ... **:DAVID**

HOGAN: Yeah.

we can, with a fair amount of safety, assume that jesus recited the hallel with his disciples the last night they were together. the night before ... **:DAVID**

HOGAN: Oh that's cool.

no. that's not the cool part. i mean, i guess that's cool, but here's where this is going ... so if we believe that scripture is inspired by god, that it is god-breathed, and if we believe that jesus was divine, that he was god incarnate, then ... **:DAVID**

HOGAN: Oh man! I totally see where this going!

!!!! ... would it be unreasonable to wonder whether god breathed out a song that he knew he would later need in his human form? did he know that something as simple as a bit of art could help shape the reality he saw with

his human eyes and heart. that in a moment
of such weight and enormity it could
make all the difference. **:DAVID**

HOGAN: No way! That is a monster of a thought. That God wrote a song for Himself? Knowing He might need it? Knowing the power art holds for us humans!?!

i think it's a beautiful thought in the least.
and if i let my mind play it all the way out,
it makes christ much more vulnerable and
accessible than i've thought of him in a long
time. i mean, to think he could need a song
as much as i do sometimes?
that is comforting. **:DAVID**

HOGAN: Here's a thought ... you know how we were just talking about working on something and how hard it is to let it go?

HOGAN: Do you think Sandy thought about that when the cancer came back?

HOGAN: Not in the sense of, you know, a project, but a life.

HOGAN: Wondering if there was one more thing to say or part to play. If she was ready to hand things over.

HOGAN: I dunno.

I wonder if she knew the weight of those few words???

HOGAN: I gotta go. The Dodsons are having a BBQ, and I'm supposed to make some brownies for it.

uh. ok. **:DAVID**

HOGAN: Late

HISTORY OF BLUEGRASS

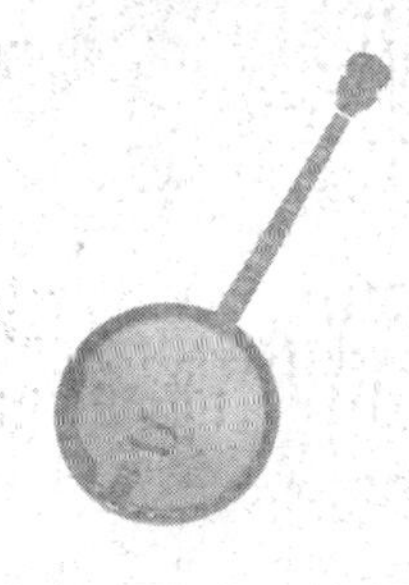

— PART 6 —

THE EARLY LIFE OF THE BLUEGRASS POOH-BAH

or

Some Depressing Childhood Memories Observed

In order to keep you on your toes, we will throw a monkey wrench right into the big fat middle of the machine that we've built. If Oprah Winfrey ever reads this and decides to bring the authors on her show, if only to later indict them for all of the horrible lies in the text, they will be able to point to this very section and say, "We never told anyone that we were right. In fact, we happily admit it when we aren't sure, and it says so right here. It also name-checks you, Oprah. How about that?" Another reason is to show that no matter how well you make your case for something, there is always going to be an exception to the rule.

There has been quite a bit of time spent suggesting that the Appalachian region and the inhabitants thereof are chiefly responsible for bluegrass music. And for the most part, this is true. But what follows is a little test: on one side is a list of artists from Appalachia, on the other side is a list of artists not from Appalachia. You pick which side is not from Appalachia.

Chet Atkins	Bill Monroe
Loretta Lynn	Lester Flatt
Dolly Parton	Earl Scruggs

Did you answer correctly?[1] So there it is. Bill Monroe, historically known as the grandfather of bluegrass, the originator, the grand pooh-bah, if you will, was not from Appalachia. He was from Kentucky.

Not only that, but Flatt and Scruggs were also from places outside of the mountainous backwoods, and they have seen a fair share of ink in this little venture. So what gives? Have the authors led you down the path of iniquity? Have you been spoon-fed lies with attestations of their veracity? Are we, in a word, *evil*?

No. An entire musical genre cannot rest on the back of one man alone.[2] And just because this cat Monroe gets most of the credit doesn't mean that Appalachia has no place in the big picture. Because it does. Elements of style, band makeup, and song repertoire all come from there, as well as many other important and historical bluegrass performers.[3] But America has never been a homogenous nation, and every region is made up of a blend of cultures and influences. This is what makes our country beautiful and proud (cue patriotic music).

The point is, Bill Monroe is sort of the lynchpin of this whole thing. He was not from Appalachia, but without the influence of said region, this whole genre of music would be getting a whole lot less attention. And Oprah can take that to the bank.

So why is Bill Monroe so important, anyhow? Earl Scruggs is way important, but he is still fated to sit one step lower than old Bill on the fabled steps of influence. Why? What makes him so special?

Presented here are three theories: **One**, He had already made a name for himself before the whole bluegrass thing hit, along with his brother Charlie, as a performer of "old-time music," which is a nice way of saying "hillbilly" music, a term that brings to mind all sorts

---

1. Answer key: The list on the right.
2. Unless your name happens to be Frank Zappa, in which case no one ever knew what you were doing in the first place.
3. Neil Rosenberg, *Bluegrass: A History*, p. 13.

of fun stereotypes.[4] In other words, he was there first. **Two**, he had what we now call "pop sensibility," which basically means that he was able to take all sorts of influences outside of the foundational old-time music, mix them together, and then sell them commercially with great success. The fact that you are sitting here reading about the guy says something, right? The **third** theory is this: It is difficult to find good stories about Earl Scruggs. It is not difficult to find them about Bill Monroe, which is what follows—a story ...

A road ran from the railroad depot in Rosine, Kentucky, down through the small town of Horton, and eventually to the larger town of Beaver Dam. This road was used for both traffic and commerce, the crops of the farmers, the coal from the mines nestled in the surrounding hills, the timber from the forest, and a special form of crippling emotional distress to a young boy named Bill on one of the larger farms along its route.

This young boy, one of eight children, had been born with a condition called esotropia, in which his left eye turned in rather than looked out. Of course, that particular medical term did not exist back then. Rather, he would have been dubbed "cross-eyed" or, even more brutal, "hug-eyed." His older siblings, the ones who should have been helping to raise and socialize the youngster, could not be bothered with such a social liability. They ignored him on a good day, teased him on a bad, and occasionally resorted to some physical abuse if alcohol made its way into the equation.

The nature of the problem is that if not done early in life, the person's vision will be permanently impaired due to atrophied nerve endings. Bill's was not corrected until late in his teens.[5]

---

4. Incidentally, Monroe despised the term *hillbilly*, unlike, say, modern hillbillies, who seem to show an enormous amount of pride in being separate from the masses and for some reason often sport Caesar-style haircuts, the tips dotted with grown-out bleach, and immaculate pencil-thin facial hair. K-Fed e.g.

5. This is a medical-ish diagram of how someone with esotropia would observe a banjo.

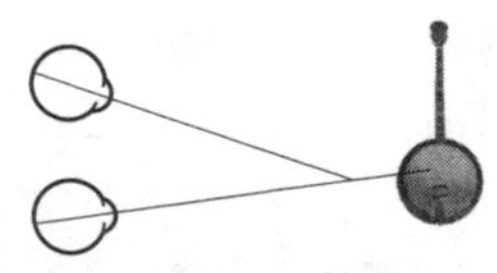

Esotropia is, obviously, a terrifying and debilitating condition.

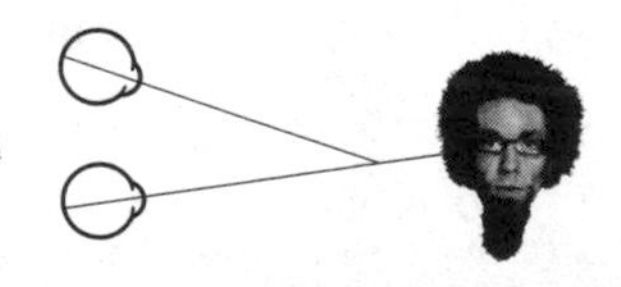

There is something curious that happens, however, when one of the senses does not work just right. Oftentimes, one of the other senses will become much more acute in order to compensate. In Bill's case, his hearing became very sensitive and keen. Kind of like Superman, just without the ability to fly and stop bullets and look through walls. Think of it like this: The quietest sound that a person can hear with normal hearing is registered at 0 decibels. This is very, very, very quiet. A soft whisper registers at 30 decibels, and a refrigerator hums at 50. With that in mind, check this out: he learned to recognize the sounds of hoofbeats and wheels upon the road that ran by their farm from miles away. That is unbelievable! If a toilet flushes at 75 decibels, a level that is probably equivalent to that of the clip-clops of a horse ... well, he could recognize an oncoming stranger by the sound of his horse before ever even seeing him ... THAT IS CRAZY!!! But superpowers always come with a curse, and his was that he also recognized that he was likely to be made fun by family and strangers alike on account of his appearance. So when he heard these sounds—the distant clapping of the approaching horses and mules—he would run away and hide in the barn, listening intently until he was sure that whoever it was had passed.

By and large, he was left alone by his family—not because they didn't like him, but because they were busy and he was too small for most of the things they were involved with. He was a proud child, unwilling to admit to the pain and loneliness he felt, his desire for human contact. He was left alone to wander the family property. He grew thoughtful, keeping his cards close to his chest, pining for affirmation, eventually deciding, "Lonesome is walking around by yourself, wondering where your brothers are."[6]

And thus is a small, highly condensed portrait of the young life of the grandfather of bluegrass. Sad, eh? If only Bill's childhood, a composition of exclusion and disregard by the family he yearned deeply to be a part of, was the exception on rural farms in the early 1900s.[7] Families were large, and life was not easy by any stretch of the

---

6. This story is paraphrased from the first chapter of *Can't You Hear Me Callin'* by Richard D. Smith. The quote is specifically from p. 13.

7. Shoot, if only the same could not be said for contemporary households.

imagination. As soon as children were old enough to work, they were out in the fields or mines, doing what they could to keep the family afloat. That Bill Monroe was the youngest didn't help his cause.

What did help him was that from very early on he was around music. It shouldn't be surprising that a boy who had to rely on his ears more so than his eyes would be drawn to the singing and playing of his family with whom he desperately wanted some sort of common ground. Much of his first musical instruction came the same way all other learning came to him, by watching and listening. His mother would play the fiddle and sing old traditional songs from the British Isles. Other relatives, such as his brothers and to a greater extent an uncle with the good fortune to be named Pen, played music and took part in square dances, which Bill soaked up like a sponge.

As if being born with a wonky eye and ignored and bullied by your own brothers weren't enough, his mother, one of the only people who had shown some amount of kindness to him, up and died when he was ten years old. This is a traumatic experience for anyone, but from the sound of it, this death was particularly ghastly. She had contracted some sort of degenerative spinal disease (accounts as to what it was exactly are conflicting), which sounds painful enough in a modern context, so you can just let your mind wander for a bit as to how this sort of thing would have gone down in the early 1900s. If fixing a jacked-up eye is a tall order, a rotting spinal cord might as well be from outer space. Apparently the pain was such that she would lie in the house and scream in agony, unable to do much else. Bill's brother Speed—another family member blessed with an awesome name—took to fleeing the house, running out into their fields to escape the cries of her dying.[8]

When she finally passed on, the house was left with an odd silence. For one, the agonizing cries had ceased, and two, so had the music—the heart of the family's musical life had gone out. The already reserved and aloof Bill took to wandering the property of the Monroe farm, heading as far away from the house as he could go. It is beautiful to note that one brother had run to the fields fleeing the noise of a

8. Smith, p. 18.

dying loved one, while another ran there to escape the silence she left behind.[9] It was in the family fields that Bill began to hone the voice that would characterize bluegrass singing.[10] While he wandered, he would sing. Loudly. He had stuff to get out and was alone in the middle of nowhere, figuring he was safe from the reach of anyone who would make fun of him. On these long walks he would hear distant railroad workers doing something called "hollering," which is a high-pitched, Swiss yodel sort of thing that field hands used to communicate with one another. It is a well-known fact that when one hears a yodel, the reflex is to yodel back.[11] So of course he would have tried this out, and to an extent integrated it into his style.

And as for his mandolin playing, for which he was considered a master? He picked that up because his musician brothers refused to give up their guitars and fiddles, leaving Bill with the only instrument left sitting around the house. How's that for a quirk of fate?

So that's the history of Bill Monroe. Was it all necessary? Yes. Just in case you tuned out and only started reading the first and last sentences of each paragraph, here's a recap: Bill was born in Kentucky, he had a gimp eye and people poked fun, his hearing ruled, the men in his life ignored him, the women were kind but they had a tendency to die, and he learned how to sing and play traditional songs on the mandolin from family members. Now, that wasn't so hard, was it?

Of course, that is just the tip of the iceberg, seeing as there are entire books written about the guy. So why concentrate on these depressing anecdotes from his childhood? It was in the suffering of Bill's younger years that he obtained many of the characteristics that bent him into the granddaddy of all bluegrass. He learned early that this life was hard. He learned that loneliness was a relentless thing, forever biting at the heels. He learned that nobody was guaranteed tomorrow.

But there was more. He learned that music was a means to heal, that the community found with it could feel like home. He also learned the traditional values of fundamental Protestantism, which

---

9. These stories are from *Can't You Hear Me Callin'*, by Richard D. Smith.

10. His style of singing was called the "high lonesome sound."

11. Sounds like a cell phone commercial. *Cut to young hip urbanite leaving voice message for a friend:* "Hey, what up, yo? Yodel back." *Cut to mass of people representing the young hip urbanite's network that is now yodeling.* This could be huge ...

would become an integral part of his routine (and of nearly every other bluegrass performer) until the end of his days. In those younger years, he learned a wealth of traditional old-time songs from family and neighbors, and those old-time songs would soon become merely another part of the fabric of music that would come to be known as "bluegrass."

DECIBEL POINTS OF REFERENCE

*measured in dBA or decibels

- 0 The softest sound a person can hear with normal hearing
- 10 normal breathing
- 20 whispering at 5 feet
- 30 soft whisper
- 31 dead bird hitting the ground from a height of 10 feet
- 50 rainfall
- 60 normal conversation
- 110 shouting in ear
- 120 thunder

HOME

- 50 refrigerator
- 50-60 electric toothbrush
- 50-75 washing machine
- 50-75 air conditioner
- 50-80 electric shaver
- 55 coffee percolator
- 55-70 dishwasher
- 60 sewing machine
- 60-85 vacuum cleaner
- 60-95 hair dryer
- 65-80 alarm clock
- 70 TV audio
- 70-80 coffee grinder
- 75-85 flushing toilet
- 80 pop-up toaster
- 80 doorbell
- 80 ringing telephone
- 80 whistling kettle
- 80-90 food mixer or processor
- 80-90 blender
- 80-95 garbage disposal
- 110 baby crying
- 110 squeaky toy held close to the ear
- 135 noisy squeeze toys

WORK

- 40 quiet office, library
- 50 large office
- 65-95 power lawn mower
- 80 manual machine, tools
- 85 handsaw
- 90 tractor
- 90-115 subway
- 95 electric drill
- 100 factory machinery
- 100 woodworking class
- 105 snow blower
- 110 power saw
- 110 leafblower
- 120 pneumatic drills, heavy machine
- 120 jet plane (at ramp)
- 120 ambulance siren
- 125 chain saw
- 130 jackhammer, power drill
- 130 air raid
- 130 percussion section at symphony
- 140 airplane taking off
- 150 jet engine taking off
- 150 artillery fire at 500 feet
- 180 rocket launching from pad

RECREATION

- 40 quiet residential area
- 70 freeway traffic
- 85 heavy traffic, noisy restaurant
- 90 truck, shouted conversation
- 95-110 motorcycle
- 100 snowmobile
- 100 school dance, boom box
- 110 disco
- 110 busy video arcade
- 110 symphony concert
- 110 car horn
- 110-120 rock concert
- 112 personal cassette player on high
- 117 football game (stadium)
- 120 band concert
- 125 car stereo (factory installed)
- 130 stock car races
- 143 bicycle horn
- 150 firecracker
- 156 capgun
- 157 balloon pop
- 162 fireworks (at 3 feet)
- 163 rifle
- 166 handgun
- 170 shotgun

INTERLUDE

Your two authors are standing in a dimly lit theater. Outside the clouds are rolling in, thundering in the distance, promising a late season storm that will manage to flood yards in the suburbs and wash at least one soccer mom's minivan off the road. The authors look at one another briefly, exchanging a glance that says in one split of a split of a second, "*Do we know what we have gotten ourselves in to?*"

"We need to figure this out."

"I know. Good find with that whole Carl Jung thing. That should help."

"Thanks. The first paragraph is where it's at."

The first paragraph is indeed where it's at. This statement was by no means an exaggeration.

"Did you know that he was into alchemy? Oh, and at the end of his life he started to believe in UFOs."

"That's awesome."

The two authors go about the rest of their morning. The storms come in the early afternoon, flooding the streets and yards of the suburbs and washing a lady in a minivan off the road. Two teenagers see her crashed in a ditch and dive into the water to pull her out. They will go on to make the evening news; they will go on to make one of the authors wonder why he wasn't more brave back when he was a teenager.

The afternoon is spent avoiding the weather and reading essays by Carl Jung, a process that makes the readers bleary-eyed and despondent. By the close of the evening, one of the authors is right back where he was at the beginning of the day, wondering where in the world all of this is going.

His wife is watching a popular medical dramedy on the television. The one where a doctor is falling for a bedridden guy who has a bad heart and the voice of a smoker who gargles with rocks. He is at the end of the line, it seems. The author knows this because he says things like "I'm tired," but he says them the way that television characters are supposed to say them when they are just about fed up with life. The author doesn't pay much attention until he hears something that finally reminds him of the reason for this whole endeavor.

"I believe in heaven. If I have to choose between this life here and one in heaven, I'm choosing heaven."

COLUMNS, PART 6

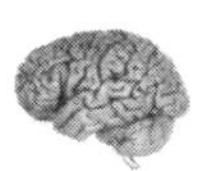

THE BIRDS HAD STOPPED DYING. THAT'S WHAT HE HAD concluded. He wasn't sure what meaning this held. But ever since he had received the second letter from Virginia, there had been no more birds appearing dead in his garden. There had been none found lying in the road. Or on the sidewalk. Or on the front lawns of the houses he passed coming to and from the church. He at first believed they had finally all perished. The death of all birds had been news the world over. But there was now rumor circulating among the other priests. Of an extraordinary phenomenon across town. Involving the gathering of birds at a hospital. And he took this as a good sign. To receive word that there were some that had survived was good. He was still entirely convinced that the ending of birds was his fault. He pressed his weight to the ends of his shoes. He clapped 4 times. Yet ever since Virginia's letter, the appearance of expired birds had stopped. Of course you and I know that the letter had nothing to do with the recent cessation of deaths. As did nothing else regarding the priest. But he did not know this. Or perhaps he was simply incapable of

THE DOCTORS HAD DONE everything they could. Tests had been run. And then more tests. And at his request, more tests. But there was consensus—there was nothing more to be done. Seven of the top specialists (in the field of heaviness) gathered in her room and announced to Steven, while he sat beside her, holding her hand, "There is nothing to be done. Put your things in order."

By this time she had acquired such a tremendous amount of

absolving himself of any blame. Virginia's letter had been good for him to read. Of course, it had also changed little. She had been correct in the letter. It was indeed more for her than him. But he felt very glad that things were most likely lighter for her before she had passed. Virginia had died on a bench in Central Park shortly after he had received it. Witnesses reported an excessive number of lifeless pigeons surrounding her. A sea of dead birds encircling her on her bench island. One of the dead birds lay with its tiny head resting in her opened palm. She had almost died in this very spot not too many years prior. He hoped he didn't die in public. He wanted to die here. In this garden. It would surprise you to know how many different individuals had confided in him that they actually hoped to die in a busy metropolitan area. That's the thing with death. Of all he had learned while wearing these clothes, this one seemed most unusual. Death comes at every one of us differently. It is the one boat we are all in. But we float in no singular way. It never ceased to be a shock to him. How people would tell him awful things that they would never tell another. A priest's clothes had a powerful effect on others. They changed people's behavior. They held the power to change people's speech. They would cause people to use words different than the ones they typically use. And if, by chance, offensive words did escape, they would immediately be followed by more words.

heaviness that the possibilities of moving her were nonexistent. This room, here in this city, would be her final location.

He would be with her.

He could not remember the exact number of hours spent listening to the sounds of the machines that sat beside her bed.

A bird tapped on the hospital window. The bird was one of the *remnants*. One that could not be killed by the weight of his tears. They had been gathering. *Gathering* was not the proper word for it. The fact of the matter was that by this time,

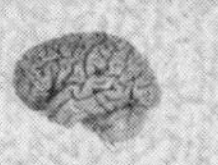

his responsibility in the matter of the birds. If the boy had been lying, a pebble would have formed for lying to a priest, of course. In this garden no less. But no pebble was found. There were always pebbles after someone left. Justin searched for days. He put off other tasks. He refused to take visitors. He did not go home. He dug and dug. Yet no pebble. Justin decided that the boy must be found. The thing the boy had said. About it being the boy's fault. The boy taking the blame. This could not be true. If it were, what was Justin to do? And so he set off into the city. He walked and walked and walked and walked. And clapped and clapped and clapped and clapped. The pain was what he needed. He was still here. He was still here. He was still here. He was still here. He would disappear into shops and businesses, asking if anyone had seen the boy with the bluest eyes and heaviest load. To his surprise most responded, "Yes." They would then relate their encounter. Each was the bizarrest of tales. All of them cannot be repeated here. But what follows is the one told to him by a seamstress in a tiny shop in the East Village. The boy had come to the shop needing thread. He asked if she had any in a light shade of purple. She was unsure. She went to the spools to search. While she searched, he sat quietly in a chair by the cash register. Eventually she found one spool in a light shade of purple. She announced this to him, and he rose from where he was

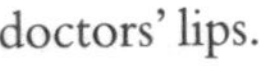

doctors' lips.

There are some deaths, which upon occurrence, arrest the considerations of the public at large. There are these moments when we all cry at once.

When Steven's mother died, all the jars shattered.

The hospital had provided seven additional rooms on his mother's floor to house the ever-growing number of jars. As the machines beside his mother's bed went silent, as she exhaled one final time, as her chest became too heavy to again inflate, the heaviest of liquids fell with the seated. Walked toward her. Reached for the spool of thread. Unwound approximately 14 inches from it. Broke the 14 inches of thread loose from the rest of the spool. Asked her how much it would be for this amount of thread. She responded, "Nothing." He insisted, "No, please let me pay you." They settled on 21 cents. He paid her. She put the small amount of change in the register. He then asked her to extend her right arm. She did so without hesitation. He plucked a needle from the needle book lying by the register. He threaded the needle with the purple thread He held a button in his hand. The exact one she had lost weeks ago from the right sleeve of the purple silk blouse she was wearing. In a series of motions, poking through the fabric, then pulling away from it, the button was returned to its original location. She was crying. All the possible places the boy could have found the button. She was crying. What had been lost had been returned. It was but a button. Yet she could not stop crying. The boy left, and she never saw him again. (Later, when the bird brought the message and laid it across her hands, she knew it was from him.) Everyone's tales were similar. They all ended in weeping. The priest's search eventually led him to the hospital where Steven's mother was being treated. She was on the 34th floor. He hated hospitals. The smell. The sterility. The circular conversations. As the elevator ascended, he pressed his weight down. The

breaking glass. The entire city shook. Steven's collected tears crashed through the hallways. Seeped under doorways. Spilled down the stairwells. Flooded into the street. The liquid was so heavy that those passing on the sidewalk became unable to lift their feet from the ground once their feet became wet. The sidewalks quickly filled with motionless New Yorkers staring up at the black cloud of birds gathering over the city, descending and ascending from this one particular floor in this one particular building. They could not move their feet. They could not take a step. They all began to cry.

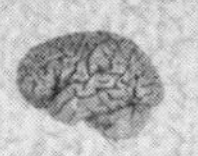

rising force helped push against the sharp edges of the pebbles. A tear formed. He smiled. He brought his hands to his face and stared at the blood-wet gloves. They were heavy and black from the blood and soil. He brought his face to rest in them. He felt the dampness against both his cheeks. He let his tears mix with their wetness. He hated hospitals. The elevator doors opened. He counted the steps to Steven's mother's room. He knew before he got to her door that they would be the same. The same exact number he had taken to Emily's room. How did he know they would be the same? As he reached the door to Steven's mother's room, he noticed the floor sagging. As if a great weight pressed upon it. He peered through the door's window. There sat the boy, next to his mother. He was holding her right hand. The machines sat beside the bed. The priest could hear the machines' noises from where he stood. He stood. There. Quietly. There were jars surrounding the mother and her son. Jars full of a clear liquid. He saw the one labeled "Nettles." It was full. There were 3 tall stacks of paper on the table beside the bed. He wanted to enter. He wanted to ask the boy what he was to do if the birds were not his fault. He reached out his right hand. He grabbed the handle of the door. He squeezed it with all of his might. Until his hand was shaking. Until his forearm was trembling. Until his chest was heaving in and out. Until there was the

Steven was holding his mother's right hand.

He could just reach the pen and paper on the table beside his mother's bed. The Lark at the hospital window again pecked against it. Steven met the bird's gaze. Steven wrote three words down. As the last word was completed and a full stop ended the sentence, the paper fell to the floor with an astonishing force, splashing into the weight of Steven's tears, and floated away from him.

The paper with the heaviest message ever sent floated down

audible sound of his tears hitting against linoleum. Steven looked up. Their eyes met. Justin slowly let go of the handle and went back to his garden.

the hallway. Down the stairwell. Out into the street. The Lark rose from the sill of the window and began the dive toward the flooded earth to retrieve the heaviest of messages.

We were all crying, and we could not stop, and the heaviest liquid was rising.

Another Lark tapped at the window. Steven took another piece of paper and began to write the three words again. The cycle would continue until everyone's message had been sent.

The Larks were flying in the New York City air.

HISTORY
OF THE
SOUL

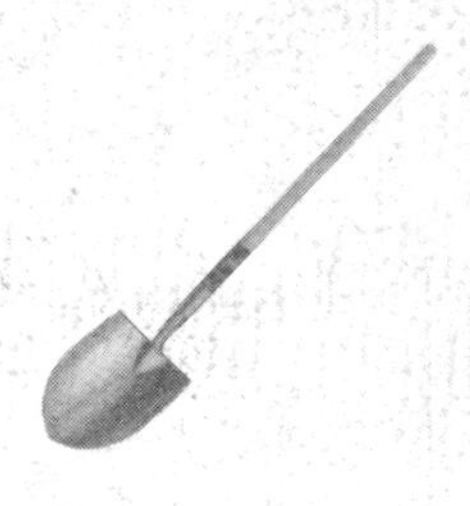

— PART 7 —

THE MOURNING AFTER

or

I'll Follow You into the Dark

What is the first thing you did when you heard the news that someone you loved died? Did the hand that was holding the phone stop cooperating? Did the phone fall to the floor? Or did you? Did you fall silent? Or start repeating one word over and over and over, such as, "No. No. No."? Or was it relief you felt, relief for a suffering that has finally passed? Were your reactions nothing more than learned responses? Were these reactions simply the summing of chemicals and a given amount of electrical pulses? If so, then why does it hurt so badly? Why do we mourn the way we do?

It's not as if we get a crash course in this sort of thing while everyone is still in good health and accounted for. There isn't a childhood moment where our parents anxiously sit us down on a couch to give us "the talk" concerning proper protocol for when someone close to us departs this realm. Death does not discriminate between those of us who are prepared and those of us who are not. If we choose to participate in human relationships, every single one of us will eventually find ourselves in a church, a funeral parlor, or standing next to a rectangular hole in the earth, trying to find the proper words for the moment. And yet somehow, in those situations, it seems we all fall in line with a certain set of activities and customs, whether we have experienced them previously or not, as if they were written in our very DNA.

It customarily plays out like this: News is received and we are stunned. Phone calls, a furious bustle of activity ensues; decisions, decisions, decisions, a complex and intricately choreographed funeral is designed and organized at lightning speed; there is a viewing of some sort, the funeral/burial/memorial takes place in the morning hours generally three days after the death; everyone congregates at somebody's house to eat food, a steady stream of casseroles having made their march to the home of the surviving family, effectively rendering the need to prepare a meal obsolete and forever ruining everyone's taste for green beans in cheese sauce with those fried onions scattered on the surface.

The family (spouse, parents, children, etc.) will by then be firmly in the "stages of grief," and everyone acquainted with them will keep track of their progress yet never say anything to them personally. Rather, talk will ensue at the local coffee shop about so-and-so's recent behavior, with phrases such as "he must be going through the anger stage right now" peppered throughout.

Okay, so that last part was a wee bit of a joke, but sometimes the truth is just funny. There are countless books written regarding the grieving process. How to do it, what it is, the good way to go about it, the bad way to go about it, and on and on ... A Google search for *grief + stages* will yield, no lie, more than four million results on the subject.[1] Nearly every single one of them lists the same basic things, the same sequence of events:

---

1. But just to put everything in perspective, a search for pop star Britney Spears yields more than sixty-one million hits. We are sure that this speaks volumes about today's society but are just too stunned to really consider the matter further.

Denial: This could not have possibly happened!
Bargaining: God, if you bring 'em back, I promise I'll never do _____ again!
Guilt: It's my fault! I can't believe I _____ed, and now they're dead!
Anger: @&%^*!
Depression: Alas, the sun shall never shine again.
Hope: Or perhaps it will ...

This process can take years. Or it can take hours, only to repeat itself over and over again. The fact is, a thing as viciously cunning as grief takes root in our emotions and imaginations, both of which can be unpredictable at best, especially when under duress. According to all four million websites,[2] everybody experiences these six stages of grief ... there is no formula—it is different and personal for each one; however, the common element is that everyone will go through each stage of the grieving process.

There is comfort in this, in the predictability of exactly how you will be miserable.

As vitally important and as well documented as these stages of grief are, there are other rituals that transpire during the observance of a death in which we all share a common yet unspoken knowledge of how to act. These acts are generally referred to as "mourning," and their cultural developments are varied, rich, and happily bizarre enough to warrant a little discussion here.

For starters, there is the language associated with the time of mourning. When someone "passes away," it seems everyone feels the need to pat you on the shoulder and exert some variation of "I'm sorry, this is so *awful*," or "Isn't it just *awful* ..." The word *awful* is defined as "very bad, unpleasant, saddening, etc." But another definition can be found in the very word itself: *awe-full* or, as the dictionary puts it, "so impressive as to inspire awe."[3] Katherine Ashenburg, author of the book *The Mourner's Dance*, writes, "That is how our ancestors saw the time between death and burial, as

---

2. *Dear Oprah,* Okay. So I did not check all four million websites, but it is no less true. *Sincerely, James Frey*
3. Dictionary.com.

a particularly dangerous, particularly dreadful interval."[4] It was generally believed that the spirit of the recently deceased would obviously become angry upon the realization of his newly departed state and therefore be prone to hanging around in order to spite the living.

Now, in our modern society, we don't place a lot of stock in the belief that our newly deceased loved ones will stick around in order to bother us due to the fact that they are ticked off at being dead.[5] However, not that long ago, this conviction held quite a bit of water, and a surprising number of customs that we still participate in today were birthed from it. Many of these traditions we now perform out of reverence and remembrance, but their origins come from a place of fear and the good old tradition of looking out for number one.

Example: When someone near to us *passes on*, it is more or less universally accepted that we will adorn ourselves in black or some alternatively dark-colored clothing—not only at the funeral, but for a given amount of time in the days that follow as well. Of late, this would be a sign of respect for the deceased, as well as a tangible testament to the sadness we feel on the inside. Shades of gloom covering shades of gloom. But it wasn't that long ago that people wore black in order to hide from the angry spirit of the dead.[6]

Here is some background on other equally odd traditions that you can share at the next office Christmas party to impress coworkers:

Speaking well of the departed: Respectful? Yes. But you guessed it, also done so as not to tick off the spirit any more than necessary.

The wake: To remind the dead that they are not forgotten. Or better yet, to trick them into thinking that they are not, in fact, dead but

---

4. Katherine Ashenburg, *The Mourner's Dance*, p. 10–11.

5. Before you offer a hearty snub of the nose to the unenlightened states of pagans past, the authors would like to point out that the first conclusion the disciples jumped to when the whole walking on water episode went down was, in fact, "A ghost!"

6. We know this little fact will come as a great disappointment to all the goth kids hanging out at Hot Topic. Guess what, kiddies? Apparently all that black is a concealing deterrent rather than an enticement to the dead. The authors would suggest wearing bright pink and orange or holding a kitten and a balloon on newly instigated visits to The Gap. It seems the possibilities of a haunting should then greatly increase.

rather just the guest of honor at a very, very depressing party.

Placing a tombstone at the gravesite: Yes, this helps to locate the deceased (you can imagine the confusion unmarked remains of friends and loved ones could potentially create), and they are also pretty. But did you know that they keep the spirit in the ground, where it is much less likely to cause trouble? Special cultural bonus fact: People of the Jewish tradition will sometimes place small stones on top of tombstones when they visit a cemetery. This was originally done for the same basic reason; they're just going the extra mile.

Opening a window in the room where a person died: This is a more prominent practice in European and Middle Eastern cultures. You would think it is done to let the room air out a little bit. But it is actually done in order for the spirit to escape the house.[7]

Covering the mirrors: Vanity is not appropriate. Neither is the dead accidentally seeing their reflection or, worse yet, the reflection of those who are still alive. Do you sense a theme here?

And these are but a few of the many customs associated with the

---

7. Personal aside: Before he was a married homeowner in the suburbs, Hogan lived downtown in an apartment building filled with some of the strangest characters to ever grace central Texas. One man in particular was large and spherical, never wore a shirt, and drove an electric wheelchair down the hall every day to the mailbox because he was too weak to make the trip on foot. His skin was covered in warts and sores and smelled of nicotine and cancer.

One day a peculiar, sweet smell, not unlike old trash, began to seep into Hogan's apartment. It wasn't bad at first, but over the next week or so it began to become more and more pungent. One night, upon returning home after a date with his wife-to-be, they were met with a street full of police cars, an ambulance, and the CSI. The cops would not allow anybody inside the building. Wanting to know what happened, Hogan asked some of the neighbors standing on the sidewalk. One guy finally had an answer: "You know that old guy who drove the scooter all over the hallway? Yeah, apparently he died. The landlord found him in his living room after he hadn't picked up his mail in a while. He'd been in there, dead, for like two weeks or more."

The smell that permeated the apartment building was so thick that you could almost see it. There were also some flies, which is just plain gross. One really creepy part is that the dead guy had just bought a new SUV, and it stayed parked, untouched, in the parking lot for well over a year.

All to say—there is something to be said for opening a window.

mourning process. There are, of course, many variations on these. For instance, in medieval Europe it was customary to wear white during mourning rather than black. Then again, the whole ghost thing seems to be a bit more popular in Europe, so they probably weren't all that concerned with scaring them off.

But what is the real underlying purpose of all of these customs and variations thereof? According to anthropologists, most cultures viewed the interval between death and burial as a very volatile one for the departed, and therefore most of the customs were born out of a desire to placate the deceased. To think there was a time people cried not only out of sadness but also out of fear is unsettling.

Maybe there is another way of looking at this. Rather than viewing our previous customs as born solely out of self-preservation, we could acknowledge that fear and awe are incredibly close sentiments. At the edge of life, between the living and the dead, between the material and the immaterial, there is unavoidable awe. In Hebrew, the same word is used for "fear," "awe," and "terrible."[8] Perhaps all this absurdity of tradition points to the simple fact that death scares us. It has always scared us. It is beyond our finite understanding, and the crazier these customs appear, the more deeply that reality can be felt. No matter how tightly packed our doctrine, at the edge of a rectangular hole in the ground (regardless of how many flowers surround it) there are leaks. It is there, more than at any other moment, that we see clearly how dimly we see.

Granted, much of the fear has now been replaced by things of a more sentimental nature. This transference of fear has coincidentally come to us as slowly and as subtly as the soul's exit. It is now not the souls of those departed that we worry about, but our own. It is at the grave that our wonder begins. It is there that we *need* to believe in something more, something bigger and grander than our hands can touch (or dissect) or that our eyes can see (with or without the aid of magnification). It is there that we need all our notions of heaven to be real. It is *our* souls that need the comfort. We go through the motions

---

8. Ashenburg, p. 12.

and rituals not because it is expected of us or because we're scared of spirits flying about, wreaking havoc on the living, but because we are scared of the possible finality of it all. We do all of this to remember.

To remember.

What was the last conversation you shared? Your last meal together? What words do you wish had exited your mouth? What would you say now if given the chance? What is your most loved memory? When was the moment you felt closest? What were the things they'd get excited about? What makes you think of them? When do you miss them the most? Wouldn't you rather feel this sadness, bear this weight, and mourn their absence than never have been touched by them?

Upon death, we hold a wake to remind us of how precious a person's life was, not to trick the dead spirit into thinking they are alive. We order tombstones, not to keep the deceased in the ground or even just to show where a person is laid to rest, but as a monument of love. In the Jewish tradition, stones are now carried to the grave, not to add additional weight, but to remember. To demonstrate the felt presence of that person's absence. We speak well of the departed because there is no use in speaking ill of them. We wear black to show that under the surface, there is left an immense cavern. We are sad because something has been lost.

IM CONVERSATION 7

HOGAN: Yo

yes **:DAVID**

HOGAN: Sorry, had to go let
out Mike D's canines.

that's so strange to me that
dogs can't just live outside. **:DAVID**

they're gone for the day, and
the dogs can't survive? **:DAVID**

weird, right? **:DAVID**

HOGAN: They went to the
lake or something ...

that's just as strange. **:DAVID**

HOGAN: Funny thing is, one
of them went to the restroom like 3 times in
10 minutes. The other one just ate grass.

the dogs? **:DAVID**

HOGAN: No, my wife.

HOGAN: —Yes, the dogs.

you said *they*, and i thought you meant the dodsons. **:DAVID**

so who went to the lake? **:DAVID**

HOGAN: The Dodsons.

HOGAN: That would be weird seeing Mike D poop on the lawn and eat grass.

it would be weird seeing him at the lake too. **:DAVID**

that's all i'm saying. **:DAVID**

HOGAN: 🙂

oh. so now we're using those things? **:DAVID**

😮 **:DAVID**

HOGAN: Well, I thought it would be a good idea ...

nice **:DAVID**

that was me gasping. **:DAVID**

HOGAN: Good, good. It lends more authenticity to this.

fair enough. **:DAVID**

ok, so did you get what just happened? **:DAVID**

in the book, that is. **:DAVID**

HOGAN: Yeah.

HOGAN: I'm still a little uncomfortable.

how so? **:DAVID**

HOGAN: I don't know really. It's just weird to think about all of these customs, where they came from and what they used to mean.

HOGAN: And then how they are interpreted now.

HOGAN: Don't get me wrong. I like them, but it's just strange.

yeah but it's all beside the point. **:DAVID**

the point is funny. **:DAVID**

HOGAN: Funnier than, say, having a wake to trick the dead into thinking they are still alive?

HOGAN: That's a joke.

HOGAN: Sorry.

no **:DAVID**

it's exactly that funny. **:DAVID**

HOGAN: OK. Please do tell ...

so we've spent all this time trying to prove that the soul is in fact dead within western public thought, right? **:DAVID**

HOGAN: Right

and then we get to the last chapter of this soul stuff, and we spend it talking about how freaked out and scared people were after someone died, right? **:DAVID**

HOGAN: Right

ha! there you go! **:DAVID**

see? that's funny!!! **:DAVID**

the soul is dead,
and it's pissed!!! **:DAVID**

and we should be freaking scared! throwing
it a wake or something. **:DAVID**

instead we just go on behaving more and
more like it's dead! antagonizing it. just
rubbing it in! **:DAVID**

see? funny! **:DAVID**

HOGAN: Dude.

HOGAN: ☺

☹ **:DAVID**

HOGAN: Or rather ...

HOGAN: 😮

ah. you gasp. **:DAVID**

HOGAN: I'm scared.

i cry **:DAVID**

HOGAN: If you think about it, they aren't all
that different.

the point is, we need to mourn. **:DAVID**

we need a moment to all cry at the
same time. **:DAVID**

the soul has died. even among those whose whole job it is to save it **:DAVID**

i don't think they really believe that much in it anymore. **:DAVID**

and so ... **:DAVID**

☹ **:DAVID**

HOGAN: That's good. And scary!

HOGAN: 😮

exactly **:DAVID**

HOGAN: It reminds me of when Robin's grandma died last year.

HOGAN: Her grandmother was a very staunch, Old-World Catholic.

HOGAN: It was so different for me, because I had never been a part of Catholic services, really, at all.

HOGAN: It was so different, yet very much the same.

how so? **:DAVID**

HOGAN: Well, I've been to a lot of funerals.

HOGAN: At least, it seems like I have.

HOGAN: Anyway, the soul seemed to play a much bigger part in this thing.

how so? **:DAVID**

HOGAN: Well. For one, they had a Mass nearly every week for an entire year *for her soul*!

HOGAN: That's just not something familiar to us Protestant types.

HOGAN: But even with that, there were rituals that were very much the same.

HOGAN: We went to the actual funeral Mass, and then all congregated at the church's reception hall to eat food.

HOGAN: Everybody sitting around, remembering in more personal ways.

HOGAN: Then everyone went back to the farm to tell more stories.

HOGAN: That's the part that was familiar.

that seems like it's a consistent item **:DAVID**

the getting together and telling stories **:DAVID**

remembering all the good moments **:DAVID**

lots of laughing **:DAVID**

after kyle died, every single group of friends we'd get together with would go through this same almost ceremonial event. it dawned on me that this was identical for every death i have been in proximity of; we always do the same thing. we sit around and tell stories. we remember. it wasn't like it was planned. we didn't say, "hey let's go back to the house and tell each other stories about the person who just left us." **:DAVID**

it was just what would happen. we would remember. like we were remembering for each other. assuring ourselves that we would not forget. that we would not *let* each other forget. **:DAVID** and there would be some amount of relief felt there in that moment of collective memory. **:DAVID**

but there was always that minute when everyone would get really quiet and the sadness would set in again. **:DAVID**

there is an ebb and flow that is always the same. **:DAVID**

HOGAN: And it goes back and forth so fast.

like this ... **:DAVID**

☺ **:DAVID**

☹ **:DAVID**

☺ **:DAVID**

HOGAN: Right! One minute you are all eating and laughing and shooting guns; the next it's just silent, crying.

HOGAN: And then back.

wait! shooting guns!!!!? **:DAVID**

what!? **:DAVID**

i've never shot guns in that moment! **:DAVID**

HOGAN: Well, that's how you roll in Hobson, Texas.

huh **:DAVID**

who knew **:DAVID**

forget what i said about consistency. **:DAVID**

HOGAN: Dude, I guess sometimes you just need to fire off a few rounds in memory of what was lost.

HOGAN: Hey ... that's just what happened.

HOGAN: It was new to me as well.

HOGAN: The gun part, that is.

well, it sounds like a fun idea. maybe we should all just shoot a gun in memory of the soul. **:DAVID**

HOGAN: Or to scare it off ...

HOGAN: Sorry. Going back to that last chapter.

right **:DAVID**

something weird i just thought of. **:DAVID**

HOGAN: Yeah?

when toni's aunt died—sandra, you know the mom of the disney world girls? **:DAVID**

HOGAN: Right.

anyway, she died in toni's house. hospice care. in toni's parents' bed! sandra was toni's mom's sister. i remember making the drive from waco to texarkana wondering how in the world you could let your sister die in your bed and ever be able to sleep in it again. her mom is way more courageous than me. **:DAVID**

but we were all there. the whole family. the girls. other close friends. waiting. of course everyone was telling stories, and there was that ebb and flow of laughter and tears. but this went on a couple of days. sandra lying in the room next to the stories. there was an intensity to it. it was as if she were gone but she wasn't yet. her breathing was labored and rattley and filling up the whole house. the girls would go sit on the bed and watch her. listening. watching. waiting. and the stories in the next room. laughter. tears. laughter. tears. laughter. **:DAVID**

but then there was another thing. people became really industrious. toni organized all of her mom's cabinets. she went through, throwing away all the old tupperware. cleaned out the refrigerator, throwing out old food. there would be three mustard bottles and everyone would convene to decide which one was the most recently purchased. it helped. it gave us control. it made things better for a bit. **:DAVID**

and then you would hear her rattled breathing and see the girls sitting beside her on the bed. **:DAVID**

tears. laughter. tears. **:DAVID**

HOGAN: Oh my God, I never heard that story ...

all the mundane things we did to convince ourselves that we were in control of something, anything. we are always so predictable. but the whole time, deep down, it was known that something bigger was taking place. thank god for that labored breathing. it was like she was breathing us back into the reality of the moment, that a soul was in a state of flux. that the line between here and there was blurring in the room next to us. eternity was breathing with us under the same roof. heaven was in the rattling breath. **:DAVID**

but you're right. **:DAVID**

of course the real point is that to declare the

soul dead is ludicrous. **:DAVID**

HOGAN: That whole standing over a coffin business blows a very obvious and undeniable hole in that thing.

you can argue intellectually until you're blue in the face, but when you've seen a body ... there is an undeniable substance to life. it is a thing that is observably absent when you're staring at your friend in a casket, when they're lying there with makeup on, even when their hair has been meticulously fixed by their brother-in-law in the same "unkempt" manner as they themselves did every day, even with all the flowers ... **:DAVID**

i'm just saying you don't need a magical soul-weighing box to know to the depth of your still-living, breathing self that the thing that was the smiles and the hugs and the tears and the laughter, that thing that was the person you loved is not what is lying there in that satin-lined container. **:DAVID**

i guess after all of this stuff we've written, it just comes down to something really simple. **:DAVID**

HOGAN: Yeah. What exactly?

we're bluegrass folks! **:DAVID**

HOGAN: OK ...?

we're bluegrass plain as day. **:DAVID**

HOGAN: How do you mean?

we're simple **:DAVID**

uncomplicated **:DAVID**

we're fiddle and banjo **:DAVID**

we use wikipedia for
crying out loud!!! **:DAVID**

HOGAN: Ah!!! Absolutely.

HOGAN: Oh there is nothing more
bluegrass than Wikipedia!

the eschatology of bluegrass is simple and
entirely compelling. **:DAVID**

there was this guy **:DAVID**

jesus **:DAVID**

he was born of earth and heaven **:DAVID**

he knew suffering **:DAVID**

what it meant to be alive and feel
the weight of it **:DAVID**

what it meant to be here **:DAVID**

then he went to be with god **:DAVID**

if we follow him ... **:DAVID**

we follow him **:DAVID**

:DAVID

HOGAN:

☺ **:DAVID**

HOGAN: ☺

HOGAN: we need to recognize the ...

HOGAN: ☹

HOGAN: but look forward to the ...

HOGAN: ☺

exactly! **:DAVID**

take kyle ... **:DAVID**

we mourn him. **:DAVID**

it is obvious. **:DAVID**

i mean, look, we're writing
a freaking book! **:DAVID**

but we believe ... (we have to ... we're
bluegrass folk) ... that he went
somewhere better **:DAVID**

to a world absent of
antagonists. **:DAVID**

if it's not cancer or electricity, it's any number
of other things that plague the mortal state of
things. **:DAVID**

it's true; what we want is rebirth. **:DAVID**

we want something beyond what we are
currently experiencing. **:DAVID**

we want new life. **:DAVID**

and there kyle
was, standing in it! **:DAVID**

the whole weight of his person
immersed in a metaphor **:DAVID**

chest deep in burial **:DAVID**

the christian representation of movement from
mortal death to the residence of god **:DAVID**

to follow jesus leads you to the grave. **:DAVID**

it leads you to death. **:DAVID**

you must follow him up the hill. **:DAVID**

and there was kyle, standing in a metaphor.
and became it. **:DAVID**

and it was what he said at the end, the
very end that was so simple and profound:
*someone help me. someone
please help me*. **:DAVID**

the supplication of humanity. he enunciated
our plea while standing in the figurative
response to it. **:DAVID**

HOGAN: Ah ... our situation as humans.
The guttural cry for rescue.

it's not until the hands are thrown up **:DAVID**

until you realize we're all in the same boat **:DAVID**

none of us is getting out of here alive **:DAVID**

HOGAN: Our suffering state.

maybe our western american life isn't one we
could classify as full of suffering, but we live in
spaces full of antagonists. **:DAVID**

this space itself is one. it is the whole. **:DAVID**

HOGAN: The container just isn't big enough
... the body isn't big enough for the soul, the
coffin isn't big enough for the soul, science
isn't big enough for the soul, religion isn't big
enough for the soul ...

a place that has no room for the soul is too
small a place. **:DAVID**

wow. sorry. i have said way too much. i just couldn't stop typing. **:DAVID**

HOGAN: No. No I'm feeling ya!
It's not half-full *or* half-empty.

HOGAN: Bluegrass people just need a bigger glass.

i think they *have* a bigger glass. **:DAVID**

they have a faith born from suffering. **:DAVID**

it is the faith of the suffering. **:DAVID**

it is the faith grabbed hold of, solely because of this guy jesus **:DAVID**

who knew what it meant to suffer **:DAVID**

it is the faith of slaves. **:DAVID**

HOGAN. I like that. I want that.

me too. i want talk of heaven. i want talk of movement from here and now to that ever-after kingdom. **:DAVID**

i want a king who brings peace and tramples the unjust. **:DAVID**

i want the place that those people's songs were taking them. **:DAVID**

it was *real*. **:DAVID**

they were singing themselves to a real place somewhere that they were really going. a place that sounded to them just as impossible as the belief of something waiting for us after death. **:DAVID**

HOGAN: And it made the here and now a little more bearable.

exactly! **:DAVID**

HISTORY OF BLUEGRASS

— PART 7 —

BILL MONROE, IN CONCLUSION

or

Darth Vader Sings!

These days, it seems that country music has a stigma. It's hard to put a finger on one thing in particular, a specific point that gives it this stigma, but rest assured, if you ask enough people what type of music they enjoy listening to, at least half of them will say something to the effect of "I like everything. Except for country, that is." In fact, at the very beginning of this project, the brave and fearless authors were at a business lunch with the publishers of this book when someone spoke up and said point-blank, "I have never really listened to bluegrass. In fact, I have actively tried *not* to listen to bluegrass music."

Hmmm.

We include this exchange to not only point out the daring gallantry of our publisher, but to also acknowledge that we the authors are, in fact, aware of this sentiment. And it is a valid one. Bluegrass is by no means the largest selling genre of music within the world of commercial compositions and many individuals share the attitude of our publisher, bearing associations of these backwoods musical articulations with Frontierland, Disney World USA or Six Flags or the local Jamboree at the Autumnal Crafts Festival.

But the larger issue seems people in our generation and those book-ending us—people in their late teens to early thirties—seem to automatically deny the quality or pleasurable benefit of country music and its offshoots. It is assumed this is largely in hopes of portraying the apposite element of hip-ness for the express purposes of impressing those around them. And by "those around them," it is meant "opposite sex." Granted, there are a number of artists who have been embraced as of late, especially by those in the Christian community—by "a number of artists," it is meant "Johnny Cash."

Most of the people who are now claiming allegiance to the house of Cash never really listened to him before his death—and even more telling, before his movie biopic. At least it means that there is *some* accounting for taste out there, not to mention that the less people we have listening to the latest fourth-generation Pearl Jam rip-off, the better; Cash's newly born hipster cred may be posthumous, but it's hipster cred nonetheless.

But if you really get down to it, country music is impossible to ignore. Truth be told, that particular industry sells records. A lot of them. If that is true (and it is), then for every person attempting to project instinctive coolness by denying country music, there is one who really doesn't mind appearing bucolic (openly discussing their purchase of the latest Big & Rich album) and one who swears he "would never" but has and will. Hats off to the ones who are "keeping it real."

There are two reasons why country music has remained so popular for so many years, and why it will continue to remain so. The first is that it does not try to push its ideas on anyone, but merely reflects what its fans already believe. The second reason is that country music is primarily concerned with the here and now. Music journalist Chuck Klosterman writes: "While rock and hip-hop constantly try to break through to a future consciousness—and while alt country tries to replicate a lost consciousness from the 1930s—modern country artists validate the experience of living right here, right now."[1]

Thanks, Chuck.

What does this have to do with us? Good question. Bluegrass, for the most part, falls into both of these categories, but with some exception. The one that most concerns our cause is the first point: that country music reflects the views of its listeners rather than pushing an agenda on them. It was mentioned earlier that Bill Monroe learned traditional values from his family during his younger years, and this made itself very evident in nearly every performance he ever did. According to the historians who study such things, a Bill Monroe set list looked almost identical from night to night. It basically went like this:

Opening segment
Monroe solo portion
Guest segment
Hymn time (*!)
Closing segment

It should be noted that, apparently, there are scholars really concerned about the structure of set lists. The mere existence of such a list proves this. They make the composition of a set list sound quite academic, but the authors of this book know better. To be fair though, there are in fact those who earn master's degrees in musicology and are infinitely interested in this stuff, despite how dull it may seem. Good for them. Somebody has to do it.[2]

Also important to note is that while portions of the set would be altered or dropped altogether depending on the amount of time given, the hymn portion of the evening was never left out because it "constituted an essential statement of values."[3] Sure, he may have

1. From his excellent book, *Sex, Drugs, and Cocoa Puffs*, p. 179–180. Specifically, the chapter "Toby over Moby." Check it out if you ever have the desire to know why teenage girls are the new teenage boys.

2. Or do they?

3. Neil V. Rosenberg, *Bluegrass: A History*, p. 233.

only performed a couple of religious songs each night, but they were there, every time, and we can't overlook that.

The religious element of music was one of the core things that Monroe adapted into his playing, thereby establishing it as one of the primary pieces of bluegrass. By securing his place as the pivotal personality of the art form, the art form in turn reflected all of the influences exerted upon him and incorporated them to an extent that the genre and personality became synonymous.[4] It is most certain that God popped up in many of the old-time folk songs brought over from the British Isles by our Appalachian immigrants, as religion was one of the main reasons they came over in the first place. But the real influence for Monroe in this respect, and for all the bluegrass performers after him, was church music and the old spirituals.

Early in his musical journey, Bill met a character by the name of Arnold Schultz, who many believe introduced him to African American music. Now, if Schultz was the well-rounded musician he is reported to be, it is safe to assume he had a working knowledge of all the old slave spirituals. Monroe undoubtedly would have been exposed to some of these, and possibly some of the marvelous stories that went with them. And here we come to the pivotal point.

... Pause for dramatic effect ...

The African American spiritual is one of the most important musical forms that we have to this day.

You would be hard-pressed to find a type of popular music that hasn't, in one way or another, come from the spiritual. The blues, gospel, jazz, rock, and hip-hop all have deep ties to the original spiritual. And what is bluegrass but old-time country songs mixed with jazz and gospel?

You: Oh my gosh! Are you serious?
Us: Yes.

---

4. When confronted with the statement that bluegrass was defined by his band (when Scruggs was still on board), Bill Monroe responded by saying "d--- lies!" (Rosenberg, p. 10).

But we aren't done. What is jazz but an evolution of the blues? And what is blues but an evolution of the spiritual?

And what is the spiritual? Many things, but mostly it is a song of sorrow. The slaves sang spirituals to comfort themselves out in the fields and take their minds off the backbreaking work they were forced to do. The songs were remarkable compositions, referencing the stories from the Bible that they most connected with. In and of itself, this is amazing because Christianity was a tool the slaveholders used to control their acquisitions. By stripping the slaves of their own personal faith and imposing Christianity on them, the slaveholders thought they would have more control. By and large, the slaves were not impressed with their masters' religion because they saw firsthand the ones doling out the brutality and hypocrisy. What they were impressed with, however, was this character named Jesus—a person like them who was no stranger to suffering, who was abused and killed at the hands of His oppressors, even though He was the son of the supreme God. They latched onto that, as well as to the faith and the hope that heaven was not far away. These songs transported them to places that their bodies could not go.

A radio program called "Speaking of Faith" featured a guest on one particular show by the name of Joe Carter. Joe is a performer and educator, and he knows his stuff. And "his stuff" turns out to be a remarkable amount of knowledge about spirituals. He and the host of the program, Krista Tippett, began talking about the transcendent nature of the spiritual. What follows is a portion of that interview along with some parenthetical color commentary appearing in microscopic print.

Mr. Carter: I think that the sorrow [the slaves felt] became the entrance, the open door, into a whole new world of experience. The slaves could not experience the normal world. They couldn't go out and go shopping, they couldn't buy a house, they couldn't do all the things that the normal white person did. They were slaves. You know, they were whipped, and they had chains, and they found the secret door to take them into that world where the tears are wiped away.

(For the most part, this is not new news. This is okay though because when Mr. Carter talks, he has this really deep voice, sort of like James Earl Jones. It's oddly comforting unless you get the mental image of Darth Vader discussing this particularly dark time in American history, at which point the whole thing gets comically eerie.)

Ms. Tippett: But the tears are cried first, aren't they?

(Tippett has a soothing motherly voice. When she makes this statement, you can almost hear watery tears. Her response is both authentic and appropriate.)

Mr. Carter: Yeah.

(Word.)

Ms. Tippett: You know, you talked about the secret power of these songs. And I think so much of what we're learning now in our advanced day is how important it is to embrace suffering in life in order to move forward. And maybe they did not have a choice.

(Thank you, Ms. Tippett, for summing up the entirety of this book. If you were lazy, you could just stop right here. But you are not, so keep reading.)

Mr. Carter: No, they didn't.

(Slaves, remember? This is why this guy is an educator. He is incapable of speaking anything but the truth.)

Ms. Tippett: But it's almost like there's healing in that moment even though it doesn't take the pain away, you know?

(Again, thank you, because you continue to reinforce the overall theme of the book. This could not have been done without you. A saint. That is what you are.)

This is really significant. These spirituals both acknowledged the suffering in this life and in the same breath looked out toward the Glory Land. Again, complete paradox. Hope placed in the future inadvertently brings hope into the present, in turn making the present tolerable. This is a VERY IMPORTANT ASPECT OF BLUEGRASS. The themes of suffering and salvation are paramount to the music.[5]

BUT WAIT, THERE'S MORE! Yes, the primary function of these spirituals was in fact this "looking out past physical suffering to a heaven that was not yet seen," but these songs had a secondary function that is equally amazing. Many of the songs contained hidden codes or messages that the master would not understand but that all the slaves would be familiar with. These codes were there to communicate details for escape: how to get out, when and where to go, how to hop on the Underground Railroad, etc. The master enjoyed hearing the slaves singing, but never listened to the words. And if he had, none of it would have made sense in the way it did to those doing the singing.

Here's another section of the transcript between Joe Carter and Krista Tippett:

Mr. Carter: My grandfather was a storyteller, and he would regale the family every time we were together with slavery stories. I mean, that's what he always talked about. And there was a slave by the name of John who was the star of all of his stories. And you never knew whether the story was true or not, but it was always funny and it got your attention, and grandpa was a good storyteller. But there was also always a moral at the end of the story. But the one theme that went

---

5. One major note concerning the innovative way Bill Monroe played, and therefore the way his band played as well, is that of the influence of jazz music. Before Monroe, the old-time songs rarely saw solo breaks or jams, both of which are standard elements of jazz music. Before these were implemented, you basically had two options: 1) You could play straight through an old song consisting of some verses and choruses and be done. 2) You could play an instrumental song, say, in the square-dance style, which people could get down to. That was about it. Then Bill Monroe moved from Kentucky to Chicago to work in the factories and found himself in the middle of the jazz movement. At this time, Chicago was essentially the jazz hub of the world, and to Bill's fresh ears it was revolutionary. The influence of jazz provided bluegrass with the *paradoxical* ability to elevate the individual (in the solo breaks), while simultaneously exhibiting the necessity of the group (errr, every time you *aren't* taking a solo, or when those harmonies are knocking you out of your chair), all within the same song. These jazz solos, which are free and loose, sit within very structured arrangements, a concept that inspired Bill to tweak the songs he was familiar with to include improvised sections by each member of the band. It gave the old-time country tunes a completely new vibe and raised the bar for musicianship and ability within the band.

through all of these stories was that by the end of the story, John had outsmarted the master. He was always ahead of the master. So there was this concept: "The master doesn't really understand us. We play a role for him and he sees us in a certain way, and we'll play that role as much as we can so that we won't get whipped. So we've got to understand his thinking, but he can never understand our thinking." And so all of the spirituals, all of the songs were masks, as well as, you know, these transcendent wonderful moments. They were also signals for escape. This was one of my grandmother's favorite songs.

(Darth Vader sings ...)

Steal away, steal away, steal away to Jesus
I've got to steal away, steal away home
Ain't got long to stay here
Steal away, steal away, steal away to Jesus
I've got to steal away, steal away home
Ain't got long to stay here
My Lord, He calls me, calls me by the thunder
The trumpet sounds within my soul
Ain't got long to stay here
Green trees are bending, poor sinner stands atremblin'
The trumpet sounds within my soul
Ain't got long to stay here

Ms. Tippett: You know, it's a religious idea that there is a better life after this one, right? It's a piece of doctrine. But there is something so miraculous happening when you are listening to this music or singing it. You know, for that moment, you're actually transported to that better life, right?

Mr. Carter: Yeah.

Ms. Tippett: I mean, you're singing, "Soon I will be done," but I think in singing that song, you can go through another day of this misery, right?

Mr. Carter: Exactly.

Ms. Tippett: It makes you strong for a little while. It's almost like the eternal becomes part of the present.

Mr. Carter: I think that's it.

Ms. Tippett: It's amazing.

Mr. Carter: I think that is it. It's like you get into the stream of that living water and there's no past, present, and future. It's just right now, and right now everything is all right.[6]

(We now need another contemplative pause and a line to sit these words on before they fall right off the page ...)

---

6. From the transcript of the radio show "Speaking of Faith," the episode "Joe Carter and the Legacy of the African-American Spiritual." *http://speakingoffaith.publicradio.org/programs/joecarter/transcript.shtml.*

COLUMNS, PART 7

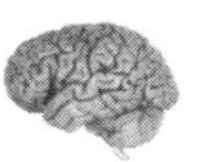

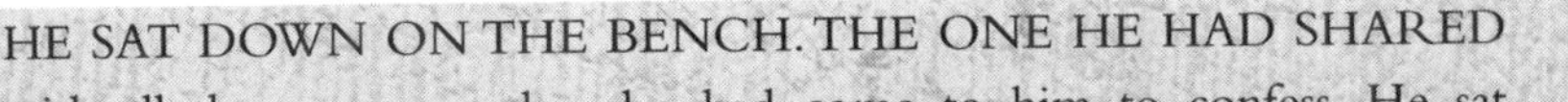

HE SAT DOWN ON THE BENCH. THE ONE HE HAD SHARED with all the many people who had come to him to confess. He sat staring at the garden. Breathing in its air. This world that seemed to burst alive with vivid color. He could feel his insides filling with its dark reds. With its brilliant oranges. With its glowing greens. All this color. Right here in the middle of this city. Right here in the middle of this cold grey concrete and stone. His eyes were following the trees that came pushing from the earth, their trunks coming up through the dirt. Lifting their green hands up into the blue of the sky. That's when he saw it. The Lark. It was circling. Dark and black against the bluest of skies you have ever seen. It held something in its beak. He thought, "I knew this was coming." The Lark Descending.

THE FIRST LARK FLEW.
The message was heavy but the
Lark's wings were strong. This was
what the Lark had been made for.

The Lark reached the church.
The bird circled above the
courtyard, above the garden.

The Lark Descending.

Into the concrete and stone.

It fell toward the earth. Pulled by a weight greater than gravity. It reached the garden's floor and laid the message across his feet. He felt the weight pressing down. But it felt like the sunshine in the morning. The way the light would wake him. It was a soothing weight. Like someone holding your feet. Not at all what you would have suspected. He wanted you to know this. He reached down and picked up the heaviest message ever sent. He sat down. He closed his eyes. He knew things would be forever different after this moment. He thought of his mother. He thought of his father. He thought of his buried child. He thought of her. He thought of all those who had come to him. Telling him they could not go on. Begging him for some small relief. Begging him for answers he still did not have. He knew this was the moment he had been waiting for. Opening his eyes slowly, he let them fall to the paper and follow the ink.

THE LARK WATCHES HOPEFUL

THE WEIGHT FALLS TO THE FLOOR

pebbles
+
needles
=
1.6180339887

IT IS FINISHED

THE GREEN PASTURES

"You look a little pensive, Lawd. Want a cigar, Lawd?"

"No thank you, Gabriel."

"You look awful pensive, Lawd. You've been sitting here, looking this way, an awful long time. Is it something serious, Lawd?"

"Very serious, Gabriel. I'm just thinkin'."

Gabriel holds up his hand. The angels stop singing.

"What about Lawd?"

"Somethin' the boy Hezdrel told Me, about Hosea and himself, how they found mercy. Mercy. 'Through sufferin',' he said. I'm tryin' to find it too. It's awful important, Gabriel. To all the people on My earth." The slow expression of a dawning begins to grow on His face. De Lawd rises from His chair. "Did he mean that even God must suffer? Listen! There's someone else on that earth."

An unnamed angel with a long white beard stares off into the distance. "Oh look at Him," the white-bearded angel says. "They're gonna make Him carry it up that high hill. They're gonna nail Him to it. Oh that's a terrible burden for one man to carry."

God smiles.

"Yes," He says.

The angels start singing again.

... THE BEGINNING

the day after kyle's funeral, the band boarded a privately chartered flight from waco to greenville, north carolina, where we were to play a concert that same night—picking back up the tour where we had left off. now this was not how we as a band typically "roll." typically we're bouncing through the heat-infested air between waco and dallas on a tiny american eagle prop plane that is, of course, opened to the general public and that is always packed full of fellow wacoans, all headed for connecting flights (on reasonably larger planes), each of us destined to various distant and, most likely, differing locales. but the day after kyle's funeral, we were on a lear jet. good friends of ours had shared the same sadness that had taken up residence in our chests, and they wished to help. they held the simple belief that a simple group of musicians singing simple songs made a difference in the great big world. so they chipped in as they were able. i don't know the details of how our good friends were connected to this particular plane, but the pilot informed us that terry bradshaw owned it. i kept looking around, wondering which seat mr. bradshaw might like to sit in. i'm certain he had no idea we were invading his space at this moment. but super bowl quarterbacks aside, i'll be honest here—a lear jet sounds a lot cooler than it is. a lear jet is a really, really tiny metal cylinder, not especially fit for someone over six feet tall as am i. with my legs folded and stuffed out of everyone's way, i decided that if i were a rapper and was attempting to obtain some cred regarding my bling, this was definitely not something i'd have thought to include in my rap song. maybe a lear jet feels differently when you aren't staring out its window at the various locales marked by your recent tears.

that morning my wife and i visited his grave. i stood in the exact place i did the previous day, leading the mass of graveside people in "amazing grace" on a borrowed guitar. he had been there, just a few feet away from me. the casket was closed, and i still couldn't look. it was still too dangerous. i was the one who was supposed to be leading, and these words were too much. the song felt like it was coming out of the ground through my feet, up my legs, through my chest, up my throat, and out into the air, and as soon as the syllables broke, they were met by all these other voices that were immediately surrounding me. all around me, so many people. all these people. i could look at them. they were like me. and their words were hitting mine in the air, and it felt like the whole ground was groaning, shooting these words up through our bodies into our mouths, and as our breath mingled and collected under the tent, it rose over our heads, and we exhaled there together, our gasping words surrounded him, and grace was in our breathing, hovering in the air.

toni and i stood there, unmoving. the ground was quieter the morning after. it had less to say. the sunlight through the trees was the kind that only happens early in the day, not too very soon after dawn breaks. it was warm and new where it hit the skin, but the air around the light was still cold, left over from the night. i could hear noise from kids playing on the playground across the street. i still can't believe there is a playground so close, with a perfect view of it from the gravesite. the laughter was so near, it was difficult to resist smiling. one of the kids playing had on bright yellow shoes, the color of the sunshine. she looked so happy.

it really is just perfect. it's the most beautiful cemetery i've ever been in. i realize it sounds like a juxtaposition to use *beautiful* and *cemetery* so closely, but it's immediately serene, peaceful. just what you'd hope. completely cinematic. the grave itself was a pile of flowers. i had expected to see dirt. that red texas clay-dirt that i've seen blanketing every other freshly covered grave i've stood beside. early morning, kids laughing, and a mound of flowers. i'm certain the mound of dirt was somewhere under the flowers, but driving up to it, it just looked like a three-foot-high pile of flowers, perfectly mirroring the rectangular shape of the hole he was in. i've never seen flowers piled three feet high in the shape of a rectangle. there were potted flowers that outlined the perimeter of the rectangle, and they were all leaning over and inward, none of them sitting up properly, resting against the mound as it rose from the grass. it was so strange, absolutely foreign to look at. a slight bit unnerving. these flowers leaning against flowers. it gave the impression that as he went into the ground, his beauty had drug all this on top of him. as if you'd spread a cloth over a table that had a rectangular hole cut in it, and then placed something with substantial weight over the hole, and then let go. it would drop past the surface of the table, pulling the tablecloth through the hole with it as it sank. this is what had happened here overnight. the weight of his passing pulled at our surface, and the flowers filled the hole, piling on top of each other, jamming the hole shut to keep the world from caving in on itself. it was the weight. i had felt the weight. there were six of us carrying it. taking it from the church. putting it in the car. placing it here above the ground. and it was impossibly heavy. the flowers didn't have a choice in the matter. this is where they had to be. they had been pulled by the force of his departure and wanted to be near him, and they saved us all in the course of their aspired proximity. it was beauty summoning beauty and falling, laying on itself until the hole was clogged. there is grace in observing a bunch of dying flowers falling over each other to be near a beauty that is too terrific a weight to keep on the surface for very long.

i was staring out of the plane window thinking all of this. i could see the church where the funeral had been. i could see the cemetery. i could see my house. and that's when i decided that i genuinely prefer public transportation. i like commercial airlines. i like us crammed in together so uncomfortably. having to listen to each other complain about the space being too small. having to put up with kids coughing while they're kicking my chair. having to wait. on you. on the plane from detroit that was delayed. having to be reminded that we are connected. having to watch you board and being forced to wonder for a bit what your life is like. having you so close to me while i scroll through my ipod looking for a song as the plane's wheels are leaving the ground. all of us so unavoidably aware that we are sharing the same air. i was staring out of the window of a plane, and i was reminded that we are all going somewhere.

typically, we only get to sing in the face of death once a year. easter. we sing at easter, and i'm always surprised at the magnitude of my emotions. once a year i stand and sing in the knowledge that death doesn't win. that it is not the ultimate negative outcome. that it is not the ultimate calamity. and i stand and sing in defiance. and the magnitude of things turning in my chest surprises me. that night, in greenville, north carolina, after staring at a mound of flowers covering the pile of dirt that covered the casket that held my friend, i stood in front of a room full of people whom i did not know and asked them, "so is that it? does death win? is death the final outcome of things? do we believe there's more?" they were real questions. i wasn't sure. and as i opened my chest to these people i didn't know, the answer grew and grew and grew, and the room filled with a noise of enormity, growing to a level of defiance i have not felt before. and i don't know how long i'll stand here in this defiance, but for now i have found a deeper part of the soul to sing from. i am here, naked, exposed, angry, brought down at the knees, and i am singing at the top of my lungs that WE WIN! we were someplace other than here that night. we were between here and there. the whole room existed someplace outside of the earthly. not quite heaven, but really, really close. simple people. singing simple songs. on our way to freedom. singing ourselves into a kingdom that was here and now and eternal.

APPENDICES

or

The Ever After

Some glad morning when this life is o'er
I'll fly away.

To a home on God's celestial shore,
I'll fly away.

I'll fly away, O Glory, I'll fly away.
When I die, Hallelujah, bye and bye,
I'll fly away.

When the shadows of this life have flown,
I'll fly away.

Like a bird thrown, driven by the storm,
I'll fly away.

I'll fly away, O Glory, I'll fly away.
When I die, Hallelujah, bye and bye,
I'll fly away.

Just a few more weary days and then,
I'll fly away.

To a land where joy shall never end,
I'll fly away.

I'll fly away, O Glory, I'll fly away.
When I die, Hallelujah, bye and bye,
I'll fly away.

APPENDIX A

HEAVEN

OR PERHAPS THE MOST ESPECIALLY, PRINCIPALLY IMPORTANT PORTION OF THIS BOOK

Genesis 1:8
God called the expanse **heaven**. And there was evening and there was morning, a second day.

Genesis 2:4
This is the account of the **heaven**s and the earth when they were created, in the day that the LORD God made earth and **heaven**.

Genesis 6:17
"Behold, I, even I am bringing the flood of water upon the earth, to destroy all flesh in which is the breath of life, from under **heaven**; everything that is on the earth shall perish.

Genesis 11:4
They said, "Come, let us build for ourselves a city, and a tower whose top {will reach} into **heaven**, and let us make for ourselves a name, otherwise we will be scattered abroad over the face of the whole earth."

Genesis 14:19
He blessed him and said, "Blessed be Abram of God Most High, Possessor of **heaven** and earth;

Genesis 14:22
Abram said to the king of Sodom, "I have sworn to the LORD God Most High, possessor of **heaven** and earth,

Genesis 19:24
Then the LORD rained on Sodom and Gomorrah brimstone and fire from the LORD out of **heaven**,

Genesis 21:17
God heard the lad crying; and the angel of God called to Hagar from **heaven** and said to her, "What is the matter with you, Hagar? Do not fear, for God has heard the voice of the lad where he is.

Genesis 22:11
But the angel of the LORD called to him from **heaven** and said, "Abraham, Abraham!" And he said, "Here I am."

Genesis 22:15
Then the angel of the LORD called to Abraham a second time from **heaven**,

Genesis 24:3
and I will make you swear by the LORD, the God of **heaven** and the God of earth, that you shall not take a wife for my son from the daughters of the Canaanites, among whom I live,

Genesis 24:7
" The LORD, the God of **heaven**, who took me from my father's house and from the land of my birth, and who spoke to me and who swore to me, saying, 'To your descendants I will give this land,' He will send His angel before you, and you will take a wife for my son from there.

Genesis 26:4
" I will multiply your descendants as the stars of **heaven**, and will give your descendants all these lands; and by your descendants all the nations of the earth shall be blessed;

Genesis 27:28
Now may God give you of the dew of **heaven**, And of the fatness of the earth, And an abundance of grain and new wine;

Genesis 27:39
Then Isaac his father answered and said to him, "Behold, away from the fertility of the earth shall be your dwelling, And away from the dew of **heaven** from above.

Genesis 28:12
He had a dream, and behold, a ladder was set on the earth with its top reaching to **heaven**; and behold, the angels of God were ascending and descending on it.

Genesis 28:17
He was afraid and said, " How awesome is this place! This is none other than the house of God, and this is the gate of **heaven**."

Genesis 49:25
From the God of your father who helps you, And by the Almighty who blesses you {With} blessings of **heaven** above, Blessings of the deep that lies beneath, Blessings of the breasts and of the womb.

Exodus 16:4
Then the LORD said to Moses, "Behold, I will rain bread from **heaven** for you; and the people shall go out and gather a day's portion every day, that I may test them, whether or not they will walk in My instruction.

Exodus 17:14
Then the LORD said to Moses, " Write this in a book as a memorial and recite it to Joshua, that I will utterly blot out the memory of Amalek from under **heaven**."

Exodus 20:4
" You shall not make for yourself an idol, or any likeness of what is in **heaven** above or on the earth beneath or in the water under the earth.

Exodus 20:22
Then the LORD said to Moses, "Thus you shall say to the sons of Israel, 'You yourselves have seen that I have spoken to you from **heaven**.

Exodus 31:17
" It is a sign between Me and the sons of Israel forever; for in six days the LORD made **heaven** and earth, but on the seventh day He ceased {from labor,} and was refreshed."

Deuteronomy 1:10
'The LORD your God has multiplied you, and behold, you are this day like the stars of **heaven** in number.

Deuteronomy 1:28
'Where can we go up? Our brethren have made our hearts melt, saying, "The people are bigger and taller than we; the cities are large and fortified to **heaven**. And besides, we saw the sons of the Anakim there."'

Deuteronomy 3:24
'O Lord GOD, You have begun to show Your servant Your greatness and Your strong hand; for what god is there in **heaven** or on earth who can do such works and mighty acts as Yours?

Deuteronomy 4:19
"And {beware} not to lift up your eyes to **heaven** and see the sun and the moon and the stars, all the host of **heaven**, and be drawn away and worship them and serve them, those which the LORD your God has allotted to all the peoples under the whole **heaven**.

Deuteronomy 4:26
I call **heaven** and earth to witness against you today, that you will surely perish quickly from the land where you are going over the Jordan to possess it. You shall not live long on it, but will be utterly destroyed.

Deuteronomy 4:39
"Know therefore today, and take it to your heart, that the LORD, He is God in **heaven** above and on the earth below; there is no other.

Deuteronomy 5:8
'You shall not make for yourself an idol, {or} any likeness {of} what is in **heaven** above or on the earth beneath or in the water under the earth.

Deuteronomy 7:24
" He will deliver their kings into your hand so that you will make their name perish from under **heaven**; no man will be able to stand before you until you have destroyed them.

Deuteronomy 9:1
"Hear, O Israel! You are crossing over the Jordan today to go in to dispossess nations greater and mightier than you, great cities fortified to **heaven**,

Deuteronomy 9:14
' Let Me alone, that I may destroy them and blot out their name from under **heaven**; and I will make of you a nation mightier and greater than they.'

Deuteronomy 10:14
"Behold, to the LORD your God belong **heaven** and the highest **heaven**s, the earth and all that is in it.

Deuteronomy 10:22
"Your fathers went down to Egypt seventy persons {in all,} and now the LORD your God has made you as numerous as the stars of **heaven**.

Deuteronomy 11:11
"But the land into which you are about to cross to possess it, a land of hills and valleys, drinks water from the rain of **heaven**,

Deuteronomy 25:19
"Therefore it shall come about when the LORD your God has given you rest from

all your surrounding enemies, in the land which the LORD your God gives you as an inheritance to possess, you shall blot out the memory of Amalek from under **heaven**; you must not forget.

Deuteronomy 26:15
' Look down from Your holy habitation, from **heaven**, and bless Your people Israel, and the ground which You have given us, a land flowing with milk and honey, as You swore to our fathers.'

Deuteronomy 28:23
"The **heaven** which is over your head shall be bronze, and the earth which is under you, iron.

Deuteronomy 28:24
" The LORD will make the rain of your land powder and dust; from **heaven** it shall come down on you until you are destroyed.

Deuteronomy 28:62
"Then you shall be left few in number, whereas you were as numerous as the stars of **heaven**, because you did not obey the LORD your God.

Deuteronomy 29:20
"The LORD shall never be willing to forgive him, but rather the anger of the LORD and His jealousy will burn against that man, and every curse which is written in this book will rest on him, and the LORD will blot out his name from under **heaven**.

Deuteronomy 30:12
"It is not in **heaven**, that you should say, ' Who will go up to **heaven** for us to get it for us and make us hear it, that we may observe it?'

Deuteronomy 30:19
" I call **heaven** and earth to witness against you today, that I have set before you life and death, the blessing and the curse. So choose life in order that you may live, you and your descendants,

Deuteronomy 32:40
'Indeed, I lift up My hand to **heaven**, And say, as I live forever,

Deuteronomy 33:13
Of Joseph he said, " Blessed of the LORD {be} his land, With the choice things of **heaven**, with the dew, And from the deep lying beneath,

Joshua 2:11
"When we heard {it,} our hearts melted and no courage remained in any man any longer because of you; for the LORD your God, He is God in **heaven** above and on earth beneath.

Joshua 10:11
As they fled from before Israel, {while} they were at the descent of Beth-horon, the LORD threw large stones from **heaven** on them as far as Azekah, and they died; {there were} more who died from the hailstones than those whom the sons of Israel killed with the sword.

Judges 5:20
" The stars fought from **heaven**, From their courses they fought against Sisera.

Judges 13:20
For it came about when the flame went up from the altar toward **heaven**, that the angel of the LORD ascended in the flame of the altar. When Manoah and his wife saw {this,} they fell on their faces to the ground.

Judges 20:40
But when the cloud began to rise from the city in a column of smoke, Benjamin looked behind them; and behold, the whole city was going up {in smoke} to **heaven**.

1 Samuel 5:12
And the men who did not die were smitten with tumors and the cry of the city went up to **heaven**.

2 Samuel 18:9
Now Absalom happened to meet the servants of David. For Absalom was riding on {his} mule, and the mule went under the thick branches of a great oak. And his head caught fast in the oak, so he was left hanging between **heaven** and earth, while the mule that was under him kept going.

2 Samuel 22:8
"Then the earth shook and quaked, The foundations of **heaven** were trembling And were shaken, because He was angry.

2 Samuel 22:14
" The LORD thundered from **heaven**, And the Most High uttered His voice.

1 Kings 8:22
Then Solomon stood before the altar of the LORD in the presence of all the assembly of Israel and spread out his hands toward **heaven**.

1 Kings 8:23
He said, "O LORD, the God of Israel, there is no God like You in **heaven** above or on earth beneath, keeping covenant and {showing} lovingkindness to Your servants who walk before You with all their heart,

1 Kings 8:27
"But will God indeed dwell on the earth? Behold, **heaven** and the highest **heaven** cannot contain You, how much less this house which I have built!

1 Kings 8:30
" Listen to the supplication of Your servant and of Your people Israel, when they pray toward this place; hear in **heaven** Your dwelling place; hear and forgive.

1 King 8:32
then hear in **heaven** and act and judge Your servants, condemning the wicked by bringing his way on his own head and justifying the righteous by giving him according to his righteousness.

1 Kings 8:34
then hear in **heaven**, and forgive the sin of Your people Israel, and bring them back to the land which You gave to their fathers.

1 Kings 8:36
then hear in **heaven** and forgive the sin of Your servants and of Your people Israel, indeed, teach them the good way in which they should walk. And send rain on Your land, which You have given Your people for an inheritance.

1 Kings 8:39
then hear in **heaven** Your dwelling place, and forgive and act and render to each according to all his ways, whose heart You know, for You alone know the hearts of all the sons of men,

1 Kings 8:43
hear in **heaven** Your dwelling place, and do according to all for which the foreigner calls to You, in order that all the peoples of the earth may know Your name, to fear You, as {do} Your people Israel, and that they may know that this house which I have built is called by Your name.

1 Kings 8:45
then hear in **heaven** their prayer and their supplication, and maintain their cause.

1 Kings 8:49
then hear their prayer and their supplication in **heaven** Your dwelling place, and maintain their cause,

1 Kings 8:54
When Solomon had finished praying this entire prayer and supplication to the LORD, he arose from before the altar of the LORD, from kneeling on his knees with his hands spread toward **heaven**.

1 Kings 21:24
" The one belonging to Ahab, who dies in the city, the dogs will eat, and the one who dies in the field the birds of **heaven** will eat."

1 Kings 22:19
Micaiah said, "Therefore, hear the word of the LORD. I saw the LORD sitting on His throne, and all the host of **heaven** standing by Him on His right and on His left.

2 Kings 1:10
Elijah replied to the captain of fifty, "If I am a man of God, let fire come down from **heaven** and consume you and your fifty." Then fire came down from **heaven** and consumed him and his fifty.

2 Kings 1:12
Elijah replied to them, "If I am a man of God, let fire come down from **heaven** and consume you and your fifty." Then the fire of God came down from **heaven** and consumed him and his fifty.

2 Kings 1:14
"Behold fire came down from **heaven** and consumed the first two captains of fifty with their fifties; but now let my life be precious in your sight."

2 Kings 2:1
And it came about when the LORD was about to take up Elijah by a whirlwind to **heaven**, that Elijah went with Elisha from Gilgal.

2 Kings 2:11
As they were going along and talking, behold, {there appeared} a chariot of fire and horses of fire which separated the two of them. And Elijah went up by a whirlwind to **heaven**.

2 Kings 7:2
The royal officer on whose hand the king was leaning answered the man of God and said, "Behold, if the LORD should make windows in **heaven**, could this thing be?" Then he said, "Behold, you will see it with your own eyes, but you will not eat of it."

2 Kings 7:19
Then the royal officer answered the man of God and said, "Now behold, if the LORD should make windows in **heaven**, could such a thing be?" And he said, "Behold, you will see it with your own eyes, but you will not eat of it."

2 Kings 14:27
The LORD did not say that He would blot out the name of Israel from under **heaven**, but He saved them by the hand of Jeroboam the son of Joash.

2 Kings 17:16
They forsook all the commandments of the LORD their God and made for themselves molten images, {even} two calves, and made an Asherah and worshiped all the host of **heaven** and served Baal.

2 Kings 19:15
Hezekiah prayed before the LORD and said, "O LORD, the God of Israel, who are enthroned {above} the cherubim, You are the God, You alone, of all the kingdoms of the earth. You have made **heaven** and earth.

2 Kings 21:3
For he rebuilt the high places which Hezekiah his father had destroyed; and he erected altars for Baal and made an Asherah, as Ahab king of Israel had done, and worshiped all the host of **heaven** and served them.

2 Kings 21:5
For he built altars for all the host of **heaven** in the two courts of the house of the LORD.

2 Kings 23:4
Then the king commanded Hilkiah the high priest and the priests of the second order and the doorkeepers, to bring out of the temple of the LORD all the vessels that were made for Baal, for Asherah, and for all the host of **heaven**; and he burned them outside Jerusalem in the fields of the Kidron, and carried their ashes to Bethel.

2 Kings 23:5
He did away with the idolatrous priests whom the kings of Judah had appointed to burn incense in the high places in the cities of Judah and in the surrounding area of

Jerusalem, also those who burned incense to Baal, to the sun and to the moon and to the constellations and to all the host of **heaven**.

1 Chronicles 21:16
Then David lifted up his eyes and saw the angel of the LORD standing between earth and **heaven**, with his drawn sword in his hand stretched out over Jerusalem. Then David and the elders, covered with sackcloth, fell on their faces.

1 Chronicles 21:26
Then David built an altar to the LORD there and offered burnt offerings and peace offerings. And he called to the LORD and He answered him with fire from **heaven** on the altar of burnt offering.

1 Chronicles 27:23
But David did not count those twenty years of age and under, because the LORD had said He would multiply Israel as the stars of **heaven**.

2 Chronicles 2:12
Then Huram continued, "Blessed be the LORD, the God of Israel, who has made **heaven** and earth, who has given King David a wise son, endowed with discretion and understanding, who will build a house for the LORD and a royal palace for himself.

2 Chronicles 6:13
Now Solomon had made a bronze platform, five cubits long, five cubits wide and three cubits high, and had set it in the midst of the court; and he stood on it, knelt on his knees in the presence of all the assembly of Israel and spread out his hands toward **heaven**.

2 Chronicles 6:14
He said, "O LORD, the God of Israel, there is no god like You in **heaven** or on earth, keeping covenant and {showing} lovingkindness to Your servants who walk before You with all their heart;

2 Chronicles 6:18
"But will God indeed dwell with mankind on the earth? Behold, **heaven** and the highest **heaven** cannot contain You; how much less this house which I have built.

2 Chronicles 6:21
"Listen to the supplications of Your servant and of Your people Israel when they pray toward this place; hear from Your dwelling place, from **heaven**; hear and forgive.

2 Chronicles 6:23
then hear from **heaven** and act and judge Your servants, punishing the wicked by bringing his way on his own head and justifying the righteous by giving him according to his righteousness.

2 Chronicles 6:25
then hear from **heaven** and forgive the sin of Your people Israel, and bring them back to the land which You have given to them and to their fathers.

2 Chronicles 6:27
then hear in **heaven** and forgive the sin of Your servants and Your people Israel, indeed, teach them the good way in which they should walk. And send rain on Your land which You have given to Your people for an inheritance.

2 Chronicles 6:30
then hear from **heaven** Your dwelling place, and forgive, and render to each according to all his ways, whose heart You know for You alone know the hearts of the sons of men,

2 Chronicles 6:33
then hear from **heaven**, from Your dwelling place, and do according to all for which the foreigner calls to You, in order that all the peoples of the earth may know Your name, and fear You as {do} Your people Israel, and that they may know that this house which I have built is called by Your name.

2 Chronicles 6:35
then hear from **heaven** their prayer and their supplication, and maintain their cause.

2 Chronicles 6:39
then hear from **heaven**, from Your dwelling place, their prayer and supplications, and maintain their cause and forgive Your people who have sinned against You.

2 Chronicles 7:1
Now when Solomon had finished praying, fire came down from **heaven** and consumed the burnt offering and the sacrifices, and the glory of the LORD filled the house.

2 Chronicles 7:14
and My people who are called by My name humble themselves and pray and seek My face and turn from their wicked ways, then I will hear from **heaven**, will forgive their sin and will heal their land.

2 Chronicles 18:18
Micaiah said, "Therefore, hear the word of the LORD. I saw the LORD sitting on His throne, and all the host of **heaven** standing on His right and on His left.

2 Chronicles 28:9
But a prophet of the LORD was there, whose name {was} Oded; and he went out to meet the army which came to Samaria and said to them, "Behold, because the LORD, the God of your fathers, was angry with Judah, He has delivered them into your hand, and you have slain them in a rage {which} has even reached **heaven**.

2 Chronicles 30:27
Then the Levitical priests arose and blessed the people; and their voice was heard and their prayer came to His holy dwelling place, to **heaven**.

2 Chronicles 32:20
But King Hezekiah and Isaiah the prophet, the son of Amoz, prayed about this and cried out to **heaven**.

2 Chronicles 33:3
For he rebuilt the high places which Hezekiah his father had broken down, he also erected altars for the Baals and made Asherim, and worshiped all the host of **heaven** and served them.

2 Chronicles 33:5
For he built altars for all the host of **heaven** in the two courts of the house of the LORD.

2 Chronicles 36:23
"Thus says Cyrus king of Persia, 'The LORD, the God of **heaven**, has given me all the kingdoms of the earth, and He has appointed me to build Him a house in Jerusalem, which is in Judah. Whoever there is among you of all His people, may the LORD his God be with him, and let him go up!'"

Ezra 1:2
"Thus says Cyrus king of Persia, 'The LORD, the God of **heaven**, has given me all the kingdoms of the earth and He has appointed me to build Him a house in Jerusalem, which is in Judah.

Ezra 5:11
"Thus they answered us, saying, 'We are the servants of the God of **heaven** and earth and are rebuilding the temple that was built many years ago, which a great king of Israel built and finished.

Ezra 5:12
'But because our fathers had provoked the God of **heaven** to wrath, He gave them into the hand of Nebuchadnezzar king of Babylon, the Chaldean, {who} destroyed this temple and deported the people to Babylon.

Ezra 6:9
"Whatever is needed, both young bulls, rams, and lambs for a burnt offering to the God of **heaven**, and wheat, salt, wine and anointing oil, as the priests in Jerusalem request, {it} is to be given to them daily without fail,

Ezra 6:10
that they may offer acceptable sacrifices to the God of **heaven** and pray for the life of the king and his sons.

Ezra 7:12
"Artaxerxes, king of kings, to Ezra the priest, the scribe of the law of the God of **heaven**, perfect {peace.} And now

Ezra 7:21
"I, even I, King Artaxerxes, issue a decree to all the treasurers who are {in the provinces} beyond the River, that whatever Ezra the priest, the scribe of the law of the God of **heaven**, may require of you, it shall be done diligently,

Ezra 7:23
"Whatever is commanded by the God of **heaven**, let it be done with zeal for the house of the God of **heaven**, so that there will not be wrath against the kingdom of the king and his sons.

Nehemiah 1:4
When I heard these words, I sat down and wept and mourned for days; and I was fasting and praying before the God of **heaven**.

Nehemiah 1:5
I said, "I beseech You, O LORD God of **heaven**, the great and awesome God, who preserves the covenant and lovingkindness for those who love Him and keep His commandments,

Nehemiah 2:4
Then the king said to me, "What would you request?" So I prayed to the God of **heaven**.

Nehemiah 2:20
So I answered them and said to them, " The God of **heaven** will give us success; therefore we His servants will arise and build, but you have no portion, right or memorial in Jerusalem.

Nehemiah 9:6
" You alone are the LORD. You have made the **heavens**, The **heaven** of **heavens** with all their host, The earth and all that is on it, The seas and all that is in them. You give life to all of them And the **heaven**ly host bows down before You.

Nehemiah 9:13
"Then You came down on Mount Sinai, And spoke with them from **heaven**; You gave them just ordinances and true laws, Good statutes and commandments.

Nehemiah 9:15
"You provided bread from **heaven** for them for their hunger, You brought forth water from a rock for them for their thirst, And You told them to enter in order to possess The land which You swore to give them.

Nehemiah 9:23
"You made their sons numerous as the stars of **heaven**, And You brought them into the land Which You had told their fathers to enter and possess.

Nehemiah 9:27
"Therefore You delivered them into the hand of their oppressors who oppressed them, But when they cried to You in the time of their distress, You heard from **heaven**, and according to Your great compassion You gave them deliverers who delivered them from the hand of their oppressors.

Nehemiah 9:28
"But as soon as they had rest, they did evil again before You; Therefore You abandoned them to the hand of their enemies, so that they ruled over them. When they cried again to You, You heard from **heaven**, And many times You rescued them according to Your compassion,

Job 1:16
While he was still speaking, another also came and said, " The fire of God fell from **heaven** and burned up the sheep and the servants and consumed them, and I alone have escaped to tell you."

Job 16:19
"Even now, behold, my witness is in **heaven**, And my advocate is on high.

Job 22:12
"Is not God {in} the height of **heaven**? Look also at the distant stars, how high they are!

Job 22:14
' Clouds are a hiding place for Him, so that He cannot see; And He walks on the vault of **heaven**.'

Job 26:11
"The pillars of **heaven** tremble And are amazed at His rebuke.

Job 37:3
"Under the whole **heaven** He lets it loose, And His lightning to the ends of the earth.

Job 38:29
"From whose womb has come the ice? And the frost of **heaven**, who has given it birth?

Job 41:11
"Who has given to Me that I should repay {him?} {Whatever} is under the whole **heaven** is Mine.

Psalm 11:4
The LORD is in His holy temple; the LORD'S throne is in **heaven**; His eyes behold, His eyelids test the sons of men.

Psalm 14:2
The LORD has looked down from **heaven** upon the sons of men To see if there are any who understand, Who seek after God.

Psalm 20:6
Now I know that the LORD saves His anointed; He will answer him from His holy **heaven** With the saving strength of His right hand.

Psalm 33:13
The LORD looks from **heaven**; He sees all the sons of men;

Psalm 53:2
God has looked down from **heaven** upon the sons of men To see if there is anyone who understands, Who seeks after God.

Psalm 57:3
He will send from **heaven** and save me; He reproaches him who tramples upon me. Selah. God will send forth His lovingkindness and His truth.

Psalm 69:34
Let **heaven** and earth praise Him, The seas and everything that moves in them.

Psalm 73:25
Whom have I in **heaven** {but You?} And besides You, I desire nothing on earth.

Psalm 76:8
You caused judgment to be heard from **heaven**; The earth feared and was still

Psalm 78:23
Yet He commanded the clouds above And opened the doors of **heaven**;

Psalm 78:24
He rained down manna upon them to eat And gave them food from **heaven**.

Psalm 80:14
O God {of} hosts, turn again now, we beseech You; Look down from **heaven** and see, and take care of this vine,

Psalm 85:11
Truth springs from the earth, And righteousness looks down from **heaven**.

Psalm 89:29
"So I will establish his descendants forever And his throne as the days of **heaven**.

Psalm 102:19
For He looked down from His holy height; From **heaven** the LORD gazed upon the earth,

Psalm 104:2
Covering Yourself with light as with a cloak, Stretching out **heaven** like a {tent} curtain.

Psalm 105:40
They asked, and He brought quail, And satisfied them with the bread of **heaven**.

Psalm 113:6
Who humbles Himself to behold {The things that are} in **heaven** and in the earth?

Psalm 115:15
May you be blessed of the LORD, Maker of **heaven** and earth.

Psalm 119:89
Forever, O LORD, Your word is settled in **heaven**.

Psalm 121:2
My help {comes} from the LORD, Who made **heaven** and earth.

Psalm 124:8
Our help is in the name of the LORD, Who made **heaven** and earth.

Psalm 134:3
May the LORD bless you from Zion, He who made **heaven** and earth.

Psalm 135:6
Whatever the LORD pleases, He does, In **heaven** and in earth, in the seas and in all deeps.

Psalm 136:26
Give thanks to the God of **heaven**, For His lovingkindness is everlasting.

Psalm 139:8
If I ascend to **heaven**, You are there; If I make my bed in Sheol, behold, You are there.

Psalm 146:6
Who made **heaven** and earth, The sea and all that is in them; Who keeps faith forever;

Psalm 148:13
Let them praise the name of the LORD, For His name alone is exalted; His glory is above earth and **heaven**.

Proverbs 30:4
Who has ascended into **heaven** and descended? Who has gathered the wind in His fists? Who has wrapped the waters in His garment? Who has established all the ends of the earth? What is His name or His son's name? Surely you know!

Ecclesiastes 1:13
And I set my mind to seek and explore by wisdom concerning all that has been done under **heaven**. {It} is a grievous task {which} God has given to the sons of men to be afflicted with.

Ecclesiastes 2:3
I explored with my mind {how} to stimulate my body with wine while my mind was guiding {me} wisely, and how to take hold of folly, until I could see what good there is for the sons of men to do under **heaven** the few years of their lives.

Ecclesiastes 3:1
There is an appointed time for everything. And there is a time for every event under **heaven**--

Ecclesiastes 5:2
Do not be hasty in word or impulsive in thought to bring up a matter in the presence of God. For God is in **heaven** and you are on the earth; therefore let your words be few.

Isaiah 7:11
"Ask a sign for yourself from the LORD your God; make {it} deep as Sheol or high as **heaven**."

Isaiah 13:10
For the stars of **heaven** and their constellations Will not flash forth their light; The sun will be dark when it rises And the moon will not shed its light.

Isaiah 14:12
"How you have fallen from **heaven**, O star of the morning, son of the dawn! You have been cut down to the earth, You who have weakened the nations!

Isaiah 14:13
"But you said in your heart, 'I will ascend to **heaven**; I will raise my throne above the stars of God, And I will sit on the mount of assembly In the recesses of the north.

Isaiah 24:21
So it will happen in that day, That the LORD will punish the host of **heaven** on high, And the kings of the earth on earth.

Isaiah 34:4
And all the host of **heaven** will wear away, And the sky will be rolled up like a scroll; All their hosts will also wither away As a leaf withers from the vine, Or as {one} withers from the fig tree.

Isaiah 34:5
For My sword is satiated in **heaven**, Behold it shall descend for judgment upon Edom And upon the people whom I have devoted to destruction.

Isaiah 37:16
"O LORD of hosts, the God of Israel, who is enthroned {above} the cherubim, You are the God, You alone, of all the kingdoms of the earth. You have made **heaven** and earth.

Isaiah 55:10
"For as the rain and the snow come down from **heaven**, And do not return there without watering the earth And making it bear and sprout, And furnishing seed to the sower and bread to the eater;

Isaiah 63:15
Look down from **heaven** and see from Your holy and glorious habitation; Where are Your zeal and Your mighty deeds? The stirrings of Your heart and Your compassion are restrained toward me.

Isaiah 66:1
Thus says the LORD, " **Heaven** is My throne and the earth is My footstool. Where then is a house you could build for Me? And where is a place that I may rest?

Jeremiah 7:18
"The children gather wood, and the fathers kindle the fire, and the women knead dough to make cakes for the queen of **heaven**; and {they} pour out drink offerings to other gods in order to spite Me.

Jeremiah 8:2
"They will spread them out to the sun, the moon and to all the host of **heaven**, which they have loved and which they have served, and which they have gone after and which they have sought, and which they have worshiped. They will not be gathered or buried; they will be as dung on the face of the ground.

Jeremiah 33:22
'As the host of **heaven** cannot be counted and the sand of the sea cannot be measured, so I will multiply the descendants of David My servant and the Levites who minister to Me.'"

Jeremiah 33:25
"Thus says the LORD, 'If My covenant {for} day and night {stand} not, {and} the fixed patterns of **heaven** and earth I have not established,

Jeremiah 44:17
"But rather we will certainly carry out every word that has proceeded from our mouths, by burning sacrifices to the queen of **heaven** and pouring out drink offerings to her, just as we ourselves, our forefathers, our kings and our princes did in the cities of Judah and in the streets of Jerusalem; for {then} we had plenty of food and were well off and saw no misfortune.

Jeremiah 44:18
"But since we stopped burning sacrifices to the queen of **heaven** and pouring out drink offerings to her, we have lacked everything and have met our end by the sword and by famine."

Jeremiah 44:19
"And," {said the women,} "when we were burning sacrifices to the queen of **heaven** and were pouring out drink offerings to her, was it without our husbands that we made for her {sacrificial} cakes in her image and poured out drink offerings to her?"

Jeremiah 44:25
thus says the LORD of hosts, the God of Israel, as follows: 'As for you and your wives, you have spoken with your mouths and fulfilled {it} with your hands, saying, "We will certainly perform our vows that we have vowed, to burn sacrifices to the queen of **heaven** and pour out drink offerings to her." Go ahead and confirm your vows, and certainly perform your vows!'

Jeremiah 49:36
'I will bring upon Elam the four winds From the four ends of **heaven**, And will scatter them to all these winds; And there will be no nation To which the outcasts of Elam will not go.

Jeremiah 51:9
We applied healing to Babylon, but she was not healed; Forsake her and let us each go to his own country, For her judgment has reached to **heaven** And towers up to the very skies.

Jeremiah 51:48
"Then **heaven** and earth and all that is in them Will shout for joy over Babylon, For the destroyers will come to her from the north," Declares the LORD.

Lamentations 2:1
How the Lord has covered the daughter of Zion With a cloud in His anger! He has cast from **heaven** to earth The glory of Israel, And has not remembered His footstool In the day of His anger.

Lamentations 3:41
We lift up our heart and hands Toward God in **heaven**;

Lamentations 3:50
Until the LORD looks down And sees from **heaven**.

Ezekiel 8:3
He stretched out the form of a hand and caught me by a lock of my head; and the Spirit lifted me up between earth and **heaven** and brought me in the visions of God to Jerusalem, to the entrance of the north gate of the inner {court,} where the seat of the idol of jealousy, which provokes to jealousy, was {located.}

Daniel 2:18
so that they might request compassion from the God of **heaven** concerning this mystery, so that Daniel and his friends would not be destroyed with the rest of the wise men of Babylon.

Daniel 2:19
Then the mystery was revealed to Daniel in a night vision. Then Daniel blessed the God of **heaven**;

Daniel 2:28
"However, there is a God in **heaven** who reveals mysteries, and He has made known to King Nebuchadnezzar what will take place in the latter days. This was your dream and the visions in your mind {while} on your bed.

Daniel 2:37
"You, O king, are the king of kings, to whom the God of **heaven** has given the kingdom, the power, the strength and the glory;

Daniel 2:44
"In the days of those kings the God of **heaven** will set up a kingdom which will never be destroyed, and {that} kingdom will not be left for another people; it will crush and put an end to all these kingdoms, but it will itself endure forever.

Daniel 4:13
'I was looking in the visions in my mind {as I lay} on my bed, and behold, an {angelic} watcher, a holy one, descended from **heaven**.

Daniel 4:15
"Yet leave the stump with its roots in the ground, But with a band of iron and bronze {around it} In the new grass of the field; And let him be drenched with the dew of **heaven**, And let him share with the beasts in the grass of the earth.

Daniel 4:23
'In that the king saw an {angelic} watcher, a holy one, descending from **heaven** and saying, " Chop down the tree and destroy it; yet leave the stump with its roots in the ground, but with a band of iron and bronze {around it} in the new grass of the field, and let him be drenched with the dew of **heaven**, and let him share with the beasts of the field until seven periods of time pass over him,"

Daniel 4:25
that you be driven away from mankind and your dwelling place be with the beasts of the field, and you be given grass to eat like cattle and be drenched with the dew of **heaven**; and seven periods of time will pass over you, until you recognize that the Most High is ruler over the realm of mankind and bestows it on whomever He wishes.

Daniel 4:26
'And in that it was commanded to leave the stump with the roots of the tree, your kingdom will be assured to you after you recognize that {it is} **Heaven** {that} rules.

Daniel 4:31
"While the word {was} in the king's mouth, a voice came from **heaven**, {saying,} 'King Nebuchadnezzar, to you it is declared: sovereignty has been removed from you,

Daniel 4:33
"Immediately the word concerning Nebuchadnezzar was fulfilled; and he was driven away from mankind and began eating grass like cattle, and his body was drenched with the dew of **heaven** until his hair had grown like eagles' {feathers} and his nails like birds' {claws.}

Daniel 4:34
"But at the end of that period, I, Nebuchadnezzar, raised my eyes toward **heaven** and my reason returned to me, and I blessed the Most High and praised and honored Him who lives forever; For His dominion is an everlasting dominion, And His kingdom {endures} from generation to generation.

Daniel 4:35
" All the inhabitants of the earth are accounted as nothing, But He does according to His will in the host of **heaven** And {among} the inhabitants of earth; And no one can ward off His hand Or say to Him, ' What have You done?'

Daniel 4:37
"Now I, Nebuchadnezzar, praise, exalt and honor the King of **heaven**, for all His works are true and His ways just, and He is able to humble those who walk in pride."

Daniel 5:21
"He was also driven away from mankind, and his heart was made like {that of} beasts, and his dwelling place {was} with the wild donkeys. He was given grass to eat like cattle, and his body was drenched with the dew of **heaven** until he recognized that the Most High God is ruler over the realm of mankind and {that} He sets over it whomever He wishes.

Daniel 5:23
but you have exalted yourself against the Lord of **heaven**; and they have brought the vessels of His house before you, and you and your nobles, your wives and your concubines have been drinking wine from them; and you have praised the gods of silver and gold, of bronze, iron, wood and stone, which do not see, hear or understand. But the God in whose hand are your life-breath and your ways, you have not glorified.

Daniel 6:27
"He delivers and rescues and performs signs and wonders In **heaven** and on earth, Who has {also} delivered Daniel from the power of the lions."

Daniel 7:2
Daniel said, "I was looking in my vision by night, and behold, the four winds of **heaven** were stirring up the great sea.

Daniel 7:13
"I kept looking in the night visions, And behold, with the clouds of **heaven** One like a Son of Man was coming, And He came up to the Ancient of Days And was presented before Him.

Daniel 7:27
'Then the sovereignty, the dominion and the greatness of {all} the kingdoms under the whole **heaven** will be given to the people of the saints of the Highest One; His kingdom {will be} an everlasting kingdom, and all the dominions will serve and obey Him.'

Daniel 8:8
Then the male goat magnified {himself} exceedingly. But as soon as he was mighty, the large horn was broken; and in its place there came up four conspicuous {horns} toward the four winds of **heaven**.

Daniel 8:10
It grew up to the host of **heaven** and caused some of the host and some of the stars to fall to the earth, and it trampled them down.

Daniel 9:12
"Thus He has confirmed His words which He had spoken against us and against our rulers who ruled us, to bring on us great calamity; for under the whole **heaven** there has not been done {anything} like what was done to Jerusalem.

Daniel 12:3
"Those who have insight will shine brightly like the brightness of the expanse of **heaven**, and those who lead the many to righteousness, like the stars forever and ever.

Daniel 12:7
I heard the man dressed in linen, who was above the waters of the river, as he raised his right hand and his left toward **heaven**, and swore by Him who lives forever that it would be for a time, times, and half {a} {time;} and as soon as they finish shattering the power of the holy people, all these {events} will be completed.

Amos 9:2
"Though they dig into Sheol, From there will My hand take them; And though they ascend to **heaven**, From there will I bring them down.

Jonah 1:9
He said to them, "I am a Hebrew, and I fear the LORD God of **heaven** who made the sea and the dry land."

Nahum 3:16
You have increased your traders more than the stars of **heaven**-- The creeping locust strips and flies away.

Zephaniah 1:5
"And those who bow down on the housetops to the host of **heaven**, And those who bow down {and} swear to the LORD and {yet} swear by Milcom,

Zechariah 6:5
The angel replied to me, "These are the four spirits of **heaven**, going forth after standing before the Lord of all the earth,

Malachi 3:10
" Bring the whole tithe into the storehouse, so that there may be food in My house, and test Me now in this," says the LORD of hosts, "if I will not open for you the windows of **heaven** and pour out for you a blessing until it overflows.

Matthew 3:2
"Repent, for the kingdom of **heaven** is at hand."

EVERYBODY WANTS TO GO TO HEAVEN ...

Matthew 4:17
From that time Jesus began to preach and say, "Repent, for the kingdom of **heaven** is at hand."

Matthew 5:3
"Blessed are the poor in spirit, for theirs is the kingdom of **heaven**.

Matthew 5:10
"Blessed are those who have been persecuted for the sake of righteousness, for theirs is the kingdom of **heaven**.

Matthew 5:12
"Rejoice and be glad, for your reward in **heaven** is great; for in the same way they persecuted the prophets who were before you.

Matthew 5:16
"Let your light shine before men in such a way that they may see your good works, and glorify your Father who is in **heaven**.

Matthew 5:18
"For truly I say to you, until **heaven** and earth pass away, not the smallest letter or stroke shall pass from the Law until all is accomplished.

Matthew 5:19
"Whoever then annuls one of the least of these commandments, and teaches others to do the same, shall be called least in the kingdom of **heaven**; but whoever keeps and teaches them, he shall be called great in the kingdom of **heaven**.

Matthew 5:20
"For I say to you that unless your righteousness surpasses that of the scribes and Pharisees, you will not enter the kingdom of **heaven**.

Matthew 5:34
"But I say to you, make no oath at all, either by **heaven**, for it is the throne of God,

Matthew 5:45
so that you may be sons of your Father who is in **heaven**; for He causes His sun to rise on the evil and the good, and sends rain on the righteous and the unrighteous.

Matthew 6:1
"Beware of practicing your righteousness before men to be noticed by them; otherwise you have no reward with your Father who is in **heaven**.

Matthew 6:9
"Pray, then, in this way: `Our Father who is in **heaven**, Hallowed be Your name.

Matthew 6:10
`Your kingdom come. Your will be done, On earth as it is in **heaven**.

Matthew 6:20
"But store up for yourselves treasures in **heaven**, where neither moth nor rust destroys, and where thieves do not break in or steal;

Matthew 7:11
"If you then, being evil, know how to give good gifts to your children, how much more will your Father who is in **heaven** give what is good to those who ask Him!

Matthew 7:21
"Not everyone who says to Me, `Lord, Lord,' will enter the kingdom of **heaven**, but he who does the will of My Father who is in **heaven** will enter.

Matthew 8:11
"I say to you that many will come from east and west, and recline at the table with Abraham, Isaac and Jacob in the kingdom of **heaven**;

Matthew 10:7
"And as you go, preach, saying, `The kingdom of **heaven** is at hand.'

Matthew 10:32
"Therefore everyone who confesses Me before men, I will also confess him before My Father who is in **heaven**.

Matthew 10:33
"But whoever denies Me before men, I will also deny him before My Father who is in **heaven**.

Matthew 11:11
"Truly I say to you, among those born of women there has not arisen anyone greater than John the Baptist! Yet the one who is least in the kingdom of **heaven** is greater than he.

Matthew 11:12
"From the days of John the Baptist until now the kingdom of **heaven** suffers violence, and violent men take it by force.

Matthew 11:23
"And you, Capernaum, will not be exalted to **heaven**, will you? You will descend to Hades; for if the miracles had occurred in Sodom which occurred in you, it would have remained to this day.

Matthew 11:25
At that time Jesus said, "I praise You, Father, Lord of **heaven** and earth, that You have hidden these things from the wise and intelligent and have revealed them to infants.

Matthew 12:50
"For whoever does the will of My Father who is in **heaven**, he is My brother and sister and mother."

Matthew 13:11
Jesus answered them, "To you it has been granted to know the mysteries of the kingdom of **heaven**, but to them it has not been granted.

Matthew 13:24
Jesus presented another parable to them, saying, "The kingdom of **heaven** may be compared to a man who sowed good seed in his field.

Matthew 13:31
He presented another parable to them, saying, "The kingdom of **heaven** is like a mustard seed, which a man took and sowed in his field;

Matthew 13:33
He spoke another parable to them, "The kingdom of **heaven** is like leaven, which a woman took and hid in three pecks of flour until it was all leavened."

Matthew 13:44
"The kingdom of **heaven** is like a treasure hidden in the field, which a man found and hid again; and from joy over it he goes and sells all that he has and buys that field.

Matthew 13:45
"Again, the kingdom of **heaven** is like a merchant seeking fine pearls,

Matthew 13:47
"Again, the kingdom of **heaven** is like a dragnet cast into the sea, and gathering fish of every kind;

Matthew 13:52
And Jesus said to them, "Therefore every scribe who has become a disciple of the kingdom of **heaven** is like a head of a household, who brings out of his treasure things new and old."

Matthew 14:19
Ordering the people to sit down on the grass, He took the five loaves and the two fish, and looking up toward **heaven**, He blessed the food, and breaking the loaves He gave them to the disciples, and the disciples gave them to the crowds,

Matthew 16:1
The Pharisees and Sadducees came up, and testing Jesus, they asked Him to show them a sign from **heaven**.

Matthew 16:17
And Jesus said to him, "Blessed are you, Simon Barjona, because flesh and blood did not reveal this to you, but My Father who is in **heaven**.

Matthew 16:19
"I will give you the keys of the kingdom of **heaven**; and whatever you bind on earth shall have been bound in **heaven**, and whatever you loose on earth shall have been loosed in **heaven**."

Matthew 18:1
At that time the disciples came to Jesus and said, "Who then is greatest in the kingdom of **heaven**?"

Matthew 18:3
and said, "Truly I say to you, unless you are converted and become like children, you will not enter the kingdom of **heaven**.

Matthew 18:4
"Whoever then humbles himself as this child, he is the greatest in the kingdom of **heaven**.

Matthew 18:10
"See that you do not despise one of these little ones, for I say to you that their angels in **heaven** continually see the face of My Father who is in **heaven**.

Matthew 18:14
"So it is not the will of your Father who is in **heaven** that one of these little ones perish.

Matthew 18:18
"Truly I say to you, whatever you bind on earth shall have been bound in **heaven**; and whatever you loose on earth shall have been loosed in **heaven**.

Matthew 18:19
"Again I say to you, that if two of you agree on earth about anything that they may ask, it shall be done for them by My Father who is in **heaven**.

Matthew 18:23
"For this reason the kingdom of **heaven** may be compared to a king who wished to settle accounts with his slaves.

Matthew 19:12
"For there are eunuchs who were born that way from their mother's womb; and there are eunuchs who were made eunuchs by men; and there are also eunuchs who made themselves eunuchs for the sake of the kingdom of **heaven**. He who is able to accept this, let him accept it."

Matthew 19:14
But Jesus said, "Let the children alone, and do not hinder them from coming to Me; for the kingdom of **heaven** belongs to such as these."

Matthew 19:21
Jesus said to him, "If you wish to be complete, go and sell your possessions and give to the poor, and you will have treasure in **heaven**; and come, follow Me."

Matthew 19:23
And Jesus said to His disciples, "Truly I say to you, it is hard for a rich man to enter the kingdom of **heaven**.

Matthew 20:1
"For the kingdom of **heaven** is like a landowner who went out early in the morning to hire laborers for his vineyard.

Matthew 21:25
"The baptism of John was from what source, from **heaven** or from men?" And they began reasoning among themselves, saying, "If we say, `From **heaven**,' He will say to us, `Then why did you not believe him?'

Matthew 22:2
"The kingdom of **heaven** may be compared to a king who gave a wedding feast for his son.

Matthew 22:30
"For in the resurrection they neither marry nor are given in marriage, but are like angels in **heaven**.

Matthew 23:9
"Do not call anyone on earth your father; for

One is your Father, He who is in **heaven**.

Matthew 23:13
"But woe to you, scribes and Pharisees, hypocrites, because you shut off the kingdom of **heaven** from people; for you do not enter in yourselves, nor do you allow those who are entering to go in.

Matthew 23:22
"And whoever swears by **heaven**, swears both by the throne of God and by Him who sits upon it.

Matthew 24:35
"**Heaven** and earth will pass away, but My words will not pass away.

Matthew 24:36
"But of that day and hour no one knows, not even the angels of **heaven**, nor the Son, but the Father alone.

Matthew 25:1
"Then the kingdom of **heaven** will be comparable to ten virgins, who took their lamps and went out to meet the bridegroom.

Matthew 26:64
Jesus said to him, "You have said it yourself; nevertheless I tell you, hereafter you will see THE SON OF MAN SITTING AT THE RIGHT HAND OF POWER, and COMING ON THE CLOUDS OF **HEAVEN**."

Matthew 28:2
And behold, a severe earthquake had occurred, for an angel of the Lord descended from **heaven** and came and rolled away the stone and sat upon it.

Matthew 28:18
And Jesus came up and spoke to them, saying, "All authority has been given to Me in **heaven** and on earth.

Mark 6:41
And He took the five loaves and the two fish, and looking up toward **heaven**, He blessed the food and broke the loaves and He kept giving them to the disciples to set before them; and He divided up the two fish among them all.

Mark 7:34
and looking up to **heaven** with a deep sigh, He said to him, "Ephphatha!" that is, "Be opened!"

Mark 8:11
The Pharisees came out and began to argue with Him, seeking from Him a sign from **heaven**, to test Him.

Mark 10:21
Looking at him, Jesus felt a love for him and said to him, "One thing you lack: go and sell all you possess and give to the poor, and you will have treasure in **heaven**; and come, follow Me."

Mark 11:25
"Whenever you stand praying, forgive, if you have anything against anyone, so that your Father who is in **heaven** will also forgive you your transgressions.

Mark 11:26
["But if you do not forgive, neither will your Father who is in **heaven** forgive your transgressions."]

Mark 11:30
"Was the baptism of John from **heaven**, or from men? Answer Me."

Mark 11:31
They began reasoning among themselves, saying, "If we say, 'From **heaven**,' He will say, 'Then why did you not believe him?'

Mark 12:25
"For when they rise from the dead, they neither marry nor are given in marriage, but are like angels in **heaven**.

Mark 13:25
AND THE STARS WILL BE FALLING from **heaven**, and the powers that are in the **heavens** will be shaken.

Mark 13:27
"And then He will send forth the angels, and will gather together His elect from the four winds, from the farthest end of the earth to the farthest end of **heaven**.

Mark 13:31
"**Heaven** and earth will pass away, but My words will not pass away.

Mark 13:32
"But of that day or hour no one knows, not even the angels in **heaven**, nor the Son, but the Father alone.

Mark 14:62
And Jesus said, "I am; and you shall see THE SON OF MAN SITTING AT THE RIGHT HAND OF POWER, and COMING WITH THE CLOUDS OF **HEAVEN**."

Mark 16:19
So then, when the Lord Jesus had spoken to them, He was received up into **heaven** and sat down at the right hand of God.

Luke 2:15
When the angels had gone away from them into **heaven**, the shepherds began saying to one another, "Let us go straight to Bethlehem then, and see this thing that has happened which the Lord has made known to us."

Luke 3:21
Now when all the people were baptized, Jesus was also baptized, and while He was praying, **heaven** was opened,

Luke 3:22
and the Holy Spirit descended upon Him in bodily form like a dove, and a voice came out of **heaven**, "You are My beloved Son, in You I am well-pleased."

Luke 6:23
"Be glad in that day and leap for joy, for behold, your reward is great in **heaven**. For in the same way their fathers used to treat the prophets.

Luke 9:16
Then He took the five loaves and the two fish, and looking up to **heaven**, He blessed them, and broke them, and kept giving them to the disciples to set before the people.

Luke 9:54
When His disciples James and John saw this, they said, "Lord, do You want us to command fire to come down from **heaven** and consume them?"

Luke 10:15
"And you, Capernaum, will not be exalted to **heaven**, will you? You will be brought down to Hades!

Luke 10:18
And He said to them, "I was watching Satan fall from **heaven** like lightning.

Luke 10:20
"Nevertheless do not rejoice in this, that the spirits are subject to you, but rejoice that your names are recorded in **heaven**."

Luke 10:21
At that very time He rejoiced greatly in the Holy Spirit, and said, "I praise You, O Father, Lord of **heaven** and earth, that You have hidden these things from the wise and intelligent and have revealed them to infants. Yes, Father, for this way was well-pleasing in Your sight.

Luke 11:16
Others, to test Him, were demanding of Him a sign from **heaven**.

Luke 12:33
"Sell your possessions and give to charity; make yourselves money belts which do not wear out, an unfailing treasure in **heaven**, where no thief comes near nor moth destroys.

Luke 15:7
"I tell you that in the same way, there will be more joy in **heaven** over one sinner who repents than over ninety-nine righteous persons who need no repentance.

Luke 15:18
'I will get up and go to my father, and will say to him, "Father, I have sinned against **heaven**, and in your sight;

Luke 15:21
"And the son said to him, 'Father, I have sinned against **heaven** and in your sight; I am no longer worthy to be called your son.'

Luke 16:17
"But it is easier for **heaven** and earth to pass away than for one stroke of a letter of the Law to fail.

Luke 17:29
but on the day that Lot went out from Sodom it rained fire and brimstone from **heaven** and destroyed them all.

Luke 18:13
"But the tax collector, standing some distance away, was even unwilling to lift up his eyes to **heaven**, but was beating his breast, saying, 'God, be merciful to me, the sinner!'

Luke 18:22
When Jesus heard this, He said to him, "One thing you still lack; sell all that you possess and distribute it to the poor, and you shall have treasure in **heaven**; and come, follow Me."

Luke 19:38
shouting: "BLESSED IS THE KING WHO COMES IN THE NAME OF THE LORD; Peace in **heaven** and glory in the highest!"

Luke 20:4
"Was the baptism of John from **heaven** or from men?"

Luke 20:5
They reasoned among themselves, saying, "If we say, 'From **heaven**,' He will say, 'Why did you not believe him?'

Luke 21:11
and there will be great earthquakes, and in various places plagues and famines; and there will be terrors and great signs from **heaven**.

Luke 21:33
"**Heaven** and earth will pass away, but My words will not pass away.

Luke 22:43
Now an angel from **heaven** appeared to Him, strengthening Him.

Luke 24:51
While He was blessing them, He parted from them and was carried up into **heaven**.

John 1:32
John testified saying, "I have seen the Spirit descending as a dove out of **heaven**, and He remained upon Him.

John 3:13
"No one has ascended into **heaven**, but He who descended from **heaven**: the Son of Man.

John 3:27
John answered and said, "A man can receive nothing unless it has been given him from **heaven**.

John 3:31
"He who comes from above is above all, he who is of the earth is from the earth and speaks of the earth. He who comes from **heaven** is above all.

John 6:31
"Our fathers ate the manna in the wilderness; as it is written, 'HE GAVE THEM BREAD OUT OF **HEAVEN** TO EAT.'"

John 6:32
Jesus then said to them, "Truly, truly, I say to you, it is not Moses who has given you the

bread out of **heaven**, but it is My Father who gives you the true bread out of **heaven**.

John 6:33
"For the bread of God is that which comes down out of **heaven**, and gives life to the world."

John 6:38
"For I have come down from **heaven**, not to do My own will, but the will of Him who sent Me.

John 6:41
Therefore the Jews were grumbling about Him, because He said, "I am the bread that came down out of **heaven**."

John 6:42
They were saying, "Is not this Jesus, the son of Joseph, whose father and mother we know? How does He now say, 'I have come down out of **heaven**'?"

John 6:50
"This is the bread which comes down out of **heaven**, so that one may eat of it and not die.

John 6:51
"I am the living bread that came down out of **heaven**; if anyone eats of this bread, he will live forever; and the bread also which I will give for the life of the world is My flesh."

John 6:58
"This is the bread which came down out of **heaven**; not as the fathers ate and died; he who eats this bread will live forever."

John 12:28
"Father, glorify Your name." Then a voice came out of **heaven**: "I have both glorified it, and will glorify it again."

John 17:1
Jesus spoke these things; and lifting up His eyes to **heaven**, He said, "Father, the hour has come; glorify Your Son, that the Son may glorify You,

Acts 1:2
until the day when He was taken up to **heaven**, after He had by the Holy Spirit given orders to the apostles whom He had chosen.

Acts 1:11
They also said, "Men of Galilee, why do you stand looking into the sky? This Jesus, who has been taken up from you into **heaven**, will come in just the same way as you have watched Him go into **heaven**."

Acts 2:2
And suddenly there came from **heaven** a noise like a violent rushing wind, and it filled the whole house where they were sitting.

Acts 2:5
Now there were Jews living in Jerusalem, devout men from every nation under **heaven**.

Acts 2:34
"For it was not David who ascended into **heaven**, but he himself says: 'THE LORD SAID TO MY LORD, "SIT AT MY RIGHT HAND,

Acts 3:21
whom **heaven** must receive until the period of restoration of all things about which God spoke by the mouth of His holy prophets from ancient time.

Acts 4:12
"And there is salvation in no one else; for there is no other name under **heaven** that has been given among men by which we must be saved."

Acts 4:24
And when they heard this, they lifted their voices to God with one accord and said, "O Lord, it is You who MADE THE **HEAVEN** AND THE EARTH AND THE SEA, AND ALL THAT IS IN THEM,

Acts 7:42
"But God turned away and delivered them up to serve the host of **heaven**; as it is written in the book of the prophets, 'IT WAS NOT TO ME THAT YOU OFFERED VICTIMS AND SACRIFICES FORTY YEARS IN THE WILDERNESS, WAS IT, O HOUSE OF ISRAEL?

Acts 7:49
'**HEAVEN** IS MY THRONE, AND EARTH IS THE FOOTSTOOL OF MY FEET; WHAT KIND OF HOUSE WILL YOU BUILD FOR ME?' says the Lord, 'OR WHAT PLACE IS THERE FOR MY REPOSE?

Acts 7:55
But being full of the Holy Spirit, he gazed intently into **heaven** and saw the glory of God, and Jesus standing at the right hand of God;

Acts 9:3
As he was traveling, it happened that he was approaching Damascus, and suddenly a light from **heaven** flashed around him;

Acts 11:9
"But a voice from **heaven** answered a second time, 'What God has cleansed, no longer consider unholy.'

Acts 14:15
and saying, "Men, why are you doing these things? We are also men of the same nature as you, and preach the gospel to you that you should turn from these vain things to a living God, WHO MADE THE **HEAVEN** AND THE EARTH AND THE SEA AND ALL THAT IS IN THEM.

Acts 14:17
and yet He did not leave Himself without witness, in that He did good and gave you rains from **heaven** and fruitful seasons, satisfying your hearts with food and gladness."

Acts 17:24
"The God who made the world and all things in it, since He is Lord of **heaven** and earth, does not dwell in temples made with hands;

Acts 19:35
After quieting the crowd, the town clerk said, "Men of Ephesus, what man is there after all who does not know that the city of the Ephesians is guardian of the temple of the great Artemis and of the image which fell down from **heaven**?

Acts 22:6
"But it happened that as I was on my way, approaching Damascus about noontime, a very bright light suddenly flashed from **heaven** all around me,

Acts 26:13
at midday, O King, I saw on the way a light from **heaven**, brighter than the sun, shining all around me and those who were journeying with me.

Romans 1:18
For the wrath of God is revealed from **heaven** against all ungodliness and unrighteousness of men who suppress the truth in unrighteousness,

Romans 10:6
But the righteousness based on faith speaks as follows: "DO NOT SAY IN YOUR HEART, 'WHO WILL ASCEND INTO **HEAVEN**?' (that is, to bring Christ down),

1 Corinthians 8:5
For even if there are so-called gods whether in **heaven** or on earth, as indeed there are many gods and many lords,

1 Corinthians 15:47
The first man is from the earth, earthy; the second man is from **heaven**.

2 Corinthians 5:2
For indeed in this house we groan, longing to be clothed with our dwelling from **heaven**,

2 Corinthians 12:2
I know a man in Christ who fourteen years ago--whether in the body I do not know, or out of the body I do not know, God knows--such a man was caught up to the third **heaven**.

Galatians 1:8
But even if we, or an angel from **heaven**, should preach to you a gospel contrary to what we have preached to you, he is to be accursed!

Ephesians 3:15
from whom every family in **heaven** and on earth derives its name,

Ephesians 6:9
And masters, do the same things to them, and give up threatening, knowing that both their Master and yours is in **heaven**, and there is no partiality with Him.

Philippians 2:10
so that at the name of Jesus EVERY KNEE WILL BOW, of those who are in **heaven** and on earth and under the earth,

Philippians 3:20
For our citizenship is in **heaven**, from which also we eagerly wait for a Savior, the Lord Jesus Christ;

Colossians 1:5
because of the hope laid up for you in **heaven**, of which you previously heard in the word of truth, the gospel

Colossians 1:20
and through Him to reconcile all things to Himself, having made peace through the blood of His cross; through Him, I say, whether things on earth or things in **heaven**.

Colossians 1:23
if indeed you continue in the faith firmly established and steadfast, and not moved away from the hope of the gospel that you have heard, which was proclaimed in all creation under **heaven**, and of which I, Paul, was made a minister.

Colossians 4:1
Masters, grant to your slaves justice and fairness, knowing that you too have a Master in **heaven**.

1 Thessalonians 1:10
and to wait for His Son from **heaven**, whom He raised from the dead, that is Jesus, who rescues us from the wrath to come.

1 Thessalonians 4:16
For the Lord Himself will descend from **heaven** with a shout, with the voice of the archangel and with the trumpet of God, and the dead in Christ will rise first.

2 Thessalonians 1:7
and to give relief to you who are afflicted and to us as well when the Lord Jesus will be revealed from **heaven** with His mighty angels in flaming fire,

Hebrews 9:24
For Christ did not enter a holy place made with hands, a mere copy of the true one, but into **heaven** itself, now to appear in the presence of God for us;

Hebrews 11:12
Therefore there was born even of one man, and him as good as dead at that, as many descendants AS THE STARS OF **HEAVEN** IN NUMBER, AND INNUMERABLE AS THE SAND WHICH IS BY THE SEASHORE.

Hebrews 12:23
to the general assembly and church of the firstborn who are enrolled in **heaven**, and to God, the Judge of all, and to the spirits of the righteous made perfect,

Hebrews 12:25
See to it that you do not refuse Him who is speaking. For if those did not escape when they refused him who warned them on earth, much less will we escape who turn away from Him who warns from **heaven**.

Hebrews 12:26
And His voice shook the earth then, but now He has promised, saying, "YET ONCE MORE I WILL SHAKE NOT ONLY THE EARTH, BUT ALSO THE **HEAVEN**."

James 5:12
But above all, my brethren, do not swear, either by **heaven** or by earth or with any other

oath; but your yes is to be yes, and your no, no, so that you may not fall under judgment.

1 Peter 1:4
to obtain an inheritance which is imperishable and undefiled and will not fade away, reserved in **heaven** for you,

1 Peter 1:12
It was revealed to them that they were not serving themselves, but you, in these things which now have been announced to you through those who preached the gospel to you by the Holy Spirit sent from **heaven**--things into which angels long to look.

1 Peter 3:22
who is at the right hand of God, having gone into **heaven**, after angels and authorities and powers had been subjected to Him.

2 Peter 1:18
and we ourselves heard this utterance made from **heaven** when we were with Him on the holy mountain.

Revelation 3:12
'He who overcomes, I will make him a pillar in the temple of My God, and he will not go out from it anymore; and I will write on him the name of My God, and the name of the city of My God, the new Jerusalem, which comes down out of **heaven** from My God, and My new name.

Revelation 4:1
After these things I looked, and behold, a door standing open in **heaven**, and the first voice which I had heard, like the sound of a trumpet speaking with me, said, "Come up here, and I will show you what must take place after these things."

Revelation 4:2
Immediately I was in the Spirit; and behold, a throne was standing in **heaven**, and One sitting on the throne.

Revelation 5:3
And no one in **heaven** or on the earth or under the earth was able to open the book or to look into it.

Revelation 5:13
And every created thing which is in **heaven** and on the earth and under the earth and on the sea, and all things in them, I heard saying,

Revelation 8:1
When the Lamb broke the seventh seal, there was silence in **heaven** for about half an hour.

Revelation 8:10
The third angel sounded, and a great star fell from **heaven**, burning like a torch, and it fell on a third of the rivers and on the springs of waters.

Revelation 9:1
Then the fifth angel sounded, and I saw a star from **heaven** which had fallen to the earth; and the key of the bottomless pit was given to him.

Revelation 10:1
I saw another strong angel coming down out of **heaven**, clothed with a cloud; and the rainbow was upon his head, and his face was like the sun, and his feet like pillars of fire;

Revelation 10:4
When the seven peals of thunder had spoken, I was about to write; and I heard a voice from **heaven** saying, "Seal up the things which the seven peals of thunder have spoken and do not write them."

Revelation 10:5
Then the angel whom I saw standing on the sea and on the land lifted up his right hand to **heaven**,

Revelation 10:6
and swore by Him who lives forever and ever, WHO CREATED **HEAVEN** AND THE THINGS IN IT, AND THE EARTH AND THE THINGS IN IT, AND THE SEA AND THE THINGS IN IT, that there will be delay no longer,

Revelation 10:8
Then the voice which I heard from **heaven**, I heard again speaking with me, and saying, "Go, take the book which is open in the hand of the angel who stands on the sea and on the land."

Revelation 11:12
And they heard a loud voice from **heaven** saying to them, "Come up here." Then they went up into **heaven** in the cloud, and their enemies watched them.

Revelation 11:13
And in that hour there was a great earthquake, and a tenth of the city fell; seven thousand people were killed in the earthquake, and the rest were terrified and gave glory to the God of **heaven**.

Revelation 11:15
Then the seventh angel sounded; and there were loud voices in **heaven**, saying, "The kingdom of the world has become the kingdom of our Lord and of His Christ; and He will reign forever and ever."

Revelation 11:19
And the temple of God which is in **heaven** was opened; and the ark of His covenant appeared in His temple, and there were flashes of lightning and sounds and peals of thunder and an earthquake and a great hailstorm.

Revelation 12:1
A great sign appeared in **heaven**: a woman clothed with the sun, and the moon under her feet, and on her head a crown of twelve stars;

Revelation 12:3
Then another sign appeared in **heaven**: and behold, a great red dragon having seven heads and ten horns, and on his heads were seven diadems.

Revelation 12:4
And his tail swept away a third of the stars of **heaven** and threw them to the earth. And the dragon stood before the woman who was about to give birth, so that when she gave birth he might devour her child.

Revelation 12:7
And there was war in **heaven**, Michael and his angels waging war with the dragon. The dragon and his angels waged war,

Revelation 12:8
and they were not strong enough, and there was no longer a place found for them in **heaven**.

Revelation 12:10
Then I heard a loud voice in **heaven**, saying, "Now the salvation, and the power, and the kingdom of our God and the authority of His Christ have come, for the accuser of our brethren has been thrown down, he who accuses them before our God day and night.

Revelation 12:6
And he opened his mouth in blasphemies against God, to blaspheme His name and His tabernacle, that is, those who dwell in **heaven**.

Revelation 13:13
He performs great signs, so that he even makes fire come down out of **heaven** to the earth in the presence of men.

Revelation 14:2
And I heard a voice from **heaven**, like the sound of many waters and like the sound of loud thunder, and the voice which I heard was like the sound of harpists playing on their harps.

Revelation 14:7
and he said with a loud voice, "Fear God, and give Him glory, because the hour of His judgment has come; worship Him who made the **heaven** and the earth and sea and springs of waters."

Revelation 14:13
And I heard a voice from **heaven**, saying, "Write, 'Blessed are the dead who die in the Lord from now on!'" "Yes," says the Spirit, "so that they may rest from their labors, for their deeds follow with them."

Revelation 14:17
And another angel came out of the temple which is in **heaven**, and he also had a sharp sickle.

Revelation 15:1
Then I saw another sign in **heaven**, great and marvelous, seven angels who had seven plagues, which are the last, because in them the wrath of God is finished.

Revelation 15:5
After these things I looked, and the temple of the tabernacle of testimony in **heaven** was opened,

Revelation 16:11
and they blasphemed the God of **heaven** because of their pains and their sores; and they did not repent of their deeds.

Revelation 16:21
And huge hailstones, about one hundred pounds each, came down from **heaven** upon men; and men blasphemed God because of the plague of the hail, because its plague was extremely severe.

Revelation 18:1
After these things I saw another angel coming down from **heaven**, having great authority, and the earth was illumined with his glory.

Revelation 18:4
I heard another voice from **heaven**, saying, "Come out of her, my people, so that you will not participate in her sins and receive of her plagues;

Revelation 18:5
for her sins have piled up as high as **heaven**, and God has remembered her iniquities.

Revelation 18:20
"Rejoice over her, O **heaven**, and you saints and apostles and prophets, because God has pronounced judgment for you against her."

Revelation 19:1
After these things I heard something like a loud voice of a great multitude in **heaven**, saying, "Hallelujah! Salvation and glory and power belong to our God;

Revelation 19:11
And I saw **heaven** opened, and behold, a white horse, and He who sat on it is called Faithful and True, and in righteousness He judges and wages war.

Revelation 19:14
And the armies which are in **heaven**, clothed in fine linen, white and clean, were following Him on white horses.

Revelation 20:1
Then I saw an angel coming down from **heaven**, holding the key of the abyss and a great chain in his hand.

Revelation 20:9
And they came up on the broad plain of the earth and surrounded the camp of the saints and the beloved city, and fire came down from **heaven** and devoured them.

Revelation 20:11
Then I saw a great white throne and Him who sat upon it, from whose presence earth and **heaven** fled away, and no place was found for them.

Revelation 21:1
Then I saw a new **heaven** and a new earth; for the first **heaven** and the first earth passed away, and there is no longer any sea.

Revelation 21:2
And I saw the holy city, new Jerusalem, coming down out of **heaven** from God, made ready as a bride adorned for her husband.

Revelation 21:10
And he carried me away in the Spirit to a great and high mountain, and showed me the holy city, Jerusalem, coming down out of **heaven** from God,

APPENDIX B

(IN SUPPORT OF W)

There is no underestimating the joy of a specific thought entering your brain, like "I wonder what the Jewish belief of the afterlife has been like throughout history," then subsequently typing "afterlife" and "Jewish" and straightaway receiving a big fat page of information concerning that exact subject matter. Or "I wonder how many rubles were stolen in the Bezdany train robbery?"—"Bezdany" + "raid" = "approximately 200,000 rubles." For this simple, instantaneous entrée into the ever so slightly questionable world of free information, we have come to feel great affection for the web-based resource—Wikipedia.

Another reason: They have a really cool logo. Check it out. It is well worth your time. And another thing: Trust. This is a significant aspect of life (obviously—eBay runs on it. And it follows that eBay is a significant aspect of life), and we choose to place a portion of our trust in the accuracy of Wikipedia because, well, for one: this here book is not rocket science. The margin for error is a little greater than, say, quantum physics. And two: it is free.

You have undoubtedly noticed that we have spent perhaps a greater-than-necessary portion of our time and effort in the manufacturing of jokes concerning the reliability of this website. This is not unfounded. The first time Hogan heard about this fantastical resource was when it made the news for its display of dubious information. That said, if you look up "Wikipedia" on Wikipedia, you will get plenty of info relating to both its trustworthiness, and its lack thereof. You will also learn such super facts as: it can be found in more than 130 languages, including Swedish. Anyways, the reason that it catches flack from snooty university types is that it is a cooperative, contributed to and edited by registered users, not exclusively academics. W claims that they have trust that this practice will yield the most accurate and extensive information on a given topic. Academics, in turn, do not see things this way. But can you really doubt a resource that is so self-aware? No, you cannot.

Did we also mention that it is a free service?

But we needed our very own substantiated proof. So we looked up "David Crowder Band," a subject that we assumed we would know enough about without having to spend a large amount of time cross-referencing things. And lo and behold, W is highly, highly accurate. Like, call the police because the-cooperative-knows-too-much-about-you accurate. It's quite eerie.

So that was proof enough for us. We may crack jokes, but they spring from the vast open spaces of love for the W that we hold delicately within our chests (thoraxes). Granted, it's the sort of love that comes with sideways glances and restraining orders after having confidently concluded that we in fact must have a stalker who contributes to this, our beloved resource.

ACKNOWLEDGMENTS

The two authors, taking into account the normal procedures for writing a book, and not wishing to offend the very few who actually read such things, would like to acknowledge the following in no particular order, but in an order that was indeed thought about beforehand as to not present an affront to certain parties acknowledged: Toni, Robin, and the Lord our God, for not laughing at us upon our resolution to write this book. (The authors would like to humbly acknowledge, however, that the previously mentioned divine being may very well be laughing, but it is difficult to prove such things. They do in fact believe that said divine being has a sense of humor as evidenced by His creation of the chicken, but since Wikipedia has no categories for researching this particular subject, they will never know for sure.) Your love and patience keep our little boat afloat (and apparently keep us rhyming!?). Sophia and Giselle, for making it okay to poop and barf on the carpet; Craig Nash; Lisette; the good folks at Hole in the Roof; Barnes & Noble, Common Grounds, the Panera Bread in Waco, the chairs in Crowder's TV room; RELEVANT Media Group, because they don't like bluegrass (or dying) and decided to publish this anyway; Cara and Tia; sixstepsrecords/EMICMG; Shelley and Louie; rousing pop-culture artifacts pertaining to death from the likes of *Grey's Anatomy*; *Scrubs*; *Law and Order*—Original—*SVU*—*Criminal Intent*; *Elizabethtown*; *Plans*—Death Cab for Cutie; *A Dirty Job*—Christopher Moore; *Guero*—Beck; *Proof*; *Best Week Ever* (VH1); Kirk Cameron; *Digital Ash in a Digital Urn*—Bright Eyes; *Good News for People Who Love Bad News*—Modest Mouse; *Apologies to the Queen Mary*—Wolf Parade; *Funeral*—Arcade Fire; *www.postsecret.com*; Animal Planet's *The Most Extreme*; "When I Get Where I'm Going"—Brad Paisley; *LIFTED or The Story Is in the Soil, Keep Your Ear to the Ground*—Bright Eyes; "Till Kingdom Come"—Coldplay; "Memories"—Eisley; "Naked as We Came"—Iron and Wine; "The Big Guns"—Jenny Lewis; *Garden State*; "The Man Comes Around"—Johnny Cash; "Apocalypse Please"—Muse; "Am I Too Late"—Old 97s; "We Will Become Silhouettes"—The Postal Service.

And, to every single person who we have loved and lost too soon, who are missed and envied. You got there first.